P9-DIH-990

INTERNATIONAL RELATIONS AND THE GREAT POWERS

General Editor: **John Gooch**
Professor of International History, University of Leeds

NO LONGER
the property of
Whitaker Library

FRANCE

AND THE WORLD
SINCE 1870

J. F. V. Keiger

European Studies Research Institute
University of Salford
Manchester

Whitaker Library
Chowan College
Murfreesboro, North Carolina

ARNOLD

A member of the Hodder Headline Group
LONDON

First published in Great Britain in 2001 by
Arnold, a member of the Hodder Headline Group,
338 Euston Road, London, NW1 3BH

http://www.arnoldpublishers.com

Co-published in the United States of America by
Oxford University Press Inc.,
198 Madison Avenue, New York, NY 10016

© 2001 J. F. V. Keiger

All rights reserved. No part of this publication may be reproduced or
transmitted in any form or by any means, electronically or mechanically,
including photocopying, recording or any information storage or retrieval
system, without either prior permission in writing from the publisher or a
licence permitting restricted copying. In the United Kingdom such licences
are issued by the Copyright Licensing Agency: 90 Tottenham Court Road,
London W1T 4LP.

The advice and information in this book are believed to be true and
accurate at the date of going to press, but neither the author[s] nor the publisher
can accept any legal responsibility or liability for any errors or omissions.

British Library Cataloguing in Publication Data
A catalogue record for this book is available from the British Library

Library of Congress Cataloging-in-Publication Data
A catalog record for this book is available from the Library of Congress

ISBN 0 340 76012 5 (hb)
ISBN 0 340 59507 8 (pb)

1 2 3 4 5 6 7 8 9 10

Production Editor: Wendy Rooke
Production Controller: Martin Kerans

Typeset in 11pt Bembo by J&L Composition Ltd, Filey, North Yorkshire
Printed and bound in Great Britain by MPG Books, Bodmin, Cornwall

What do you think about this book? Or any other Arnold title?
Please send your comments to feedback.arnold@hodder.co.uk

Contents

General editor's preface

Great powers stand at the centre of modern international relations. The history of their inter-relationships once rested entirely on the formal record of diplomacy, and focused exclusively on the statesmen, diplomats and ambassadors who shaped and conducted foreign policy. Today, international historians, while still acknowledging the importance of diplomacy, cast their nets more widely. Power rests on many foundations, both tangible and intangible. National wealth is one ingredient of power, but so are ideology and national politics. Personalities have their influence on policies, so that there must always be a place for the individual in the history of international relations; but so, too, do the collective institutional forces of modern state bureaucracies, the military and naval establishments, big business and industry. Together, in varying combinations at different times, these forces and factors find their expression in external policy.

The policies of Great Powers are shaped by their unique amalgams of internal ingredients; but they also have to act and react in a particular but changing international environment. Their choices of policy are affected by the shifting balance between them, and by contingent events: wars and revolutions sometimes offer them opportunities but at other times represent setbacks to a preferred course. The aim of this series is therefore to present the histories of the Great Powers in the twentieth century from these two broad perspectives and to show how individual powers, trying to achieve their own priorities in the regional and global arenas of world politics, have sought to balance the actions and reactions of their rivals against the imperatives of domestic politics.

Few Great Powers have been tossed about more tempestuously in both international and domestic waters than was France during the first half of the twentieth century. Defeated in the war of 1870–71 and then victorious – but at what cost? – in the First World War, she crashed again to German arms, but this time in only six short weeks, in 1940. *D'une défaite à l'autre* ('From one defeat to the other'), a great historian recently subtitled a military history of those seventy years. The result was to produce one of the great conundrums of modern history – why did France collapse? – and to link international relations with domestic history as historians such as Marc Bloch and writers such as Jean-Paul Satre turned the spotlight on the last turbulent years of the once stately Third Republic in an effort to understand what was to them more a failure of social and political institutions than of military ones. Nor was the sad story of French arms yet over. Defeat in Indo-China helped seal the fate of the fragile Fourth Republic, and defeat in Algeria almost sealed the personal fate of the head of the Fifth Republic, General Charles De Gaulle. Yet, in the past thirty years France has risen above her past to present a second conundrum of contemporary histoy – how has she recovered from these vicissitudes to reach the position of independence and influence that she enjoys today?

To answer these questions, John Keiger presents us with a penetrating study of French institutions and policies in which statesmen and politicians such as Georges Briand, Raymond Poincaré, Charles De Gaulle and Georges Mitterand share the stage with the 'silent administrators' so diligently furnished by the *Grandes Ecoles* as well as with the more shadowy operatives of France's secret services. The outcome of the story he has to tell is a remarkable reversal in France's international fortunes. Where the earlier generations of politicians proved incapable of mastering the currents of international politics, the later ones have proved so adroit at doing so that we may perhaps speak now of the renaissance of France as a Great Power. As readers will discover, John Keiger's France, viewed in perspective across the century that separates us from 1900, looks very different from the dismal landscape of the five decades which divided 1870 from 1940.

John Gooch
April, 2001

Acknowledgements

This book was started a long time ago as my long-suffering, but remarkably tolerant, publisher Christopher Wheeler knows to his cost. My debt of gratitude also extends to a number of individuals who provided information, suggested avenues of investigation or gave of their time to read various versions of the typescript. It is a great pleasure to thank, in particular, two old friends who supplied advice and documentation on French defence policy and initiated me into the real workings of the French administrative elite, Pierre Serra and Jacques Roudière. John Gooch, the series editor, first invited me to write this volume and subsequently offered extremely helpful suggestions for making the typescript better than it would otherwise have been, as did Robert Tombs, Martin Alexander and Pascal Venier. The text also benefited from the most efficient copy-editing skills of Hilary Walford. An author's family usually becomes part of the writing process. Mine was supportive in a host of ways. Victoria, Emma, Laura and little Edward even suggested amendments to the text that would have made it far more amusing; alas, I dared not incorporate them. My final thanks are, as always, to my parents.

John F. V. Keiger
Manchester, March 2001

Introduction

'France, once soldier of God, today soldier of humanity, will always be the soldier of the ideal.'[1] So proclaimed Georges Clemenceau, leader and defender of the French state in the First World War. The action of states is at the heart of international relations. Diplomatic history is indispensable in studying the aims, decisions and intentions of governments, but it is insufficient to explain the influences that motivated a state's action. Any explanation calls for an understanding of what Pierre Renouvin called profound forces: geography, demography, economics, collective mentalities, which to a large extent determine a state's action and limit decision-makers' freedom to choose.[2]

States are at one level material entities, moulded and governed by geography, demography and economics. They are also shaped by more abstract concepts such as political experience, tradition and mentalities. But construction of state and nation is far from passive; it is partly invented and manufactured to promote a particular common ideal. For 200 years the French nation has imagined and projected itself as the custodian of the universalist principles of the French Revolution encapsulated in the revolutionary triptych liberty, equality and fraternity and radiated by the French language. Thus language, culture and self-image are as important in France's relations with the rest of the world as treaties and trade. France's position in the world in the twentieth century was as dependent upon how decision-makers and the average French person perceived and understood that role as the more concrete realities that underpinned it.

The history of France in the world, what Fernand Braudel called 'The France beyond France',[3] in the twentieth century is of a multitude of realities that cannot adequately be encapsulated in a single historical narrative, other than a rather flat chronological account. It is several narratives at different levels, obeying several logics moving at varying speeds. To comprehend France's position in international relations it is helpful to separate rather than amalgamate those narratives. As one of the oldest nation states, France is both inheritor and prisoner of a long past. With a greater sense of history than

most other nations, the French tend to reason historically and turn to the
past for counsel. According to a report published in 1992, France is probably
the country that directs the greatest effort towards the teaching of history.
Figures released by the French publishing association showed that in 1992
one eighth of all paperbacks published were on history, a third more than
novels.[4] Academic subjects, whether it be Politics, the Law or Geography, are
all taught through the prism of History. History, as Republican governments
from the nineteenth to the twentieth century knew only too well, was a vital
element in inventing the French nation. History is then a reflex of the
collective consciousness of the French. Little wonder that it be French
historians who have developed the notion of 'sites of memory', casting their
shadow on the consciousness of the present. Nor is it surprising that it be a
French historical school, the Annales, which should have made such a play
of studying history over the long term, *la longue durée*. By separating out
specific themes, and by looking at them continuously from the late nineteenth century to the present, certain continuities and cycles of behaviour
can be highlighted that explain France's relations with the rest of the world,
rather than have their patterns lost amid a flurry of events.

The structure of this work is therefore thematic. To a large extent the
notions of 'France' and the 'state' refer to the political elites who, almost by
definition, have had the greatest say in the running of the country. The book
begins in Chapter 1 with the determinants of France's relationship with the
rest of the world. It considers the material factors such as geography, demographics and economics that form the backdrop to France's external
relations. But it also considers more abstract concepts such as notions of the
state, national identity, France's self-perception and how others see it. Rather
like individuals, how a state views itself conditions how it sees the world and
reacts to it. All great powers tend to think of themselves as superior in some
way. But, unlike other powers, with the possible exception of the USA,
France has had a unique way of looking at the world based on the notion
that it had a mission to extend the fruits of its superior civilization and
values, borne of Revolution, to other nations – the 'civilizing mission'.

Chapter 2 looks at how these determinants conditioned the reality of
France's interaction with the rest of the world through diplomacy. It analyses
the machinery of diplomacy, the bureaucratic organization and politics of
foreign policy formulation and execution. It looks at how decision-makers
from diplomats to politicians dealt with the day-to-day issues of managing
France's relations with the rest of the world. Diplomacy is largely about the
peaceful management of a state's relations with other states, but most states,
and certainly all great powers, prepare for the eventuality of physical conflict
and war according to the maxim 'If you want peace, prepare for war'. In so
doing they have political goals around which they weave a number of
military objectives involving the planning and deployment of their armed

forces. Chapter 3 looks at how France perceived its defence over the course of the twentieth century and how it conceived and adapted a military strategy to suit its political objectives. Again the organization of defence policy making, the relationship between the military and their political masters is described as well as the bureaucratic politics of that relationship. France had particularly turbulent civil–military relations at various moments of its history. This had an impact on how it organized its armed forces, through military service and conscription. It also played a part in how it conceived its defence posture, as when from 1960 General de Gaulle consciously set about making nuclear weapons – not potentially mutinous soldiers – the prime defenders of the nation. Of course, the final test of any military strategy is the test of war. From 1870 to the 1960s France was involved in several wars, from the recurrent wars with its principal potential enemy Germany to the 'savage wars of peace' in the decolonization process. War has therefore played a considerable part in France's relations with the world beyond its shores.

The information on which states base their understanding of the world in war and peace is nowadays referred to as intelligence. Intelligence is at the crossroads of how a state perceives itself and how it perceives the wider world. France's turbulent political past explains why intelligence was gathered as much about internal 'demons' as foreign ones. In the last decade of the nineteenth century the French counter-intelligence services overstepped themselves in what became the Dreyfus Affair and French intelligence never fully recovered to this day from the discredit heaped upon it in political and public circles. This was to the detriment of foreign and defence policy making, given the importance of intelligence in knowing not only one's enemies, but also one's friends and how they will react in given circumstances. Chapter 4 will look at the machinery of French intelligence organization, for domestic and foreign purposes, and the extent to which the information gathered and its analysis were fed into policy and decision making.

What is patently clear in France's relations with the wider world from the last quarter of the nineteenth century to the present is the shadow cast by its German neighbour. For most of that time France's foreign and defence policies were predicated on how to deal with the German 'question'. For that reason, the history of France's relations with the world in the twentieth century is to a large extent the history of its relations with Germany. This explains why Chapter 5, which deals with Germany, is by far the largest, and why Germany is predominant in so many of the chapters dedicated to relations with other great powers. Thus, although Chapter 6 deals with the French notion of the 'Anglo-Saxons' – best understood as Britain and the USA – much of the rationale for their importance as allies to France has to do with a fear of Germany. There is a fundamental ambivalence at the heart of France's relations with the Anglo-Saxons that makes them adversaries and allies, sometimes at one and the same time. This can be explained, quite understandably, by France's desire to have a free hand on the international stage in order to promote a French view of the world order, occasionally at variance with that of London and Washington. Yet often simultaneously Britain and the USA are perceived as real or potential allies against a hegemonic Germany. Relations with Russia, developed in Chapter 7, have also been characterized by a similar ambivalence. Despite ideological differences since the nineteenth century ranging from autocracy to communism, French policy-makers have cultivated Russia's friendship whatever the regime as a bulwark against an over-powerful Germany in the heart of Europe. While on the subject of Europe, in these heady days of European integration, one might ask why no single chapter has been devoted to France's relations with 'Europe'. It is the logic of this work that France's stance in relation to Europe was based to a large part initially, and perhaps still, on the notion that European integration was the best peaceful means of dealing with the German 'problem'. Much of the question of European integration is therefore dealt with either obliquely or head on in a number of chapters but principally in the ones devoted to Germany and the post-cold war era.

A classic expression of how a great power related to the world in the twentieth century was through empire. France in the twentieth century has moved from having the second largest empire in the world to having only a few confetti-like dependencies, albeit strategically placed in all the oceans of the world. What motivated the development of that empire, how it was managed and how decolonization was dealt with is the subject of Chapter 8. One of the most profound peacetime adjustments France had to make on the international scene in the twentieth century was after the end of the cold war. At least since the Gaullist era of the early 1960s, France's position during the cold war was one of ambiguity, which allowed it a freer hand than most other powers. With the ending of the cold war it more than most has had to find a new role in the world. How it has attempted to do that is the subject of the final chapter, devoted to the post-cold war era.

In the course of the twentieth century France more than most other great powers saw its fortunes fluctuate wildly. From being one of the leading great powers in the nineteenth century, France had, to all intents and purposes, ceased to exist as a great power in 1940. However, in the second half of the twentieth century it was able to restore itself to a position of considerable international prominence. Some would suggest that much of that was an illusion. Of course, defining great power status is notoriously tricky, particularly when one moves from economic and military aggregates and attempts to evaluate abstract notions such as national prestige and international influence. Then there is always the degree to which believing one is a great power is enough to define one's status; it is 'performative', as devotees of cultural studies might say. Certainly, France performed the role of a great power even when on occasions it had few tangible assets with which to do so, as in 1944, and many, not least in France, came to believe in the fiction. Indeed, after the traumas of defeat and collaboration from 1940 to 1944, many French, unaware that life was imitating art, were seduced by the idea of France strutting the world stage. Yet by the beginning of the twenty-first century it could be argued that France occupies a more convincing position as a great power than in 1900. As a permanent member of the United Nations Security Council, the third greatest nuclear power in the world, the fourth most powerful economy and a leading member of the European Union, France can make a claim to being the third or fourth great power in the world. That is certainly no worse a ranking than at the beginning of the twentieth century, with the added benefit that France feels more secure now than it did then.

In terms of relations with the outside world the twentieth century was the long century for France, with its beginnings in 1871 and the defeat by Germany. In retrospect, perhaps, that was the defining moment for France's priorities in the century and a quarter to come. Its trajectory in terms of world status over that period was a fluctuating one that has seen France experience decline and renewal. Those twin experiences have themselves conditioned how France relates to the world today.

Notes

1 Quoted in Robert Tombs, *France 1814–1914* (London, Longman, 1996), p. 478.
2 Pierre Renouvin and Jean-Baptiste Duroselle, *Introduction à l'histoire des relations internationales* (2nd edn, Paris, Armand Colin, 1966), pp. 1–2.
3 F. Braudel, *L'Identité de la France*, vol. III, *Les Hommes et les choses*, part 2 (Paris, Arthaud-Flammarion, 1986), pp. 426–7.
4 *Le Monde*, 18 Mar. 1993.

1
Determinants of France's relations with the world

To understand how a state interacts with the rest of the world it is necessary to have some knowledge of its national make-up. A state's relationship with other states and the international system is conditioned by a series of material, as well as psychological, factors that limit or enhance its freedom to act on the international stage. This chapter will attempt first to analyse some of the material aspects that condition France's relations with the outside world: geography, demographics and the economy. Second it will look at some less tangible, but no less important, political and psychological components that might be said to make up France's national persona and condition its reflexes on the international stage, such as notions of the state, national identity and the way France is perceived by the international community.

Geography

Geography might be considered to be the least flexible and most deterministic aspect of France's outlook on the world. De Gaulle in *Vers l'armée de métier* remarked in 1934: 'As the sight of a portrait suggests to the observer the impression of a destiny, so the map of France reveals our fortunes.' He went on to quote Napoleon: 'The policy of a state is in its geography.'[1] Though it is easy to exaggerate the influence of geography, it has conditioned France's relationship with the rest of the world. Leaving aside the climatic conditions derived from its being part of the world's temperate zones, where all modern great powers developed,[2] its geographical position on the north-west edge of the European continent has affected its outlook. It is, and has been for several centuries, both a maritime and a continental power, the dual demands of which have not always been comfortably accommodated in its foreign and defence policies. The truism that Britain is an island and that France is not does explain much about their differing foreign and strategic priorities. Until the military development of the aircraft in the 1930s, Britain had been to a large extent in its history naturally protected against invasion. France has not, having been invaded three times in the last century and a quarter.

Territory may once have been a determinant of state power, but by the beginning of the nineteenth century this no longer conferred a decisive advantage. France, with its 536,000 square kilometres in 1900, was one of the largest territories in Europe, smaller by far than Russia, but roughly equivalent to Germany and almost twice the size of Britain.[3] Indeed, for the historian Fernand Braudel, France was a victim of the immensity and diversity of its territory. It was slow to develop a unified national economy and to engage in international exchange similar to smaller states such as Britain and The Netherlands. Today at 550,000 square kilometres (having regained Alsace-Lorraine in 1918) it remains the largest country in Western Europe, though a medium-sized one on a world scale.

Although France has a massive coastline, vulnerable to a hostile navy, its *westerly* position at the end of the European land mass renders its western regions relatively safe from land attack. Hence the idea briefly countenanced after French military defeat by the German armies in June 1940 of establishing a military redoubt in the north-west of the country to enable it to pursue the war. Though 'naturally' protected to the south by the Pyrenees and to the east by the Alps and the Jura mountains, to the north-east along 300 kilometres of frontier with Germany it is not so fortunate. Since the sixteenth century this has been the invasion route on nine occasions. Its capital and some of its most productive agricultural and industrial regions in the north-east are vulnerable from across the great plains of northern Europe. France has therefore dreamt on numerous occasions since the Revolution of extending its borders to its 'natural frontiers' along the Rhine to block invasion routes. It has been completely successful in that quest only twice: from 1795 to 1814, when France dominated Europe under the Revolution and Napoleon, and from 1919 to 1930, when the French and their allies occupied the left bank of the Rhine. On three occasions in the last century and a quarter it has had to move its seat of government from Paris across the Loire to Tours or Bordeaux when invasion threatened in 1870, 1914 and 1940. Hence the conscious shifting of certain strategic manufacturing interests such as aerospace to Toulouse in the south-west since the Second World War. On the other hand, its pivotal position on the continent has allowed it to invade other European states such as the Netherlands, Italy, Switzerland, Spain and the German states under Louis XIV, Louis XV or Napoleon. As the German geographer Friedrich Ratzel wrote in 1897, a state's history is always 'a part of the history of neighbouring states'. The relationship might fluctuate between amity and animosity,[4] as it has with Germany. Geopolitics have therefore determined the ambivalent nature of France's relationship with its eastern neighbour since German unification.

France has another dimension to its geographical position, which, since Algerian independence in 1962, has been eclipsed. France is an important

Mediterranean power and has been for centuries. This is, or was, an advantage for trading with the eastern and southern Mediterranean basin and as a maritime route to its South East Asian empire until its decolonization in 1954. The Mediterranean was also an important axis of France's African empire from the colonization of Algeria in 1830 to the push into the heart of the continent in the 1880s. In the 1920s, textbooks portrayed France as the 'heir to Rome', reviving the Roman Empire around the Mediterranean Sea. As the ferociously colonialist General Salan later put it: 'The Mediterranean runs through France as the Seine runs through Paris.'[5]

Yet from the thirteenth to the twentieth century the Mediterranean could also be a weakness, demanding that France possess two fleets anchored at Brest on the Atlantic and Toulon on the Mediterranean to ensure protection of both its seas. It was forced either to maintain two major fleets at enormous expense or to split one between the two, as was more often the case.[6] Although for the nineteenth century and the inter-war years it was one of the world's greatest naval powers, the geographical dispersion of its fleets undermined its power. This handicap was temporarily resolved by the so-called Grey–Cambon letters of 1912, when France and Britain, fearing Germany, agreed to concentrate their fleets in the Mediterranean, and the Channel and the Atlantic, respectively, to look after their respective interests. This dilemma went hand in hand with the other – 'the sempiternal hornets' nest of land war'[7] and of deciding whether to focus its strategy and defence estimates on land or on sea.

The Mediterranean also posed a strategic threat if its southern rim were to come under the control of a hostile power. In the early part of the twentieth century France feared British control of Tangiers or the establishment of a German port in Morocco. At the other end of the century following the 1991 Gulf War the threat of a hostile Islamic power along the North African coast within missile distance of Marseilles was seen as the new danger.

Thus geography has presented threats and opportunities. France has either sought to defend itself from the mastery others might seek to exercise over the continent or seas around its coastline, or to exercise its own hegemony often in order to ensure its own safety and promote its own values. This has involved France in varying attempts to secure its western, eastern and southern flanks. Anxious about repositioning its strategy in the aftermath of the cold and Gulf wars, Prime Minister Edouard Balladur warned, on 18 May 1993 in the Senate, that one of the challenges now facing France was 'to avoid weakening the Atlantic and Mediterranean facades in the face of a centre of gravity which recent history has rendered more continental'.[8] France's traditional geographical dilemma between a continental and a maritime strategy is still alive at the beginning of the twenty-first century.

Geography may have conditioned France's outlook on the world but it is not restricted to its immediate borders. In a series of concentric circles moving out from its natural borders one next encounters Europe. As the historian Marc Bloch remarked, 'There is no history of France, there is a history of Europe.'[9] From the Holy Roman Empire to Louis XIV, the French Revolution, Napoleon and even the European Community, France has sought to extend its influence over Europe. As de Gaulle's Prime Minister, Georges Pompidou, remarked on 24 February 1964, France 'by its geography and its history is condemned to play the European card'.[10]

Since at least the nineteenth century the circle beyond Europe has been France's empire – 'Greater France'. For almost a century, from the 1880s to the 1960s, many French people could not conceive of metropolitan France without the Empire. The African Empire was perceived as a natural adjunct to its metropolitan geography: Paris–Algiers–Brazzaville. Following decolonization in the 1950s and 1960s, relatively little of that empire remains. But, in addition to its 96 metropolitan departments, France has retained four overseas departments (*DOM*) – Guadeloupe, Martinique, French Guiana and Réunion – and four overseas territories (*TOM*) – New Caledonia, French Polynesia, the French Southern and Antarctic lands, and Wallis and Futuna. To these must be added the 'territorial collectivities' of Mayotte and St Pierre-et-Miquelon. This peppering of worldwide possessions represents nonetheless an area the size of metropolitan France. As a French Foreign Ministry publicity brochure proudly proclaims, this gives France the world's third largest coastal area, after the USA and Britain, and an enormous 'exclusive economic zone'.[11] What the brochure does not say is that these possessions also allow France potential military access to a series of fixed 'aircraft carriers' in every ocean of the globe.[12] From one end of the century to the other geography remains a strong determinant of France's relations with the rest of the world.

Demography

In the course of the nineteenth century demography greatly affected the relative power of states. For centuries France had been the most populous country in Europe and hence the most powerful. Yet France's share of Europe's population declined from 15.7 per cent in 1800 to 9.7 per cent in 1900 and with it its power.[13] From being the second most populous of the six great powers (Prussia/Germany, Austria, France, Britain, Italy, Russia) in 1850, France shifted to being the least populous in 1913, Italy apart. By 1938, of the world's seven powers (Austria-Hungary having been replaced by the USA and Japan), France was now last. From 1850 to 1938 its population rose by a mere six million from 35.8 to 41.9 million, whereas Britain's jumped by 20 million from 27.6 to 47.6 million and what was to become Germany doubled from 34 to 68.5 million.[14] Ironically, France's population began to grow again after the Second World War when demography played a less significant role in great power status. At the beginning of the twenty-first century France's population is ranked twentieth in the world and fourth in Europe. It is on a par again with Britain (last seen a century ago) at 58 million. However, it has fallen well behind its traditional rival Germany following the latter's climb to 81 million on reunification, a renewed source of anxiety.

Population stagnation has affected France's interaction with the rest of the world. A low population density attracted surplus populations from abroad making it effectively at the beginning of the twentieth century the only European country of immigration. With an annual average net intake of 38,500 immigrants from 1881 to 1900, by 1901 it already had an immigrant population of just over one million representing 2.66 per cent of the total, to which should be added a further 0.59 per cent of naturalized citizens.[15] The very concept of French nationality, *jus solis* (nationality by country of birth), was introduced in 1889 to give automatic citizenship to French-born children of foreign parents so as to make them eligible for military service and allow France to compete with its potential enemy Germany, where *jus sanguinis* (nationality by inheritance) survived. High immigration and one of the highest percentage immigrant populations of any European country (or elsewhere) of between 6 and 7 per cent since 1931 remained a feature of the twentieth century, albeit with a few regressions in the late 1930s and after the Second World War. By the mid-1990s 14 million individuals – a quarter of the French population – were either immigrants or the children or grand-children of immigrants.[16] Immigration has been contingent on weak demo-graphic growth, relative prosperity and, from 1954 to 1965, when massive inflows reached 220,000 for 1957 alone, a dynamic economy short of manpower. Consequently the French – along with citizens of the USA – have long been one of the most racially mixed peoples of any state, a fact not without irony given the xenophobia of certain sections of French society.

The predominantly unskilled nature of the immigrant population has not changed, though its origins have. Whereas at the beginning of the twentieth century immigrants were mainly European and predominantly Italian (419,000 in 1913) with very few from the Empire, since the 1960s the proportion of immigrants from the Maghreb and sub-Saharan Africa has increased sharply to 45.8 per cent of the total in 1990.[17] The extent to which they have been tolerated has often varied according to economic activity. In the 1880s and 1890s during the economic depression, Belgians and Italians were the main targets. In 1892 Belgian workers and their families were forced to flee by the trainload. The following year the notorious Aigues Mortes riots in the south caused the death of at least eight Italians by ston-ing, clubbing or shooting. At the end of the twentieth century intolerance manifested itself less in terms of violence than in the shape of the overtly exclusionist French National Front Party, which polled 15 per cent of the 1997 general election vote. The presence of a large immigrant population not only affects how the French perceive the outside world; it is having more direct repercussions on France's strategic posture, with fears that the largely Muslim immigrant population could provide cover for terrorist groups sponsored by potential regional hegemons along the southern Mediterranean rim.

Absence of a growing indigenous French population also reduced emigration, with consequences for colonization and France's presence in the world. At the beginning of the twentieth century French emigration was under half Britain's, thereby denying France the influence the White Dominions conferred on the British Empire, or the family ties that could be the basis for popular sympathy with empire. In 1902 France had only 814,000 citizens in the colonies and 660,000 abroad,[18] so that even within the French Empire the French were not necessarily the dominant European group. In North Africa, Spaniards were the largest group in Algeria and Morocco, while in Tunisia it was the Italians – something that affected Franco-Italian relations over Tunisia.[19] More recently, the absence of a strong physical presence of citizens abroad (only 1.7 million) led to official exhortations in 1997 for the French to expatriate themselves.[20]

France's poor demographic performance has, of course, had strategic and economic repercussions. Population size was an essential ingredient in military power for as long as military effectiveness was linked to the number of combatants rather than technology. It operated in France's favour via conscription at the time of the French Revolution when France was well populated, but with France's relative demographic decline the advantage was reversed. The Franco-Prussian War was largely between equals demographically, but, with the subsequent development across Europe of compulsory military service, France found it increasingly onerous to keep up, especially with its potential enemy Germany. It was obliged to extend the length of its military service to three years in 1913 to compensate for the relative decline of its population with all the economic and manpower drain that provoked. On the eve of the First World War, 84 per cent of Frenchmen of military age actually carried out military service, compared with only 53 per cent in Germany. Desperate exhortations to procreate equated parenthood with military service, whilst women who had fewer than four children were deemed 'no better than deserters'. Contraception was denounced because 'with a few kilos of rubber the Kaiser can suppress thousands of future soldiers'.[21]

The demographic deficit resulting from the First World War and continuing demographic stagnation reached its nadir in the 1930s, becoming an increasing source of anxiety for French politicians, though glee for potential enemies. The Italian Foreign Minister, Count Ciano, declared in January

1939: 'The political significance of France as a great power must inevitably decline, because the annual deficit in births equates to a battle lost.'[22] Marshal Pétain conveniently – and exaggeratedly – used demographics as an excuse in 1940 when attributing France's defeat to 'Too few men, too few allies, too few arms'.

Things changed after the Second World War, which saw 600,000 French deaths. A baby boom had a profound effect on French morale as well as its economy. From 1946 to 1969 the French population increased by 10 million, almost as much as between 1800 and 1946. Fear of a return to demographic stagnation and anxiety about the strategic handicap of a small population have remained a national preoccupation, explaining the natalist policies designed to increase the birth rate by high family allowances, free nursery schooling and all manner of privileges for large families. But security was not the only motivation for demographic *dirigisme*. Most commentators agree that demographic and economic trends evolved in parallel.[23] Politicians, of right and left, understood the importance of a young, dynamic population to economic well-being, itself a considerable source of power in the world.

Economy

If the ultimate test of a great power is its potential for war, then one determinant must be economic strength. For centuries France was one of the wealthiest and most powerful nations, owing to its rich agriculture and thriving commerce and trade. One of the things this enabled it to do was to wage wars. In the sixteenth century the total length of major wars involving France was 44 years, in the seventeenth it was 52 years, in the eighteenth 51, in the nineteenth 19 and in the twentieth century it was 10 years.[24] As wars have become more 'total', so the cost of waging them has risen. The economist Alfred Sauvy calculated that, in terms of lost productive capacity, the 1914–18 war cost France 21 months of national income while in 1939–45 it was 50 months.[25]

Given the importance of economic development in determining a nation's power, it is important to have an overview of the relative performance of the French economy during the twentieth century, even if the picture is a complex one and economists disagree on causes and indicators. With the Industrial Revolution the nature of a country's wealth changed. France's prosperity, and with it its power and influence, was more open to challenge. In 1850 Britain was by far the most industrialized power and France the largest industrial power on the continent. By 1870 Germany had outstripped France in terms of coal production and equalled its iron and steel output, so that in economic terms the Franco-Prussian War was a war of equals.[26] By 1913 Germany's iron and steel production was four times that of France and just over double Britain's. Despite France being one of the victorious nations over Germany in the First World War, its coal and steel production was still less than one-third that of its eastern rival in 1920 and by 1938 had slipped to merely a quarter. In terms of per capita industrialization, France was about half that of Britain in 1913 and three-fifths that of Germany; by 1938 it was still half that of Britain but also half that of Germany. But the relative power of the French economy appears worse if it is remembered that per capita indices give a rosier picture of French economic performance because of its stagnating population.[27]

By 1870 Germany had put this wealth to military use and by 1890 was clearly the greatest military power on the European continent. France had tried to keep up with the British navy and the German army at the same time, placing considerable strain on its exchequer and national energies. The percentage of its national income devoted to defence was 4.8, about the same as Germany's (4.6 per cent) though greater than Britain's (3.4 per cent). But, given that its national income was lower than the two other powers, it had to spend more to keep up. By 1914 the strain was too much and its was slipping behind the other great powers. That decline continued in the inter-war years, justifying its complaint that, having won the war, it was losing the peace. Only after the Second World War would its economy be on a par once again with a truncated Germany's (something not seen since before1870) in terms of absolute and per capita performance (as well as population). In 1950, with roughly equal populations, France's GNP was restored to the level of West Germany's, although its GNP was just over three-quarters of Britain's and less than a seventh of the USA's. But in economic (and demographic) terms the tables were beginning to turn. Anxious to shrug off the humiliation of defeat and collaboration in the Second World War, stimulated by the post-war 'bébé boom' and primed by the 2 per cent of the Marshall Aid programme (the largest share of any nation) it had received by 1951, France embarked on a modernization of its economy and infrastructure that was to produce one of the most sustained and intense periods of economic expansion since the eighteenth century, even if marred by recurrent monetary and financial crises.[28] It progressively took France away from its rural roots and established it as a modern advanced industrial democracy.

From the beginning of the nineteenth century France had experienced a number of periods of rapid economic growth: 1850–70, 1896–1913, 1920–9. But these bursts of rapid growth seemed so only in relation to the longer sluggish eras. By comparison with most other advanced societies, over the long term France's growth rate was below average.[29] However, from 1947 until the 1970s the economy grew at a spectacular annual rate of around 5 per cent, double anything experienced before. These so-called 'thirty glorious years' enabled France, at last, to better the economic performance of many other advanced states, notably Britain. By the 1990s French politicians could claim that France was the world's fourth economic power after the

USA, Germany and Japan. Economic power laid the foundations for the modernization of its armed forces and defence posture.

Nevertheless, underlying structural problems remained in the French economy, such as the traditional reliance on former colonial markets. As economic growth evaporated in the 1980s and early 1990s, other weaknesses became apparent: poor productivity, high social costs and one of the highest tax rates in the world – 44 per cent of GDP compared with 33 per cent in Britain and 15 in Japan – a distended and overweening state sector with a quarter of the workforce directly on its payroll resulting in high public borrowing and a large national debt. A political reluctance to confront these problems in the 1980s and early 1990s led to a concomitant decline in French influence and power. France was unable to use economic prosperity to continue to bolster former colonial possessions, notably in Africa. It no longer had the financial might to sustain the old Gaullist dogma of national independence by maintaining a wholly national arms procurement policy and an independent defence strategy. However, by the end of the 1990s reform was underway to reduce the size of the state sector with a second raft of privatizations and to overhaul radically the complex tax system, much of which is unchanged since Napoleon created it. A restructuring of the confetti of armaments industries was begun with greater cross-border mergers to form a powerful European defence industry able to compete with the USA. But strict labour laws, the introduction of a 35-hour week, and reluctance to erode generous state benefits and abandon the French model of *service public* remain obstacles to competition.

One of the main features of what is sometimes referred to in France as the 'French economic model', with its reliance on state planning and state inter-vention, is protectionism. France has remained for over a century one of the most protectionist liberal economies. Often identified as Colbertism after its seventeenth-century initiator, French protectionism reached a peak in 1892 with the Méline tariff, but has continued to operate up to the present. Within the European Union France continues to press for protectionist policies, notably for agriculture. The protectionist reflex has made adjustment to globalization particularly difficult for this otherwise modern trading economy and France has slipped behind more open economies. In 2000 Britain's GDP overtook France's, reversing a trend since the early 1970s. At the dawn of the twenty-first century, with only 5.3 per cent of world trade (Britain 5.1 per cent), the state of France's economy is forcing it to relive some of the problems it was experiencing at the end of the nineteenth, then as now searching for security through closer defence cooperation, notably with Britain.

The economy may be a measure of a state's international influence, but states also interact with the world through economic and financial relations. Just as the City of London helped Britain to maintain an international influence above that conferred by its domestic economy, so France retained influence through the power of its banks. Although in 1914 only 9 per cent of France's overseas investments went to the Empire, compared to Britain's 45 per cent in its empire, France was Europe's banker (Russia included), investing 25.2 per cent of total foreign investment in Europe compared to Britain's mere 6 per cent. Financial might gave France powerful leverage, not least in diplomatic terms. After 1873 foreign access to French capital through the French Bourse was granted only after permission by the Foreign Ministry, making finance a potent instrument of diplomacy.[30] Finance played an important role in securing and bolstering the Franco-Russian alliance of 1894, which was the cornerstone of French security up to the First World War. Since 1947 the franc zone has provided financial stability and support to many of France's ex-colonies in exchange for diplomatic support, notably in the United Nations. In the 1990s Paris continued to grow as a financial capital, even if that no longer conferred the direct political and diplomatic leverage of a century earlier. In 1999 the Paris Bourse overtook the Frankfurt exchange for the first time in decades to become the largest on the European continent by capitalization, even if that was still only half the London Stock Exchange.[31] General de Gaulle always believed that finance and currency were important to international power and used them as instruments of diplomacy in the late 1960s in refusing to support the dollar and the pound sterling. However, beyond economics and material determinants other elements of a more abstract nature related to collective mentalities influence France's relations with the rest of the world.

The notion of collective mentalities and cultural values can be obscure phenomena, especially when applied to states. At their worst they can be simplistic and descend into national stereotypes. France, like most countries, is a raft of complex and contradictory mentalities often pulling in different directions. There is therefore no one coherent and fixed idea of what France is, but rather a kaleidoscope of images whose shape and colour mutate according to the angle of vision. But it is possible to detect certain traditions, attitudes, ideas and values, albeit perhaps characteristic of the elites, which have moulded the unspoken assumptions that underpin how France has perceived and reacted to the rest of the world. Three more abstract determinants in particular deserve mention for having influenced France's relations with the rest of the world.

The state

Throughout the nineteenth and twentieth centuries France was a land where state intervention and control were far greater than in most democratic states, although the ideologies for its justification changed. The bureaucrats and technocrats of the elite *grandes écoles* continue to obey the rules of an administrative law whose principles go back centuries. Its primary idea is that over and above individual interests there exists a 'general interest' that only the state can divine, and which it has the job of defending. The Revolution, then Napoleon and the Republics reinforced the notion of the state's monopoly on 'general interest'. But French citizens have retained an ambivalent attitude towards the state, both suspicious of, and dependent on, it. In many ways the solutions proposed by the state for French societies ills have become part of the problem. According to Stanley Hoffmann, a major preoccupation of French political history has been the attempt to strike a balance between stability and change, between playing a powerful role in the world and ensuring order at home, between the struggle against an authoritarian state and a state with a monopoly on the 'general interest'. The French state has been held responsible for having produced a 'bureaucratic phenomenon', a façade behind which the administration decides. This in turn has given rise to a 'stalemate society', where change is opposed by the elites until revolution radically overhauls the system.[32] Disagreements may continue over whether state intervention in France has been a good or a bad thing. Some suggest that it was a conservative force under the Third Republic denying the executive any real power and concentrating it in the hands of the legislative. Others suggest that it was expansionary under the Fourth and Fifth Republics – for instance, in the way it controlled and prioritized economic development through the system of five-year plans.[33] Nevertheless, particular conceptions of the state's role have clearly affected France's relations with the rest of the world. Amongst its citizens there has developed a culture, a reflex that the state will always provide a solution. The notion of the state as an active agent in wealth creation through foreign trade was already apparent in the mercantilist policies of the sixteenth and seventeenth centuries under men such as Colbert. Some have suggested that an over-reliance on the state explains the intense disillusionment that characterized large elements of French society in the 1990s. When confronted with increasing intervention from the European Union and 'globalization', the state was unable to intervene or was ineffective when it did so, provoking the impression that French national identity was being eroded.

At the core of the modern French state has been the law and the lawyer. Indeed, the importance of the law in France is all-pervasive. Even if the political class of many states has had close links with the law, in France it has been taken to extremes. Under the Third Republic (1870–1940) there was an overwhelming number of lawyers in French political life, especially *députés* and ministers – nearly half of *députés* elected in 1880 were from law faculties. In the 1906 Chamber the figure was still 40 per cent. It is not surprising that until 1914 the regime was known as the *République des juristes*. Even though this number declined after 1919, lawyers remained the largest socio-professional group until the end of the Third Republic and probably up to the Fifth Republic. According to Georges Burdeau, no one is better qualified than a lawyer to introduce order, prioritize objectives and develop compromises. But when it is a question of creating a new world, their competence is taxed. Certainly the presence of lawyers in French political life will have done nothing to reduce the obsession with constitution writing (16 different constitutions since 1789).[34] Nowadays the number of legally trained members of the political and administrative class has marginally diminished. However, criticism of a similar conservative and blinkered outlook is now reserved for the graduates of the École nationale d'administration (ENA) – the elite administrative training school – who populate the political and administrative class. The beliefs and unspoken assumptions of that French political and administrative class have, not unsurprisingly, had a profound impact on foreign policy formulation and execution and how France relates to the world.

National identity and the civilizing mission

One area where the state's influence has been pervasive is in the creation of a national identity. Robert Tombs has remarked that, if Italy in Metternich's phrase was merely a geographical expression, then 'France' was a political one given its unusual diversity of culture, family structure, belief and economic activity. Consequently, 'The nineteenth century saw a prolonged effort by the State to create in reality the organic national unity which the Revolution had proclaimed in theory.'[35] That reality was to a certain extent a construct, so that notions of 'France' and Frenchness were in many ways 'imagined'. Until wall maps were issued to schools in the 1880s, maps of France were practically non-existent. Significantly, most maps were of the regions, so that it was only on the eve of the First World War that people became familiar with the shape of France, the national hexagon, and their own position in it.[36] One of the many means used by the state to foster national unity was in how France imagined and defined itself in relation to the rest of the world.

One artifice was by emphasizing France's greatness. Indeed, the history of France's international relations over the nineteenth and twentieth centuries might be described as a tremendous over-investment in greatness. Paradoxically, in attempting to create a 'one and indivisible' nation, the Revolution created more divisions: between republican and royalist, catholic and anticlerical, and so on. Conflicting ideas about what the nation signified could only be countered by appeals to a more abstract and consensual notion of what being French meant. The idea of French greatness was nothing new, having been built on French cultural and political hegemony during the seventeenth and eighteenth centuries. In the eighteenth century Montesquieu had summarized it as 'this general passion the French nation has for glory'.[37] In the nineteenth century Alexis de Tocqueville understood the necessity for France to be involved in impressive enterprises to counter the centrifugal forces of political and material division. In 1840 he told John Stuart Mill: 'National pride is our greatest remaining sentiment.'[38] In the twentieth century General de Gaulle understood its potency as a unifier. At the beginning of his War Memoirs, referring to 1940, when the French state, let alone the economy and armed forces, was divided and devastated, he proclaimed:

> The positive side of my mind convinces me that France is not really itself except in the front rank, that only vast undertakings are capable of offsetting the disintegrating elements of its people. In short France cannot be France without greatness.

It follows that, almost independently of its material power, France has a right to international status because it is France; it is predestined to greatness. This aspect of the collective mentality has had a real impact on France's relations with the rest of the world.

The starting point was the conviction that French civilization was in important ways universal. The Enlightenment developed this, but the French Revolution gave it a particular spin. For democrats the French nation was above all the revolutionary nation, the prophet and standard-bearer of political progress and thus in a new way the universal civilization.[39] The concrete ideals of the Revolution – liberty, equality, fraternity – were to be established first in France, then in Europe, and eventually throughout the colonies and the world. They were encapsulated in the Universal Declaration of the Rights of Man and the Citizen. France was now at the apex of civilization. Robespierre proclaimed: 'The French people seems to have advanced 2000 years beyond the rest of humankind; one would be tempted to regard it . . . as a different species.'[40] Just as the birth of Christ was seen by the Catholic Church as the dawn of a new era and was marked by a new calendar for Western civilization, so the Revolutionaries began a new calendar to mark this momentous occasion for humanity. Revolutionaries of the mid-nineteenth century, such as Louis Blanc and Auguste Blanqui, insisted that all workers were brothers, and thus equal, but that Paris was the 'ville lumière', the font and capital of civilization. As with the Catholic Church, Messianism also flowed from this conviction of universalism: France had a duty and mission to bring the fruits of its civilization to less fortunate nations. Popular historians in the nineteenth century such as Jules Michelet relayed the message: 'France, Glorious Mother who is not ours alone!' or 'The Fatherland, my fatherland, alone can save the world.'[41]

This was accompanied by the idea that France, and the French, were essentially altruistic. This allowed the French to define themselves by what they were not. The French, said Louis Blanc, are an 'inspired nation'. The English, 'the anti-France', were not:

The principle of egotism is incarnate in the English people, the principle of devotion in the French people. England has set foot in no country without setting up its counting-houses. France has nowhere passed without leaving the perfume of her spirituality.[42]

France stressed its unity with desperate wish-fulfilment and its greatness as a diversion from inner divisions. Some would suggest with minimal success. Fernand Braudel in his *Identité de la France* remarked: 'Division is in the house of France, whose unity is merely an envelope, a superstructure, a wager.' He concurred with the remark that 'France is not a synchronized country; it resembles a horse each of whose feet would appear to move at different speeds'. These divisions have had dramatic consequences if the historian Marc Ferro, quoted by Braudel, is to be believed:

> France ... does not so much have the genius of arms as that of civil war. Except in 1914, it has never known the experience of a long and truly patriotic war ... Each of the wars waged by the nation with the greatest pride in its military glory has been more or less tinged with civil strife. What is clear for 1939–1945 was so also for the Revolution and the Empire, or the time of Joan of Arc and of the Burgundians, for Henri IV, the League and the time of Richelieu. Even in 1870, a party was to be found which, secretly or openly, desired the defeat of those who governed the country.[43]

Notwithstanding the apparent failure of policies designed to promote unity, the strategy of diverting the French people's attention abroad has not relented.

Belief in France being able to conceptualize what is in the interests of humanity was still alive at the end of the twentieth century. On 31 December 1967 General de Gaulle's New Year radio message to the French stated: 'Our action aims to attain linked objectives, and which, because they are French, respond to the interests of mankind.' On the left, the leader of the French Socialist Party, François Mitterrand, told the French National Assembly on 27 June 1975: 'This indefinable genius which allows it [France] to conceptualize and to express the deep needs of the human spirit'. During a trip to Belgium on 21 October 1975, the centre-right President of the Republic, Valéry Giscard d'Estaing, was unembarrassed about telling his audience: 'France is what is best.'[44] Back in 1966 the pro-European Jean Monnet club did not consider such utterances too kindly: 'The image that France has of itself has more to do in most cases with mythology or psychoanalysis than with political science. Nationalism is the reassuring temptation of a frustrated and divided people.'[45]

The civilizing mission has permeated French society and become a strand of the collective mentality. It has, in part, achieved its objective of developing a consensus and a degree of unity. Not only politicians and permanent officials believe in it. Opinion polls in the 1970s showed that the French believed that what characterized them above other nations was intelligence. The civilizing mission has also become important to understanding how France perceives itself in relation to the rest of the world. On 15 April 1961 President de Gaulle stated:

> France must fulfil its mission as a world power. We are everywhere in the world. There is no corner of the earth, where at a given time, men do not look to us and ask what France has to say. It is a great responsibility to be France, the humanizing power *par excellence*.[46]

Perceptions of France by others

How France perceives itself is inextricably linked to how it is perceived by other nations. This symbiosis has shaped its national identity and given it an international identity that has legitimized a world role. From medieval times until the twentieth century France was perceived by others as a warlike nation, which had always played a prominent role in European and world affairs. At times that role was perceived as hegemonic, at others it was believed that France would attempt to restore its hegemony over Europe. Even setting aside the Revolutionary and Napoleonic wars, in the century after 1815, France was characterized by war more than any other major European country. It was involved in eight wars or expeditions in Europe engaging in conflict with all the other continental Great Powers and fighting innumerable colonial campaigns at a cost of some 350,000 French soldiers lives, a toll exceeded only by Russia.[47] Indeed through revolution and war, both as cultural obsessions and periodic events, the French were made aware of belonging to the nation. This has shaped the collective memory. Certainly the French imagine themselves historically as a fighting nation from de Gaulle through Napoleon to the Revolutionary armies and the struggles of Vercingétorix against the conquering Romans, mythologized in popular culture today in the cartoon strips of *Asterix the Gaul*. The self-image is also that of France as oppressed nation or champion of the oppressed. The external perception of France as warlike nation could be an advantage in deterring potentially hostile nations, but also a disadvantage. Bismarck feared that France would attempt to restore its military power in Europe in the years following the 1870 Franco–Prussian War and kept it quarantined from diplomatic alliances for two decades. After the First World War Britain and the USA believed that France had a natural inclination to restore its supremacy over the European continent and that consequently they could not allow too great a diminution of German power. On the other hand, Churchill's belief that France as a military power was vital to European stability played an important part in it being elevated to victor status after the Second World War, despite four years of collaboration with Germany.

France's international identity and personality have also been based on the specific profile it has successfully projected of itself since the French Revolution in international eyes: that of the purveyor of universalist values and of culture through the medium of the French language. In the eighteenth century the writer Joseph de Maistre understood the power of the French language: 'What is referred to as the art of speaking is eminently the talent of the French, and it is by the art of speaking that one rules over men.'[48] Ever since the French Revolution language and national identity have been tightly meshed internally and externally. In the name of unity and equality, local languages and dialects were quashed to cement *la patrie française* via a linguistic community. Externally, France's international identity and role were founded and promoted on the basis of it being the fount of universalist values inextricably linked to French culture and language. As Braudel remarked: 'France is the French language.'[49] In 1941, when asked to describe what France represented, the writer Paul Valéry replied: 'The first thing to examine if one wishes to understand the mental life of this people and its development . . . is its language, the primary fruit of a nation.' This is where the notion of *Francophonie* has been so important in promoting a certain image of France through its language. The term itself is attributed to the nineteenth-century geographer Onésime Reclus, who wanted to bring together the people and territories where French was spoken. As a Republican and patriot Reclus believed that France could spread its ideals of liberty, equality and fraternity through French language and culture. The term fell into disuse, but was revived in 1962. By the late 1960s it was being used in official circles and had entered most dictionaries. The timing of this revival is significant in coinciding with the end of empire and the development of a post-colonial strategy. Francophonie took over where the empire had left off. Some 200 years after Joseph de Maistre, French President Valéry Giscard d'Estaing reiterated the importance of the French language and Francophonie to France as a world power:

> There is an interdependence between the economic power of a nation and the radiation of its culture . . . This is why the spread of French culture in the world must be ceaselessly reinforced and extended. This is why this linguistic and intellectual community one calls *francophonie* must be considered an essential element of our political policy.'[50]

A further element of France's international identity is its claim to be the country of rationality and clarity. A self-perpetuated nationalistic myth originating in the eighteenth century developed around the notion of French classicism.[51] According to this conceit, while Counter-Reformation Europe basked in the Baroque form, France pursued the classical with its

multiple rules to tame imagination and passion and distil them into a purer
state. This emphasis on form over content in everything from philosophy to
literature and gardens has been projected and perceived as quintessentially
French. The French were proud to utter Rivarol's claim of 1783 that
'Anything that is not clear is not French'. Elegance of style and form came
to be seen as intrinsically French, from writing to fashion. As the writer Paul
Valéry claimed in his 1927 *Images de la France*: 'France is perhaps the only
country where questions of pure form, a preoccupation with form for form's
sake, have persisted and dominated in the modern era.'[52] Obsession with
form and seeming clarity has had an impact on domestic and foreign politics.
On the negative side, the French appear obsessed with codifying and constitution making, and as having a legalistic outlook that has contributed to
an obsession with rules, regulations and a bureaucratic mentality. On the
positive side, the rational and clear French approach has produced models of
clarity such as the Napoleonic Code, still today the basis of much of the
Roman system of law on the European continent. At the international level
this preoccupation with form has clashed most often with its Anglo-Saxon
opposite of a pragmatic, empirical preoccupation with content over form,
which is at the heart of legal systems based on Common Law. Preoccupation
with clarity arguably explains the French predilection for the written record:
'legalistic at heart they only have faith in what is written down.' Emphasis on
the written could be so easily at odds with the English tendency towards the
notion of 'My word is my bond'. Cultural clashes along these lines have been
apparent between Britain and France over the sealing of an alliance before
the First World War and within the European Community, where a French-
dominated legal system and *modus operandi* have perplexed and frustrated
Britain.

It was Pierre Renouvin who brought to the study of international history
the notion of what he called 'profound forces' underpinning a state's relations
with the wider world. He chose geography, demography, economic and
financial issues as well as collective mentalities as key influences on decision
making. Of course, a case could be made to include other determinants.
However, it is important to understand how France integrated such elements
into organizing officially its relations with the wider world by looking at
how foreign policy was formulated and executed.

Notes

1 Charles de Gaulle, *Vers l'armée de métier* (Paris, Presses Pocket, 1989), p. 19.
2 On this, see Pierre Renouvin and Jean-Baptiste Duroselle, *Introduction à l'Histoire
   des Relations Internationales* (Paris, Armand Colin, 1966), pp. 7–22.
3 Max Tacel, *La France et le monde au XXe siècle* (Paris, Masson, 1989), pp. 9, 16.
4 Quoted in Renouvin and Duroselle, *Introduction*, p. 22.

5 Quoted in C. M. Andrew and A. S. Kanya Forstner, *France Overseas: The Great War and the Climax of French Imperial Expansion* (London, Thames & Hudson, 1981), p. 250.

6 See Fernand Braudel, *L'Identité de la France*, vol. 1, *Espace et histoire* (Paris, Arthaud-Flammarion, 1986), pp. 292–6.

7 Braudel, *Identité*, I. 294–5.

8 *Le Monde*, 20 May 1993.

9 Quoted in Braudel, *Identité*, I. 14.

10 Quoted in Alfred Grosser, *Affaires extérieures: La Politique de la France, 1944–1984* (Paris, Flammarion, 1984), p. 193.

11 *France, 1996* (Paris, La Documentation française et Ministère des affaires étrangères, 1996), p. 9.

12 See the 1994 French *Livre blanc sur la défense* (Paris, Sirpa, 1994), pp. 67–8, which cites protection of these overseas possessions as one of six scenarios for the intervention of France's armed forces.

13 Tacel, *France et le monde*, pp. 19–20.

14 Figures conflated from tables in A. J. P. Taylor, *The Struggle for Mastery in Europe 1848–1918* (Oxford, Oxford University Press, paperback edn, 1971), p. xxv, and Paul Kennedy, *The Rise and Fall of the Great Powers* (London, Unwin Hyman, 1988), p. 199.

15 Tacel, *France et le monde*, p. 20.

16 *France 1996*, p. 18.

17 *France 1996*, p. 18.

18 Tacel, *France et le monde*, p. 21.

19 René Girault, *Diplomatie européenne et impérialismes, 1871–1914* (Paris, Masson, 1979), p. 27.

20 *Le Monde*, 26–27 Oct. 1997.

21 Quoted in Tombs, *France*, pp. 53–4.

22 Quoted in Renouvin and Duroselle, *Introduction*, p. 31 n. 2.

23 François Caron, *An Economic History of Modern France* (London, Methuen, 1979), p. 183.

24 Cited in A Gueslin, *L'Etat, l'économie et la société française XIXe–Xxe siècle* (Paris, Hachette, 1992), p.11.

25 Gueslin, *L'Etat*, p. 12.

26 Taylor, *Struggle for Mastery*, p. xxx.

27 Tables in Kennedy, *Rise and Fall*, pp. 200–1.

28 Maurice Parodi, `Histoire récente de l'économie et de la société françaises, 1945–1970', in Georges Duby (ed.), *Histoire de la France* (Paris, Larousse, 1970), p. 557.

29 Parodi, `Histoire récente', p. 557.

30 Girault, *Diplomatie européenne*, table p. 42, pp. 43, 38.

31 *Financial Times*, 11 Nov. 1999.

32 Stanley Hoffmann, *Sur la France* (Paris, Seuil, 1976), pp. 12–13, 52–4 and *passim*.

33 Caron, *Economic History*, pp. 364–5.

34 Georges Burdeau, preface to Yves-Henri Gaudemet, *Les Juristes et la vie politique de la IIIe République* (Paris, PUF, 1970), pp. 5–6.

35 Tombs, *France*, p. 302.

36 Eugen Weber, *Peasants into Frenchmen: The Modernization of Rural France* (London, Chatto & Windus, paperback edn, 1979), p. 334.

37 Quoted in Jean-Baptiste Duroselle, 'Changes in French Foreign Policy since 1945', in Stanley Hoffman *et al.*, *In Search of France* (New York, Harper Torchbooks, 1963), p. 316.

38 Quoted in Douglas Johnson, 'Entente and Mésentente', in Douglas Johnson, François Bédarida and François Crouzet (eds), *France and Britain: Ten Centuries* (Folkestone, Dawson, 1980), p. 267.

39 Tombs, *France*, p. 313.

40 Quoted in Tombs, *France*, p. 1.

41 Quoted in Christopher Andrew and A. S. Kanya-Forstner, *France Overseas: The Great War and the Climax of French Imperial Expansion* (London, Thames & Hudson, 1981), p. 26; Tombs, *France*, p. 313.

42 Quoted in Andrew and Kanya-Forstner, *France Overseas*, p. 26.

43 Sanche de Gramont, *Les Français, portrait d'un peuple* (1970), p. 454; Marc Ferro, *La Grande Guerre, 1914–1918* (1969), p. 24, all quoted in Braudel, *Identité*, I. 104.

44 All quoted in Grosser, *Affaires extérieures*, pp. 319–20.

45 Quoted in Guy de Carmoy, *Les Politiques étrangères de la France 1944–1966* (Paris, La Table Ronde, 1967), p. 500.

46 Quoted in Duroselle, 'Changes in French Foreign Policy,' p. 353.

47 Tombs, *France*, p. 34.

48 J. de Maitre, *Correspondance*, 13 Dec. 1815, in *Œuvres completes . . . Nouvelle édition, contenant ses œuvres posthumes et toute sa correspondance inédite* (Lyons, 1884-7).

49 M. Rosenblum, *Mission to Civilize: The French Way* (San Diego, Harcourt Brace Jovanovich, 1986), p. 8.

50 David C. Gordon, *The French Language and National Identity* (The Hague, Mouton, 1978), p. 57.

51 See essays by C. E. J. Caldicott, G. Spielmann and others in Philip Tomlinson (ed.), *French Classical Theatre Today: Teaching, Research, Performance* (Amsterdam, Rodopi, 2001).

52 Quoted in Philippe Moreau Defarges, *La France dans le monde* (Paris, Hachette, 1994), p. 16.

2
Foreign policy formulation and execution: From Quai d'Orsay to Elysée

During the course of the twentieth century France lived under four different regimes: the Third, Fourth and Fifth Republics, with the unpleasant interlude of the Vichy regime from 1940 to 1944. For most of that period the foreign policy process did not alter dramatically, though in practice responsibility within the matrix shifted. The formulation and execution of foreign policy, the 'official mind' of diplomacy, preserved through its structure, bureaucracy and unspoken assumptions a good deal of independence from outside influences. So who makes foreign policy, officially and unofficially, in France and how? To a large extent the initiators, agents and influencers can be divided into two groups. First, there are what might be called the forces from below, comprising the Foreign Ministry and its diplomats and bureaucrats who execute foreign policy, the parliament, the military and finally the media and commercial, financial and industrial influences. Second, there are the forces from on high, which initiate foreign policy to a greater or lesser extent, beginning with the President of the Republic followed by the Président du conseil (later to be called the Prime Minister under the Fifth Republic) and finally the Foreign Minister.

THE FORCES FROM BELOW

Ministry of Foreign Affairs

The building from which foreign policy has traditionally been carried out is the Ministry of Foreign Affairs situated in the elegant building on the left bank of the Seine at 37 Quai d'Orsay. The Ministry has had the dual function of foreign policy formulation and execution – the former largely the prerogative of the permanent officials in the central administration, the latter devolved to the diplomats in the embassies of the foreign service. Since the late nineteenth century both bureaucrats and diplomats of the Ministry have been members of the diplomatic corps and theoretically were supposed to serve terms of duty abroad and in the central administration to guard against diplomats 'going native' and to ensure that the central administration got to understand foreign affairs 'in the field'. In practice, until the First World War such rotations of duty were not strictly carried out. As communications with embassies improved through better transport, telegraph and telephone, the power of the ambassador and his staff declined while that of the central administration, or 'bureaux', close to the reins of power, increased.

Bureaucrats

Gone are the days when 'bureaucratic politics', the role of permanent officials in policy formulation and execution, were overlooked in international history. Ministers rely on their officials for expertise and for the spadework of policy formulation. The officials' power resides in the advice they give to their political masters, which is partly contingent upon the mass of paperwork with which ministers are confronted. In 1947 alone France signed 160 international agreements.[1] In the 1980s 1000 telegrams arrived at the Quai d'Orsay every day, the most important of which were selected by the Minister's officials for his attention.[2] The volume of telegrams has continued to increase, leaving enormous scope for officials to influence policy making and its execution, directly or indirectly, wilfully or passively. At the beginning of the twentieth century, a diplomat confessed to having been told by one of his seniors at the beginning of his career: 'The incompetence of our parliamentary ministers . . . is their principal quality, it puts them at the will of the "bureaux".'[3]

The central administration at the Quai d'Orsay fluctuated in influence according to the power of the Minister and his longevity in office, which could be a matter of months under the unstable governments of the Third and Fourth Republics. In 1912 the experienced British ambassador in Paris reflected on the likely fortunes of the new incumbent at the Quai d'Orsay.

> So far as I am aware, M. Poincaré has no special aptitude for foreign affairs. In view of the enormous demands made on the energy and time of the head of Government in France, it is likely that any one holding that post as well as that of Foreign Minister, without previous experience of foreign affairs, will be very dependent on the officials of the Quai d'Orsay.[4]

This had not been the case from 1898 to 1905, when the Foreign Minister had been the very competent and experienced Théophile Delcassé. But from 1906 to 1911 the instability of French governments and ineffectual foreign ministers gave the 'bureaux' a free rein.

French permanent officials, like their British or German counterparts, were, and remain, prisoners of certain unspoken assumptions and ingrained prejudices, which they bring to decision making. These unspoken assumptions could be socially or educationally induced. Socially, many of the diplomats at the beginning of the twentieth century were from the Parisian upper *bourgeoisie*, if not the aristocracy (despite republican purges in the 1880s), with a discreet preference for the brothers, sons or nephews of diplomats. When competitive examinations were introduced in 1868 for the recruitment of attachés to the Foreign Ministry, the educated Parisian social elite was best placed to meet the challenge. The institution that most effectively prepared for the exam was the École libre des sciences politiques. Created in 1872 to fashion an administrative elite, which would prevent further military defeats, it was rapidly colonized by the Parisian elite, who could afford its high fees. The teaching was nationalistic, anti-German and often sceptical of republicanism, ideas often carried over into the 'bureaux'. Although British Foreign Office officials shared a common social background and education from the major public schools and the universities of Oxford and Cambridge, it was membership of a certain social order not the university curriculum that produced its cohesion and determined it modes of thinking. With 'Sciences po', the nature and aims of the education were far more narrowly focused on subjects such as history, international public and private law and economic geography, though little on economics and commerce. In effect, the School trained and equipped a new technocracy with similar ways of thinking and doing things. Gradually, the School gained a monopoly of recruits to the diplomatic career, so that from 1905 to 1927 some 80 per cent of recruits to the Foreign Ministry were graduates of the School.[5]

The School's Vichyite sympathies during the Second World War led to its nationalization in 1945. But the newly named Institut d'études politiques continued to act as the antechamber for the civil service and government. Since 1945 it has been aided and abetted by the Ecole nationale d'administration (ENA) – a super Sciences po, which accepts only 100 students a year. By 1997 ENA graduates included two of France's three previous presidents, six of the previous eight prime ministers, nearly all foreign ministers and between 20 and 50 per cent of government ministers since 1976, not to mention over two-thirds of the ministerial *directeurs de cabinet* as well as the leaders of all three of France's main political parties. This led one French political leader to remark: 'Ireland has the IRA, Spain has ETA, Italy the Mafia, but France has ENA.' High-flying jobs in the diplomatic service have been virtually conditional on having graduated from Sciences po and ENA, given that the subjects and modes of thinking required of candidates for the Foreign Office's highly competitive examination are closest to their teaching. The gravest charge made against the ENA in the 1990s was that of having a blinkered way of thinking and of doing things – *la pensée unique* – the consequence of which was that in foreign affairs, as elsewhere, new perspectives on old problems did not emerge.

During the 1997 presidential campaign Jacques Chirac, an ENA graduate, excoriated 'the dictatorship of a technocratic elite, allergic to reform, cut off from all reality, more talented at flattery than decision making'. However, once elected, he also chose *énarques* for the key posts on his staff and appointed another *énarque*, the former Foreign Minister Alain Juppé, to be Prime Minister.[6]

The 'bureaux' have been self-reproducing products of these institutions (to an extent not witnessed in the foreign offices of other great powers) and have not been embarrassed at various moments in France's foreign relations in promoting policies that ran contrary to those of their political masters. They were partly responsible for French hostility towards Germany before the First World War, even when official policy sought détente with it. In April 1911, Ambassador Jules Cambon told his brother Paul, ambassador to London: 'All these wretched people are sabotaging foreign policy as they have sabotaged the organization of the Ministry.'[7] Their obstructionism and aggressive actions led to the diplomatic showdown with Germany in 1911 at Agadir, which narrowly missed becoming war. In the inter-war years they helped promote a policy sympathetic to Germany even after Hitler had come to power in 1933.

Amongst the seemingly faceless bureaucrats, certain individuals came to have a control of foreign policy that rivalled that of the Minister. The Political Director at the Quai d'Orsay effectively headed the organization before the First World War, though his power did not go unchallenged by other departmental directors and the Minister's private office. For that reason the post of Secretary-General was created in 1915 to maintain continuity in foreign affairs and give overall responsibility for the coordination of work to one person along the lines of the Permanent Under-Secretary at the British Foreign Office. With the dual mandate of being head of the administration and permanent adviser to the Minister, the Secretary-General was expected to be the voice of neither one nor the other, but rather the central organ of policy formulation. He quickly became one of the most powerful personalities in French external policy.

During the inter-war years two men of considerable influence successively occupied the Secretary-General's chair. Both were protégés and disciples of the pliant and moderate former Premier and long-standing Foreign Minister, Aristide Briand, ultimately convinced of the need for compromise with Germany in the 1920s. The first was Philippe Berthelot, who occupied the post from September 1920 until December 1921 and then again from April 1925 until February 1934. He had exercised considerable influence over the Quai before and during the First World War when he had crossed swords with the likes of Premier and Foreign Minister Raymond Poincaré. By the 1920s Berthelot, unlike many politicians, was also convinced of the need to abandon confrontation for conciliation of Germany. His successor as

Secretary-General from 1934 to 1940 was the diplomat Alexis Léger. Under the pseudonym of St John Perse, he was part of a galaxy of talented diplomat-writers such as Paul Claudel and Jean Giraudoux able to combine the leisurely office hours with their literary inclinations. Léger surrounded himself with officials sympathetic to Germany, enabling a 'pro-Munich' ethos to triumph over the anti-Munich stance of other permanent officials in the so-called Protestant clan grouped around René Massigli. Certain of Léger's disciples took their pro-German sympathies to their logical end: Charles Rochat became Secretary-General under Vichy, for which he was sentenced to national disgrace at the Liberation.[8]

The Secretary-General was depicted as the power behind the throne. It has been said with some exaggeration that 'Foreign Ministers reigned but did not rule'.[9] This is not surprising, when foreign ministers came and went with the proverbial transience of Third Republican governments. Léger has been described as the 'permanent master of French foreign policy'.[10] Despite the unusual power it bestows on one individual, the post of Secretary-General is the only such office to have survived in the Ministry since 1915, largely because of the advantages it confers in terms of continuity and coordination.[11] When matched and controlled by equally competent political masters, as has been the case under the Fifth Republic, the Secretary General's functions are an essential ingredient in foreign policy making.

But over-powerful officials have not been the only problem in the French Foreign Ministry. A 1933 parliamentary report indicted the Quai d'Orsay for inadequate intelligence services, lack of administrative coherence and that hoary problem of insufficient coordination between the central administration and the diplomats on the ground.[12] Senate commissions in 1933 and 1938 came to the same conclusions. After the Second World War the National Assembly created a parliamentary commission to investigate events that led to defeat in 1940. The report was seriously critical of the foreign service, for being too wedded to the system rather than to political realities, and of permanent officials, for acting as barriers between the minister and diplomats in the field. Thus officials like Léger afforded little attention to ambassadors like André François-Poncet in Berlin, who warned of Germany's aggressive intentions in the years immediately preceding the war. In the hands of socially conservative officials, the Quai d'Orsay remained an inefficient machine where distrust of the modern means of communication such as telephones and mechanical cipher machines reigned at a time when the number of foreign missions increased between 1914 and 1939 from 404 to 526 just as the personnel was being reduced.[13]

Under the Fourth Republic the Quai d'Orsay's power began a gradual decline. The prestige of the Secretary-General, expected to promote the interests of his department, was undermined by a high turnover – four in the 12 years of its existence – and the fact that the post was given to only two career diplomats. The veteran political observer of French politics André Siegfried believed that the Quai was weakened because it 'had not known how to defend its personnel, which had become heterogeneous, against the intrusion of foreign elements, inspectors of Finance, academics or mere resistance personnel'.[14] At the Liberation the new political class was sceptical of functionaries who had continued to serve through the Occupation, even if some had rallied to 'la France Libre' in the nick of time. Approximately 150 officials from the Foreign Ministry were purged at the Liberation. But friction remained between those diplomats who had climbed the career ladder by the normal route and those who had been catapulted into high office through the Resistance in London or Algiers. Although in 1952 only a quarter of plenipotentiary ministers were career diplomats, during the course of the Fourth Republic almost half of the 16 key posts at the Quai were held by officials from outside the diplomatic service,[15] breaking the *esprit de corps* that had been the Quai's strength (though not France's) in the inter-war years.

Nevertheless, the bureaucratic politics of the Quai continued to exert tension on policy making. Whereas the inter-war years were characterized by the tension between Secretary-General and minister, under the Fourth Republic, like the pre-First World War period, tension was between different factions within the 'bureaux' – the anglophilia of some diplomats, the anglo-phobia of a number of General de Gaulle's supporters, but most serious of all, the acute differences of opinion on colonial policy and European integration. This explains contradictory remarks about the Quai during this period. Charles-André Julien claimed that 'the Sub-directorate for protectorates at the Ministry of Foreign Affairs determined Tunisian and Moroccan policy or rather ensured that there was not one'. On the other hand, Gilbert Grandval, Resident General in Morocco, praised the same department's 'luminous clairvoyance'. Meanwhile foreign ministers, such as Antoine Pinay and Christian Pineau, voiced suspicions about the Quai for what they claimed was permanent officials' hostility to the European Defence Community (EDC), while other sources were critical of it for being pro-EDC in 1954. In reality, the question of German rearmament divided the Quai as much as it did the nation.[16]

Under the Fifth Republic the influence of the bureaux has declined, owing to greater political stability ushered in by the 1958 Constitution and greater permanence of foreign ministers. Most of all, their control of the policy process has been arrested by the pre-eminent role in foreign affairs of the President of the Republic with his parallel team of advisers at the Elysée Palace who receive copies of Foreign Ministry telegrams. The bureaux have been progressively reduced to mere technicians limited to producing a stream of briefing papers.

Ambassadors

The influence of ambassadors under the Third, Fourth and Fifth Republics was inversely proportional to the Foreign Minister's. Prior to the First World War France had 10 embassies abroad staffed by ambassadors of whom the so-called *grands ambassadeurs* had considerable influence over their foreign ministers and foreign policy. Their permanence in the capitals of the great powers conferred on them independence, a prestige and power that far outweighed that of their transitory political masters, a fact enshrined in the protocol that theoretically, at least, gave them precedence over their own ministers. Thus Camille Barrère served in Rome from 1898 to 1925, Jules Jusserrand in Washington from 1902 to 1924 and Paul Cambon in London from 1898 to 1920, often making them household names. Some such as Paul Cambon had scornfully turned down offers of the foreign affairs portfolio, knowing that they could often impose policies of their own.

In the inter-war years ambassadorial heads of missions increased to 14, plus another 37 legations, of which only Austria, Czechoslovakia, Yugoslavia and Romania were of any real importance, while only one legation covered the whole of Central America. Apart from the Vatican, Switzerland, Belgium, Argentina, Brazil, Turkey and Spain, embassies were still reserved for the great powers of Britain, Germany, Italy, the Soviet Union, the USA, Japan and, sign of the times, Poland. But ambassadors were what counted, even if their influence was in decline. No ambassador stayed in post longer than André François-Poncet in Berlin from October 1931 to October 1938. The problem during the inter-war years was that some of the most far-sighted ambassadors in strategic capitals such as Berlin, Warsaw or Moscow who warned of impending dangers were short-circuited in negotiations by incompetent or unsympathetic ministers or a hostile Léger.[17] In many ways, it was a repetition of what the French ambassador in Berlin, Jules Cambon, had experienced, in seeking détente with Germany from 1907 to 1914.[18]

Under the Fourth Republic ambassadorial influence continued to decline with improved transport and communications and the greater centralization of policy making at the Quai d'Orsay. A more personal diplomacy conducted directly by heads of government and foreign ministers, albeit underway in the inter-war years, was increasingly the trend among the great powers.

Under the Fifth Republic the trend towards 'summitry' has accelerated as foreign policy making has shifted away from the Foreign Ministry to the President of the Republic. De Gaulle took Article 13 of the new constitution, whereby the President appoints ambassadors and 'envoyés extra-ordinaires', to mean that they were his personal envoys. These envoys, rather than ambassadors, became household names, such as Jacques Foccart for African affairs under de Gaulle and Pompidou, or the ubiquitous Jacques Attali for President Mitterrand from 1981 to 1991.

Though new roles have been found for diplomats in acting as permanent representatives to international organizations such as the European Union, the work is more liaison and administrative than political. Consequently, the prestige of the diplomatic service has continued to wane, as it has with other powers. Traditionally, the diplomatic service was the prestige corps for the ENA elite. High-flying ENA graduates have followed the general shift of power to the executive or to the Finance Ministry at the expense of the Foreign Ministry. The Finance Inspectorate, Council of State and Court of Accounts have outdistanced diplomacy as choice destinations.

Parliament

The lingering fear of Bonapartist coups d'état constitutions limited the executive's power while bolstering that of the legislative under the Third and Fourth Republics. Parliament's pre-eminent role led to unstable governments with an average life span of nine months for the Third Republic and six months for the Fourth, making both into *régimes d'Assemblée* in which the *député* was king. But the *député*'s interest lay in getting re-elected and therefore of concentrating on domestic issues liable to produce more immediate and tangible benefits for his constituents. This explains the *clientèlisme* that so characterized both Republics. There was little mileage to be gained from an interest in foreign affairs and so parliament took little interest in them. Parliament's absence of influence over foreign affairs was largely its own choosing. Cabinet ministers, let alone parliament, were not informed until 1914 of the details of the Franco-Russian Alliance of 1892–94, the cornerstone of French foreign policy, which bore a commitment to war.

Ironically, the parliamentary regime with the greatest potential for controlling foreign affairs was not interested in them. Under the first half of the Third Republic the upper chamber, the Senate, had no Foreign Affairs Commission until 1915, with treaties and agreements being studied by the Customs and Colonies Commission. A request in 1907 for such a commission was rejected. Things were marginally better in the lower house, the Chamber of Deputies, where a Foreign Affairs commission sat. Although its reports were thorough, they were of little interest to other parliamentarians and so carried little weight. A further opportunity for parliament to influence foreign affairs was through parliamentary questions, whether written or oral, but these, along with parliamentary debates on foreign affairs were severely limited. To a large extent parliament was a rubber stamp in foreign policy.

Things improved slightly after the First World War, but the parochialism of French politics remained. This was so despite the average Frenchman's heightened interest in foreign affairs owing to the impact on his everyday life of phenomena such as the League of Nations, disarmament, reparations, Wilsonian and Briand ideals. From 1919 to 1940 the French parliament remained more interested in domestic than foreign affairs. Senator Charles Reibel, member of the Senate Foreign Affairs Committee, could justifiably declare in 1939: 'On the whole, our country hardly follows foreign affairs.'[19] The Munich crisis came and went without parliament even being consulted. Parliamentary committees played a role, but that was almost exclusively restricted to information gathering rather than influencing policy making; they were 'channels of information about foreign policy, rather than agencies in making it'.[20]

Though the legislative dominated the executive under the Third and Fourth Republics, foreign affairs were an exception. Under the first two legislatures of the Fourth Republic from January 1947 until December 1955 of the 87 votes of confidence held only 18 concerned foreign affairs in the broadest possible sense. Debates on foreign affairs were rare; none took place on the 1950–53 Korean War. Parliamentary oral questions had to be put down eight days in advance, virtually eliminating them as ways of reacting immediately to foreign events, and the parliamentary foreign affairs commissions lost much of the authority they wielded under the Third Republic. The parliament was not even called upon to ratify the granting of independence to Tunisia and Morocco in 1955–56. Overall the Fourth Republic parliament 'suffers foreign policy more than it contributes to making it'.[21] Isolated cases such as the French Assembly's debate and final rejection of the 1954 European Defence Community Treaty were exceptions that proved the executive's rule.

The Fifth Republic's 'reversal of the previous relationship in the executive's favour has merely served to bring the formal position into line with the real situation'. A few parliamentary questions apart, the legislative has been content with *a posteriori* oversight, leaving the formulation and execution of foreign policy to the executive. Even that oversight is of a largely symbolic nature: debating a government foreign policy declaration (where no vote is taken) parliament may be asked to ratify a treaty but cannot unilaterally amend its provisions. More thorough scrutiny of foreign policy can come from the Foreign Affairs and Finance committees of the Assembly and Senate, when they hear testimony from the Foreign Minister or his junior several times a year, or at discussion of the Foreign Ministry's budget. Even then, according to one expert, eminent parliamentarians are likely to be little better informed than are readers of *Le Monde*.[22]

Military

The role of the military increased in late-nineteenth-century Europe as societies became more militarized. Military service, the greater emphasis on plans for war, such as the German Schlieffen Plan and the notorious French Plan XVII, and the need to mobilize rapidly in order to strike an immediate and decisive blow at the enemy demanded greater integration of the military in foreign policy making. Their expertise was called upon in the expanding areas of espionage, counter-espionage and intelligence assessments of potential enemies (see Chapter 4 on intelligence). In France, generals were made ambassadors to key posts: three were dispatched to Russia between 1871 and 1886. Nearly every embassy gained a military attaché, sometimes two or three for the different services. Their reports, ranging from defence to economic, social and political issues, were passed to their service chiefs only after first being presented to the ambassador. During the inter-war years the role of the 26 military, 10 naval, and 11 airforce attachés (created in 1920) was most important (as was that of the financial attachés like Jacques Rueff in London). Officially they were not allowed to spy on the country to which they were accredited, but some did (Commandant Fustier was expelled from Brussels in 1939).[23] Nevertheless, what this apparently positive picture hid was the poor liaison and coordination of diplomacy and defence in the policy-making process, which dogged France for at least half of the twentieth century.

Before the First World War the coordination of French strategy and foreign policy was fitful and inadequate. An attempt had been made in 1906 to bring the two together through the Conseil supérieur de la défense nationale, a committee composed of defence chiefs, ministers and civil servants. However, in the eight years leading up to the war it met only 15 times and even then only really discussed the conduct of operations. It had no planning section until 1921. Lack of coordination between foreign and defence policy led to the Quai d'Orsay failing to inform the General Staff of the details of the 1902 Franco-Italian convention, which neutralized Italy's position in the hostile Triple Alliance. As a consequence, for seven years two army corps were pointlessly stationed in the Alps.

Harmonization of defence and foreign policy making remained a problem during the inter-war years. A centralized structure existed for this purpose but, as was so often the case with French institutions, it was used erratically. Until 1936 the *haut comité militaire* and the *conseil supérieur de la guerre* were supposed to coordinate defence policy, but their unwieldy size, sporadic meetings and a preference for unofficial channels of communication made this difficult. The *haut comité militaire* had been created in 1932 with a view to streamlining decision making by bringing together the Premier, service ministers, chiefs of staff, and vice-presidents of the supreme councils of the armed forces, but the Foreign Minister had the status only of an observer and only eight meetings had been held by January 1935. In 1936 Premier Léon Blum reformed it to produce the Comité permanent de la défense nationale, of which the Foreign Minister was a member, but it met a mere 13 times in the three years before the Second World War.[24]

The consequence of defence and diplomatic lack of coordination was that in the inter-war years, according to Jean–Baptiste Duroselle, France had strategies that were at odds with each other. The Quai d'Orsay's was based on reliance on Britain and France's East European allies, whom it would be necessary to defend in the event of attack. The military's strategy by the 1930s was chiefly designed around a defensive posture and a fortress France protected by the Maginot Line.[25] They had little faith in the military worth of their eastern allies, as Pétain told Foreign Minister Pierre Laval in 1935, when the latter confessed to thinking they represented 'something substantial'.[26] Moreover, with no offensive strategy, France was unable to come to the aid of its eastern allies when Germany began to pick them off. France could only huddle behind its fortifications and wait for the German attack. As Robert Young has put it: what 'was needed was allies who would go to war for France but who would not make France go to war'.[27] In that way, absence of coordination between diplomacy and defence contributed to the catastrophic defeat of 1940.

With that defeat firmly in mind, General de Gaulle, as head of the post-war provisional government of the Republic, passed the 1946 decree reorganizing French defence into a unified structure that dispensed with the separate service ministries and placed defence squarely in the hands of the Premier. Within a year of de Gaulle's resignation in 1946, the new Fourth Republic, suspicious of centralized control and blessed from the outset with the imperfections of its predecessor, diffused and dispersed power to other ministers, to parliament and to the generals. The Defence Minister was denied control of the Indochina and Algerian Wars, which racked France from 1946, thereby undermining political control and coordination with French diplomacy until the demise of the regime. The interministerial Defence Committee descended into confusion and paralysis at the hands of quarrelling government coalition partners, leaving the way open for the military to take matters into their own hands, choosing which ministers to obey and finally refusing to obey at all. Absence of coordination, absence of organization and absence of order quickly succeeded each other, until in 1958 a military revolt brought the whole regime to its knees.[28]

Under the Fifth Republic, coordination of defence and foreign policy was aided considerably by the vesting of responsibility for both in the hands of the President with his seven-year mandate. Apart from foreign policy being constitutionally the President's *domaine réservé*, he also chairs the Defence Council and according to the decree of 18 July 1962 controls 'the overall framework of national defence'. Though the same decree created the General Secretariat of National Defence (SGDN) nominally under the Prime Minister's office, the fact that its main function was to service meetings of the Defence Council put it firmly in the grasp of the Elysée. The 14 January 1964 decree gave sole responsibility for firing France's nuclear weapon to the President, while that of 10 December 1971 gave

him authority over the Joint Chiefs of Staff.[29] Even when the President has
been of a different political persuasion from his Prime Minister, under so-
called *cohabitation*, as from 1986 to 1988, 1993 to 1995 and 1997 to 2002,
presidential coordination and control of foreign and defence policy appear
to have been maintained, though tested on occasions. This has much to do
with the consensus reigning in French foreign and defence policy since at
least the late 1970s. As Prime Minister Jacques Chirac told *Le Monde* on 8
July 1987 after a year of *cohabitation* with President François Mitterrand:
'Since we are fortunate enough in France to have general agreement on
these matters, there have been no difficulties between the President and the
government.'[30]

Media

The relationship between a government's foreign policy making and the
media, whether printed, audio or visual, is an ambivalent one. Since the
advent of a widened franchise in the nineteenth century (France had
universal male suffrage from 1848) and a mass popular press from the 1880s,
both have craved the support of a similar constituency, that elusive entity
'public opinion'. Most French politicians (and newspaper editors) would not
have disagreed with the Whig Foreign Secretary Lord Clarendon in 1869:
'Governments no more than individuals can afford nowadays to despise
public opinion . . .'.[31] How one defined public opinion is a moot point. Many
politicians equated the press with public opinion, so that, if governments had
the support of the press (and later the other media), they carried public
opinion. Conversely, so much press coverage was given over to politics and
foreign affairs that newspapers needed the politicians. This symbiotic
relationship was taken to an extreme in France, where the press and politics
seriously overlapped under the Third Republic.

Following the rapid introduction of the telephone to the press after 1885,
foreign news was covered more widely, aided by the development of the
large news agencies, of whom Reuters in London and Havas in Paris
dominated the world. The geographical extent of Havas's news agencies, the
quality of its information and the solicitude shown to its correspondents by
foreign, as well as French, governments put it in a commanding position as
far as influencing policy making was concerned. This was soon the case for
many French national newspapers. At its creation in 1883 *Le Matin* devoted
some 50 per cent of its coverage to foreign affairs. This was more than most
of the major French dailies, for which a still substantial average of 15–20 per
cent was the norm. How foreign affairs were covered was of considerable
concern to French politicians and diplomats. Few politicians, and no
ministers, felt they could survive without tame newspaper editors. This was
made easier by most successful politicians under the Third Republic having

been, or continuing to be, journalists or newspaper proprietors. Many foreign ministers, in France and abroad, feared the pen of the former diplomat turned foreign news editor of the influential daily *Le Temps*, André Tardieu, later to become Premier in the inter-war years. The German Chancellor, von Bülow, said of him: 'There are 6 great powers in the world, the 7th is M. Tardieu.'[32] The influence that he and other journalists exercised over weak foreign ministers or adoring permanent officials and diplomats was considerable. His articles were read by foreign powers and often perceived as the semi-official voice of the Quai d'Orsay. Raymond Poincaré, as Premier and Foreign Minister in 1912, always eager to court press praise, regularly consulted him on policy issues.

The press was also used to influence foreign policy making in a negative way. Members of the 'bureaux', diplomats or politicians regularly leaked sensitive material to the press to sabotage foreign policies with which they disagreed or to promote their own ideas. Ministers would also use the press to test out potential policies on public opinion. In the first half of the twentieth century Paris had the reputation as the 'leak' capital of Europe, much to the annoyance of foreign diplomats and governments, who rejected Paris for London as the venue for the ambassadorial conference to settle the First Balkan War in December 1912. Things changed little in the inter-war years, provoking Neville Chamberlain's acerbic remark in 1938: 'France suffers from two faults, which reduce by a half the value of her friendship; she cannot keep a secret more than half an hour, nor a government more than nine months.'[33]

During the inter-war years foreign ministers received twice a day the diplomatic correspondents of the major dailies, as well as seeing the foreign press corps regularly, as General de Gaulle would do under the Fifth Republic. Foreign affairs journalists might be offered decorations such as the *légion d'honneur* as sweeteners by the Quai d'Orsay.

It could be said that such practices were unexceptional for any power. The difference was that the Third Republic's press was known to be corrupt and open to 'subsidies' from its own government and foreign powers intent on influencing French foreign policy. Before the First World War it was generally acknowledged that Russia and Italy had certain newspaper editors in their pay. Partly for that reason the French press played a considerable role after the inception of the Franco-Russian Alliance in promoting a sanitized and flattering picture of the autocratic Tsar, his regime and society to Republican France, home of the Universal Declaration of the Rights of Man. A high-ranking Russian permanent official was permanently posted in Paris to distribute these funds and could justifiably write to his minister about the 'abominable venality of the French press'.[34] The French government might turn a blind eye to these practices, where they benefited French foreign policy. However, they appear to have been unaware of the scale of German moneys dispensed to newspaper editors. One such recipient was Ernest Judet of the influential Paris daily *L'Eclair*, who was eventually accused and tried in 1920 for receiving money from Germany and for consorting with the enemy. Many parliamentarians were also 'subsidized' by foreign governments before, during and after the First World War to promote policies in flagrant contradiction with official policy.[35] In the 1920s the USA was said to have spent 'enormous sums in the French press to influence public opinion'. From 1935 Italy became a principal banker of French newspapers. It was also alleged that British Intelligence and the Trades Union Congress made payments to certain newspapers.[36] Newspaper policy could follow the highest bidder and change radically as a consequence. Because this could influence public opinion and limit policy-makers' freedom of manœuvre, the French government was also active in providing subsidies from its notorious secret funds (*fonds secrets*).

To this end a formal Foreign Ministry press department was established in 1920 (though one existed before the First World War as part of the *cabinet du ministre*). From 1925 to 1930 every major ministry had a press office with a group of journalists on its payroll who received their 'handouts'. Pierre Laval and André Tardieu encouraged senior government departments to distribute monthly 'envelopes' to journalists and newspapers. The Havas news agency was a particular target for its intrinsic influence, but also because it had majority stakes in Radio Luxembourg and other radio stations. During the inter-war years much of the French press was owned by right-wing political or business interests and was thus fairly pro-Munich and sympathetic to Foreign Minister Georges Bonnet. The influential *Le Temps* was by this time owned by powerful coal, iron and steel interests and was very pro-Munich, even though its Prague correspondent, Hubert Beuve Méry, resigned in October 1938 over Munich. He was to become the paper's editor after the Second World War, when, following its punishment for having continued to publish under the Occupation, it re-emerged as *Le Monde*. In the post-war period *Le Monde* was often regarded as a semi-official organ of the French government, albeit more independent than its predecessor.[37] Thus the pro-German policy of the Daladier government went unchallenged, especially after decrees in 1939 restricted the press's freedom to give offence to foreign powers.

The idea that news should be controlled continued at the Quai d'Orsay under the Fourth Republic through the Service d'information et de presse, which gave regular press briefings. However, few important foreign correspondents and French journalists ever attended these gatherings, preferring to approach the minister's Cabinet directly. The three most influential newspapers for foreign affairs in reverse order were: *France-Soir*, for its remarkable network of foreign correspondents who were themselves often involved in international negotiations; *Le Figaro*, for being the semi-official organ of the Foreign Ministry, supporting for instance the EDC; *Le Monde* for its more guarded support of official foreign policy. French radio, the RTF, was firmly under government control and was allowed no independence or impartiality. Even so, these organs represented only a small sample of the media. Many others were severely critical of various foreign-policy initiatives, or lack of them.[38] For all their attempts to marshal information effectively, governments were not able to manipulate public opinion to anything like their satisfaction. This was partly because it was not always clear what their own views were, so divided were the parties that made up the government coalitions and the permanent officials who serviced them. These divisions and contradictory views were not restricted to foreign affairs; the problem was the general weakness of the Fourth Republic regime, whose demise would not be long in coming.

Under the Fifth Republic the media have had very little influence on policy making. General de Gaulle took little notice of their views and exploited the opportunities offered to him by the media quite unashamedly to promote the President's views on foreign policy. Press conferences were, according to de Gaulle's own admission, arranged in advance by his press officer to confirm an aspect of his foreign policy and 'rouse the national spirit'.[39] The state-run radio and television organization, the ORTF, was the mouthpiece of government. De Gaulle's successor to the presidency, Georges Pompidou, warned that being a journalist at the ORTF was not like being a journalist elsewhere. State control over the media has all but gone. Today journalists are allowed to set the questions themselves at the presidential press conferences, but searching questions are usually dodged without a murmur, such is the profession's self-censorship. Now when the Foreign Minister wants to explain the government's official position on an international question, he receives a number of hand-picked French or foreign journalists for an informal chat. Routine contact with the press is through the head of the Quai's press office, who holds a daily press conference. With decision making closeted away in the Elysée, it is now much harder for the media to play any part in the policy-making process.

Financial, industrial and commercial influences

The degree to which financial, industrial and commercial interests influence policy making is unclear. French banks were certainly influential on French foreign policy at the end of the nineteenth and early twentieth centuries when France was Europe's banker. They and the Paris Bourse were instrumental in bringing about a Franco-Russian rapprochement through loans in the 1880s, providing the opening France needed to escape from diplomatic isolation. France used finance as a lever in attempting to draw Italy out of the Triple Alliance between 1898 and 1902. In the decade before the First

World War, French banks and financiers encouraged closer relations with Germany through lucrative joint investment projects with their German counterparts in the Ottoman Empire, Scandinavia, South America and China.[40]

Similarly, a number of large industrial and commercial companies from steel and coal to insurance were happy to encourage better political relations with Germany, as trade between the two countries continued to grow in the decades before the First World War. They successfully lobbied French diplomats for a rapprochement with Germany until Franco-German relations suffered after the 1911 Agadir incident. In the 1930s French industrial interests, such as iron and steel and the perfume magnate François Coty, provided support for the French 'fascist' *ligues*. Their encouragement of closer relations with Nazi Germany contributed indirectly to a pro-Munich foreign policy.

Under the Fourth Republic the Confédération générale des petites et moyennes entreprises was opposed to the Schuman Plan for a European coal and steel community and the EDC. Its attitude was protectionist, but with a large admixture of nationalism, characteristic of the 1950s populist Poujadist movement. The Banque de Paris et des Pays Bas had interests in Morocco, which it attempted to defend against Moroccan independence. The Banque d'Indochine and the Compagnie de Suez encouraged the 1956 Franco-British expedition against nationalization of the Suez Canal by Colonel Nasser. Marcel Boussac, the cotton magnate, and the French cotton industry appear to have torpedoed a Franco-Italian customs union. The Schuman Plan was also opposed by the chemical, mechanical and steel industries, which saw in it the decline of their trade. But overall, according to Alfred Grosser, there was certainly no concerted effort of French 'bosses' or capitalism in any one direction, whether over policy in Indochina, Morocco or Algeria.[41]

Under the Fifth Republic the role of financial, industrial and commercial interests in policy making is less clear. However, one particularly strong lobby is that surrounding arms manufacture in the military-industrial complex. General de Gaulle was insistent that France should reclaim its national independence from the American dominated Western bloc, partly through a national arms procurement policy supplied by an indigenous defence industry. Economies of scale and the huge sums needed for capital development projects could be acquired and sustained only by an aggressive and occasionally unscrupulous arms export policy. The sale of corvettes to Israel, nuclear power stations to Pakistan and South Africa and Mirage jet fighters to unpopular and repressive foreign regimes may have made France into the world's third largest arms exporter by the 1970s, but it flew in the face of world opinion, if not arms embargoes, and gave a negative international image of the country and complicated foreign policy making. Imperatives imposed by the defence industry steered policy-makers in directions in which they did not wish to go. In the 1980s, President François Mitterrand may have believed in European defence cooperation and in the need to make defence budget savings, but the defence industry lobby won the day in imposing on him and a reluctant military establishment the French *Rafale* combat aircraft with its astronomical price tag, ending French participation in the five-nation European fighter aircraft.[42]

Many of the financial, commercial and industrial interests are themselves used as instruments of policy, most notably in the former French Empire and the francophone zone. This was easy because of the 1945 nationalization of banks, large swathes of industry from energy to defence, Air France and Renault. Companies such as Air France, Elf or Total were until privatization in the 1990s used as foreign-policy intermediaries or as parallel intelligence networks, according to the former head of France's foreign intelligence services from 1981 to 1982.[43]

THE FORCES FROM ON HIGH

These then were the influences on foreign-policy formulation and decision making. To a degree this is the unofficial mind of French decision making. What then of the official mind, that of the political masters in the executive and their role in the process?

French foreign policy making from the Third Republic to the present is to all intents and purposes the work of a triumvirate of President of the Republic, Premier and Foreign Minister. Over the course of the twentieth century power oscillated between these individuals and their staff.

President of the Republic

It is often believed that under the Third Republic the President of the Republic had a purely ceremonial role. The veteran 'toppler of governments', Georges Clemenceau, likened the usefulness of the office to the prostate gland. He believed that the presidential function should remain limited to 'opening flower shows' and harangued parliamentarians at presidential elections 'to vote for the stupidest candidate'. Unlike the lower chamber, the President was not elected by universal suffrage and was politically irresponsible. However, the role of the President according to the three constitutional laws of 1875 was potentially powerful, especially in foreign affairs. The President commanded the armed forces; he appointed to all military and civil posts (which included ambassadors); foreign envoys and ambassadors were accredited to him; he negotiated and ratified treaties, and informed parliament of them only when the interests and the security of the state allowed (the Franco-Russian Alliance was ratified by the President alone). Even though many of these prerogatives demanded a ministerial countersignature, with a seven-year mandate, the right to choose the head of government, to suggest a foreign minister and to chair Cabinet meetings, the President could effectively make foreign affairs his domain.[44]

However, throughout much of the Third Republic there was a gap between theory and practice. The coup d'état of 16 May 1877 taught the embryonic Republic a lesson: the presidential right of dissolution fell into disuse and henceforth Presidents of the Republic were expected to be feeble creatures. And for much of the Third Republic they were; only occasionally did strong personalities revive the dormant powers, like President Raymond Poincaré from 1913 to 1920. Unusually, before becoming President he had been a leading politician, who had made his mark as Premier and Foreign minister. He made the President's role much more like that of his successors under the Fifth Republic. Having outlined the main tenets of his foreign policy in 1912, once in the Elysée from 1913 he ensured that the grand designs of his policy were rigidly adhered to by a judicious selection of premiers and foreign ministers.

To a large extent, presidential influence on foreign affairs was conditional on the President being able to control the head of government and Foreign Minister. When in 1917 the direction the war was taking obliged Poincaré to appoint the forceful and independent Clemenceau to the premiership, the President's power over foreign policy was severely reduced.

With Alexandre Millerand's election to the Elysée in 1920, an attempt was made to reactivate Poincaré's successful use of the presidential role in foreign affairs. This worked so long as the Chamber and government were of similar political colouring as the President. Even then it provoked several confrontations, ironically with Poincaré himself. When the latter returned as Premier and Foreign Minister in 1922 he was reluctant to carry out Millerand's demand that France occupy the Ruhr in 1923 to secure German reparations. Poincaré succumbed, but further high-handedness from the Elysée in the 1924 elections led the incoming left administration to force Millerand's resignation. This would be the last attempt under the Third Republic by the President to play an active role in foreign policy making.

Under the Fourth Republic, once again the constitution conferred on a politically irresponsible President of the Republic substantial possibilities for action. He chose the names of candidates for Président du conseil (the premiership), chaired Cabinet meetings and drew up the minutes, appointed ambassadors, generals and members of the Conseil supérieur and of the Comité de défense nationale, over which he also presided. He was to be kept informed of treaty negotiations, then signed and ratified them; foreign envoys and ambassadors were accredited to him. The President 'commands the armed forces', although this prerogative was removed by the law of 7 December 1954. He had the responsibility of representing the interests of the Union française, the French equivalent of the British Commonwealth. The only limits imposed on these powers were that they required a countersignature of the Premier and a minister.

The first president of the Fourth Republic, Vincent Auriol, made full use of these powers in attempting to steer policy towards a more severe treatment of Germany and in favour of retaining France's colonies. Though Auriol was not always successful, he has been described by a historian of the presidential office as 'the most influential personality in the country, which, apart from Thiers, was not the case of any of his Third Republic predecessors'.[45] However, his successor, René Coty, was more in the tradition of the majority of his Third Republican predecessors: ageing grey men unwilling to overstep the tradition of inaction in foreign affairs and to do anything other than support government policy. Only under the Fifth Republic have constitutional theory and practice been brought squarely into line over foreign affairs.

The 1958 Fifth Republic constitution set out to change the power distribution between executive and legislature to the clear benefit of the former. That shift was hammered home by the 6 November 1962 constitutional amendment whereby the President of the Republic was to be elected by direct universal suffrage, conferring on him greater legitimacy than the National Assembly. It was helped by the first incumbent being General de Gaulle, a tested exceptional leader of international stature. Foreign and defence policy were his keys to France's revival as a power of the first rank. It is in the foreign and defence realms that the President's role has significantly increased. He is responsible for the general direction of foreign policy and for taking major decisions of international importance. According to Article 5, 'he is the guarantor of national independence, of territorial integrity, of respect for Community agreements and of treaties'. Article 15 stipulates that the President is 'chief of the armed forces' and chairs the 'conseils et comités supérieurs de la défense nationale'. Since 1964 he has had sole responsibility for firing France's nuclear weapon. De Gaulle's successors Georges Pompidou (1969–74), Valéry Giscard d'Estaing (1974–81), François Mitterrand (1981–95) and Jacques Chirac (1995–2002) have all attempted to maintain the Gaullist mystique of distance to keep foreign and defence policy part of the presidential 'reserved domain'. Even during cohabitation from 1986 to 1988 and again from March 1993 to May 1995 the President's virtual monopoly of foreign and defence policy was not successfully eroded. In March 1995 the right-wing victory in the Chamber did, however, give rise to speculation that socialist President Mitterrand was taking steps to reinforce the technical means at his disposal for directing foreign policy from the Elysée, in the event of the new Foreign Minister wishing to take over foreign policy. Rumour had it that he would have vetoed the appointment of an anti-European foreign minister. Following President Chirac's miscalculation in dissolving the National Assembly and calling early elections in March 1997, in the hope of reinforcing his right-wing parliamentary majority, which led to a substantial left-wing victory, the President experienced a marginal loss of authority in foreign policy making. Even so, with general consensus on the main tenets of France's diplomacy, this had little visible impact.

Given the President of the Republic's prominence in foreign affairs, it is not surprising that his staff at the Elysée have acquired considerable influence, led by the Secretary-General, often a diplomat. His role has become increasingly focused on foreign affairs.[46] Under de Gaulle and Pompidou presidential staff, civilian and military, averaged 45. But under Giscard d'Estaing numbers dropped to around 31 and rose again under Mitterrand to some 47.[47] Both Pompidou and Giscard were suspicious of the Quai d'Orsay and concentrated even more power at the Elysée. The Elysée staff organize the interministerial councils and committees, where coordination takes place between the President's diplomatic advisers and the Premier's and Foreign Minister's personal staff. They receive copies of diplomatic telegrams and have become a foreign office in miniature.

Prime Minister

Under the Third and Fourth Republics the Prime Minister was supposed to coordinate foreign policy with other government departments. In reality, his interest in foreign affairs was usually slight, as domestic politics were what made or broke parliamentary majorities. At the beginning of the century, when discussion in Cabinet turned to foreign affairs, Premier Emile Combes famously remarked: 'Leave that, Gentlemen, that is the business of Monsieur le Président de la République and Monsieur le Ministre des Affaires Etrangères.'[48] The only real exception to this unspoken rule was when the Premier combined his office with that of the Foreign Ministry. Between 1871 and 1918 28 per cent of premiers did so; from 1919 to 1939 this rose to 53 per cent and dropped to 15 per cent from 1944 to 1958.[49] But the sheer weight of business of the two offices overwhelmed the most industrious individual and lead to other agencies exercising greater influence over policy making and execution, as happened under the Fourth Republic.

Under the Fifth Republic the Prime Minister has held no other office. Although his role has been strengthened, in foreign policy making this is less so. His role has largely been to coordinate the overall policy of the government as determined by the President, even though constitutionally he has important powers in foreign and defence policy (Articles 10 and 21). Most premiers have accepted taking a back seat in these areas. Jacques Chirac attempted to challenge presidential dominance during cohabitation under Mitterrand but was unsuccessful.

The Cabinet rarely discussed foreign affairs under the Third Republic. Under the Fourth Republic, party loyalties in shifting coalitions made any discussion of foreign affairs (and other issues) divisive. This led to immobilism and a tendency for officials, at home and abroad, to take matters into their own hands. Under the Fifth Republic there is even less scope for the Cabinet, chaired by the President, to influence policy making, even though it receives a weekly summary of foreign affairs from the Foreign Minister. The Cabinet generally ratifies decisions taken at the Elysée.

Minister of Foreign Affairs

Under the Third and Fourth Republics the Foreign Minister theoretically had sole responsibility for foreign policy. In reality, and depending on personalities, he shared responsibility with the President of the Republic, the Premier and, increasingly as the century progressed, with a host of other 'technical' ministries. His power was also determined by the permanent hazard of ministerial instability, even if the Foreign Ministry portfolio was a good deal more stable than most. Delcassé remained at the Quai d'Orsay from 1898 to 1905, achieving a great deal by tightening France's diplomatic alliances; Aristide Briand pursued a conciliatory policy towards Germany from 1925 to 1932.

It might be considered a sign of relative longevity that, from 10 September 1944 until 13 May 1958, France had 25 governments, 17 premiers, but only seven foreign ministers (two of whom were also premier).[50] Even so, few seem to have made much of a mark on foreign policy.

Under the Fifth Republic the Foreign Minister is responsible for the detailed implementation and defence of the President's policy through day-to-day diplomatic activities. When he formed his 1958 government, General de Gaulle stated that he was giving four posts to civil servants who 'would be more directly under my wing': the Foreign Ministry went to Ambassador Couve de Murville and defence to engineer Pierre Guillaumat. The aim was to deny both any responsibility for policy formulation. Couve was in place for 10 crucial years during which France's national independence was underlined. He recognized in his memoirs how he and the General were in agreement and that at their Friday morning meetings they discussed only 'ways and means and timing'.[51] Things have continued in this vein with President Mitterrand asserting in 1983, after jettisoning his outspoken Overseas Development Minister, 'It is I who determine France's foreign policy, not my ministers.'[52]

Ironically, over the twentieth century, as the Foreign Ministry's spheres of interest have extended, for instance to Europe, so the Foreign Minister's power has declined. With the spectacular increase in summitry and the importance of personal chemistry between leaders, the President of the Republic's control of policy making remains supreme.

Despite different regimes the same agents have continued to participate in foreign policy making. Fluctuations in their degree of influence have been more a result of individual personalities and styles of leadership than theoretical constitutional prerogatives. This was true of the President of the Republic under the Third and Fourth Republics. Under the Fifth Republic the President's constitutional powers, in theory and in practice, have been aligned and nowhere is that more true than in foreign and defence policy making. The Fifth Republic has legalized the *de facto* position whereby under the Third and Fourth Republics foreign affairs was the prerogative of the executive. Today the French President's powers in foreign and defence policy extend well beyond those enjoyed by any other democratic leader.

Notes

1 Alfred Grosser, *La IVe République et sa politique extérieure* (Paris, Armand Colin, 1961), p. 75.
2 J. E. S. Hayward, *Governing France: The One and Indivisible French Republic* (2nd edn, London, Weidenfeld & Nicolson, 1983), p. 245.
3 Comte de Saint Aulaire, *Confession d'un vieux diplomate* (Paris, 1953), p. 31.
4 Quoted in J. F. V. Keiger, *France and the Origins of the First World War* (London, Macmillan, 1983), p. 53.
5 Keiger, *France and the Origins*, pp. 25–43.
6 *The Economist*, 9 Aug. 1997, pp. 32–4.
7 Quoted in Keiger, *France and the Origins*, p. 36.
8 Jean-Baptiste Duroselle, *La Décadence 1932–1939* (Paris, Imprimerie Nationale, 1979), pp. 269–75; Anthony Adamthwaite, *France and the Coming of the Second World War 1936–1939* (London, Frank Cass, 1977), p. 137.
9 Adamthwaite, *France and the Coming*, p. 138.
10 Quoted in Adamthwaite, *France and the Coming*, p. 138.
11 Hayward, *Governing France,*, pp. 244–5.
12 Adamthwaite, *France and the Coming*, p. 139.
13 Adamthwaite, *France and the Coming*, pp. 137–40.
14 Quoted in Grosser, *IVe République*, p. 68.
15 Grosser, *IVe République,*, pp. 22–3, 69.
16 Quoted in Grosser, *IVe République*, p. 72.
17 Duroselle, *Décadence*, pp. 276–81.
18 J. F. V. Keiger, 'Jules Cambon and Franco-German Détente 1907–1914', *Historical Journal*, 26/3 (1983), pp. 641–59.
19 Adamthwaite, *France and the Coming*, p. 125.
20 Quoted in Adamthwaite, *France and the Coming*, p. 135.
21 Grosser, *IVe République*, pp. 81–101.
22 Hayward, *Governing France*, pp. 246–7.

23 Duroselle, *Décadence*, pp. 281–7.

24 Adamthwaite, *Grandeur and Misery: France's Bid for Power in Europe 1914–1940* (London, Arnold, 1995), pp. 157–61.

25 Jean-Baptiste Duroselle, *Tout empire périra: Une vision théorique des relations internationales* (Paris, Publications de la Sorbonne, 1981), p. 65.

26 Martin Alexander, *The Republic in Danger: General Maurice Gamelin and the Politics of French Defence, 1933-1940* (Cambridge, Cambridge University Press, 1992), p. 215.

27 R.J.Young, 'The Aftermath of Munich:The Course of French Diplomacy, October 1938 to March 1939', *French Historical Studies*, 8/2 (Fall 1973), pp. 305–22.

28 Hayward, *Governing France*, pp. 265–66.

29 Jolyon Howorth, 'The President's Special Role in Foreign and Defence Policy', in Jack Hayward (ed.), *De Gaulle to Mitterrand: Presidential Power in France* (New York, New York University Press, 1993), pp. 152–3.

30 Howorth, 'The President's Special Role', p. 160.

31 Quoted in Paul Kennedy, *The Realities behind Diplomacy: Background Influences on British External Policy, 1865–1980* (London, Fontana, 1981), p. 51.

32 Rudolph Binion, *Defeated Leaders,* New York, Columbia University Press, 1960, p. 237.

33 Quoted in Grosser, *IVe République*, p. 60.

34 Girault, *Diplomatie européenne*, pp. 49–50.

35 J. F.V. Keiger, *Raymond Poincaré* (Cambridge, Cambridge University Press, 1997), pp. 195–201.

36 Adamthwaite, *France and the Coming*, pp. 143–4.

37 Adamthwaite, *France and the Coming*, pp. 144–5.

38 Grosser, *IVe République*, pp. 76–8, 161–71.

39 Hayward, *Governing France*, p. 247.

40 Raymond Poidevin and Jacques Bariéty, *Les Relations franco-allemandes 1815–1975* (Paris, Armand Colin, 1977), pp. 158–61, 180–2.

41 Grosser, *IVe République*, pp. 151–5.

42 Edward A Kolodziej, *Making and Marketing Arms: The French Experience and its Implications for the International System* (Princeton, Princeton University Press, 1987), pp. 59–60; Howorth, 'President's Special Role', pp. 180–1.

43 Pierre Marion, *La Mission impossible: A la tête des service secrets* (Paris, Calmann-Lévy, 1991).

44 Jean-Marie Mayeur, *La Vie politique sous la Troisième République 1870–1940* (Paris, Seuil, 1984), pp. 98–101.

45 A. Dansette, *Histoire des Présidents de la République* (Paris, 1953), p. 326, quoted in Grosser, *IVe République*, pp. 47–8.

46 Howorth, 'President's Special Role', pp.174–80.

47 Anne Stevens, 'The President and his Staff', in Hayward (ed), *De Gaulle to Mitterrand*, pp. 80–1.

48 Quoted in Grosser, *IVe République*, p. 40.

49 Hayward, *Governing France*, p. 243.

50 Grosser, *IVe République*, pp. 62–4.

51 Quoted in Hayward, *Governing France*, p. 243.

52 Quoted in Howorth, 'President's Special Role', p. 168.

3
Strategy and defence

Constraints on strategy

How France best organizes its military might for its own security and to promote its national interests is pivotal to an understanding of its relations with the world. But, as with any country, France's defence posture is affected by a national strategic culture, a set of assumptions, attitudes and policies towards defence and security that arise from history, geography, political culture, self-perception, as well as how others perceive it. As General de Gaulle remarked in *La France et son Armée*, the French are 'a people whose genius, whether in eclipse or in glory, has always found its faithful reflection in the mirror of its army'.[1]

In democracies, military power is controlled by civilian authorities that determine what they consider to be vital national interests. In general one might expect there to be consensus on the fundamental issue of a nation's security such as the avoidance of war, or, in the event of war, maintenance of territorial integrity. However, there may be political differences of opinion on how best to organize strategically for the supreme eventuality of war. There may be an even greater divergence of opinion on peacetime defence and security priorities and how they should be aligned with national interests: conquest or status quo, grandeur or resignation, politics or the economy, overseas or European priorities.[2] Then there is the extent to which strategically desirable postures fit with what is economically feasible, so that strategy is as much about economic constraints as political ones. The permutations are rendered more complex by the choices afforded by technical developments, notably when nuclear weapons became so important to French security after the Second World War. These are examples of the choices or dilemmas that have faced French decision-makers since 1870. The extent to which France should or should not try to 'punch above its weight' in the world is as dependent on how France perceives itself and the world as on more objective military and diplomatic priorities.

Strategy, being about the calculation of aims, means and risks, needs first to be decided upon, then formulated and finally executed. Its implementation is the result of coordination between diplomats and military –the former persuade and negotiate; the latter represent 'the big stick' to threaten war or military action. The military must, therefore, be consulted on strategy, and the degree to which their influence is felt will vary according to political circumstance and the extent to which military force is being applied. Not surprisingly, the French military's influence increased markedly during the First World War, and from 1939 to 1940 and after the Second World War when wars of decolonization were being fought in Indochina and then Algeria.

Although these issues apply to most states, in France's case long-standing troubled civil–military relations have complicated them. Since the Revolution France has often been governed by soldiers, from Napoleon to de Gaulle – but not by the army. But in no other major European country of the nine-teenth century, other than Spain and Russia, has armed force been so frequently used at home. Paradoxically, despite political instability, the army never attempted to impose its own political solution, even standing aside at crucial moments in the face of challenges to the political order, earning itself the label of 'la grande muette'. This can be explained partly by France living through the nineteenth century in a state of at least cold war with its neigh-bours, making the army's overriding task that of defending the frontiers; and partly by soldiers' realization that their interests and those of the army were better furthered by steering clear of political involvement.[3] Nevertheless, a large body of republican opinion continued to regard the military with suspicion, even though republicanism was by no means absent from their ranks. Incidents such as Boulangism, when the popular War Minister General Boulanger looked like staging a coup in the 1880s to do away with the republican regime, or the Dreyfus Affair of the 1890s, when the army became associated with reactionary ideals, reinforced negative perceptions of the military, particularly on the left. These perceptions were reinforced in the twentieth century when military cynicism towards the political authorities led to displays of insubordination, mutiny and even the demise of the regime in 1958. Mutual suspicion between civilian and military authorities affected French military strategy and defence.

The French army has also been since the nineteenth century a far more heterogeneous body than in Britain and Germany. The imperatives of continental preparedness and colonial warfare on a power of dwindling demographic strength, together with the political nicety of ensuring that the army did not become a Pretorian Guard, imposed the necessity of mass conscription. Military service, born with the French Revolution, intended to forge a nation of soldier-citizens, became the 'blood tax' that from 1889 was to be paid, in theory, by all citizens of the nation. Though unpopular, it was presented as the national melting pot of Republican values, a guarantee against military dictatorship, surviving until 2002 and determining the nature of the army and what it could be expected to do. This political function complicated its strategic activities and occasionally made it almost inoperable, as was evident during the 1991 Gulf War. Whole regiments had to be stripped of their conscripts and reassembled with only professional soldiers to allow them to fight in a modern overseas war, as casualties among conscripts would have been politically damaging. Not for the first time did the French have to confront the issue of whether they were creating an army to be politically reliable or militarily effective.

The French army's revolutionary roots have also affected strategy. The Revolution's notion that the French conscript army was superior because it encapsulated the unique unity and brotherhood of the nation influenced, at various moments, French military thinking and defence planning until the First World War with emphasis laid on spontaneity, not planning; guts, not brains; morale, not numbers; cold steel, not advanced technology,[4] and a supercilious disregard for potential enemies.

Of further significance was that for most of the period from 1870 until 1962 French strategic priorities faced the dilemma of a continental versus an overseas commitment. France conspicuously refused to choose between the two, often with dire consequences.

The evolution of France's defence posture up to 1918

The primary determinant of French strategy for at least three-quarters of a century after 1871 was Germany. To have one clear potential enemy, against which the entire national resources could be concentrated, might be considered an advantage. But until July 1918 France was largely reacting to German initiatives. Everything, it could be said, started with the Franco-Prussian War. In material terms this may have been a war of equals, but in strategic terms France fought it in a desperately inferior position. French strategy had taken insufficient account of the Prussian army reforms. In 1857 Moltke the elder had established the General Staff (non-existent in France at this time); a better use was made of reserves and armaments, especially artillery, and the railways. All were woven together into more efficient mobilization, concentration and deployment. By comparison the French were using an out-of-date military system. Even though they possessed a roughly equivalent population to the Germans, French forces would be outnumbered two to one. Yet their self-perception – derived from historical military complacency – was of overwhelming superiority. That in turn determined French strategy, which was so characterized by the 'offensive' that it was said that maps of French territory were not even issued to officers who asked for them at the outbreak of the Franco-Prussian War. Such was the collective psyche of the offensive that French travel agents were taking bookings for Emperor Napoleon III's triumphant entry into Berlin. This had disastrous results: the French armies of the Second Empire were defeated in a mere six weeks. Henceforth Germany would provide the essential impetus for French strategic planning.

But Germany was not France's only security threat. In keeping France isolated diplomatically, Bismarck also sought to sublimate France's energies by encouraging it to develop the empire with the potential bonus of bringing it into conflict with other powers. France obliged. By the late 1880s it was challenging Britain in Egypt and West Africa, and Italy in North Africa. This heightened France's strategic dilemma. It was obliged to divide its defence attention between the so-called blue line of the Vosges on its eastern frontier, while developing its maritime forces to compete with the Royal Navy and Italy. This dispersal of effort was all the more foolhardy as France attempted to take on powers where they were strongest: Germany on land in Europe and Britain at sea abroad. Ironically, provoking Italy, 'the least of the great powers', was the most costly in defence terms. It risked invoking the Triple Alliance and bringing in Rome's German ally; for the army it meant stationing several divisions along France's south-eastern frontier and for the navy it highlighted the age-old strategic dilemma of having to maintain sizeable naval forces in both the Mediterranean and the Atlantic.

France's poor choice of adversary from a strategic point of view appears rarely to have been the fault of the military. The transience of Third Republican governments little interested in defence and foreign affairs allowed permanent officials, diplomats, colonial governors and colonial lobbyists to pursue policies that lacked overall strategic coherence and led to Germany, Britain and Italy being at various times, occasionally simultaneously, adversaries. Party politics and ministerial instability also had a direct impact on strategic planning through the high turnover of ministers of War and Marine. Some were appointed on purely political grounds, others, more dangerously, because they had firmly held beliefs about strategy. Though the navy attracted large sums of money, the varying strategic views of its ministers ensured that it was badly spent. Building programmes went first on a *guerre de course* (commerce-raiding) strategy of small ships and then on battleships, so that in the 1880s and 1890s the French navy had a motley collection of craft that was no match for its British or, later, German counterparts. Politics also took their toll of the army as it lurched from one political preference to the other. War Minister General Boulanger attempted to radicalize the army from 1886 to 1888, while seeking a war of *revanche* against Germany. A succession of incompetent war ministers aligned the army with the reactionary elements of French society – notably the church – to defend the miscarriage of justice that was the Dreyfus Affair at the end of the 1890s. The resulting discredit heaped on the military ushered in a new republican purge under the anti-clerical General André from 1900 to 1904, whereby officers' career advancement was measured by how little they attended church according to records (*fiches*) kept by the soundly republican Freemasons. The sacrifice of military efficiency and morale to politics only began to be reversed just two years before the outbreak of the First World War.[5]   Despite this handicap, France's defence posture vis-à-vis Germany began to improve from 1882, at least psychologically. Gradually the construction of new fortifications along its eastern border, the adoption of new artillery and the steady progress of the military laws of the early Third Republic allowed the French to countenance the possibility of a defensive war with some confidence. The 1891 Franco-Russian Alliance reinforced French security and allowed it to adopt for the first time since 1870 an offensive strategy in Lorraine supported by the new 75 mm gun adopted in 1898, which was superior to German artillery pieces. From this point onwards French strategy, as outlined in its 20 different campaign plans from 1875 to 1914 (though only 17 were numbered), was increasingly offensive, so that the infamous Plan XVII used in 1914 was said to be 'so offensive that even the customs officers attack'. But the more offensive they became, the less the plans prepared for a German attack through Belgium. Plan XVII concentrated the army along a line from only Maubeuge to Belfort, unlike its predecessors IV to XV, and even XVI, which had covered the eventuality of a surprise attack through Belgium. A further problem with Plan XVII was that it was primarily a concentration plan, whereas its German counterpart was both a concentration and an operational plan.[6]

The problem was that French military strategy of the 'outright offensive' was predicated on the irrational belief of French superiority over Germany. French strategists attempted to defy perhaps not gravity, but numbers, by cultivating the old Napoleonic dictum of 'the morale is to the physical as two to one'. The idea that the offensive was the best way of mobilizing morale appeared vindicated during the revolutionary wars, most notably at the Battle of Valmy in 1793, but then the French had numbers on their side. Yet by 1905, in the event of general mobilization, Germany was able to field about half as many troops again as France. Fortunately, although the military prepared for the eventuality of war, the politicians did not want to start one. The problem was partly France's inaccurate assessment of its potential enemy Germany before 1914, based on poor intelligence and inadequate use of it, and partly the inappropriate and inflexible strategy of the offensive. Thus the French High Command misjudged both the strength and the direction of the German attack and quite wrongly based French strategy on offensive operations, the élan of the infantry and an early victory. As one military historian has observed: 'Rarely had a military organization entered a conflict with such a serious and complete misunderstanding of the nature of the fighting that their troops would undergo.'[7] One is tempted to add, at least not since 1870. The slaughter of the Battle of the Frontiers in eastern France in August 1914 was the devastating consequence.

Reinforcing France's belief in its own superiority was the contribution that the Empire was thought to make, supported by its being in 1914 the fourth ranking naval power (by fleet tonnage) in the world. Talking up 'Greater France' of a 100 million inhabitants, as many contemporaries did, could not but encourage hubris. Of course the Republic had inherited from Napoleon III's Second Empire a second army, the African army, made up of colonial troops and units from metropolitan France, professional and conscript. The Third Republic had also developed a third army, the colonial army, made up of professionals. Although these helped reinforce France's military position, they were no compensation for France's demographic inferiority vis-à-vis Germany and for the fact that France strained to keep up militarily by conscripting 80 per cent of its eligible youth, with all the economic and political drawbacks. Against France's five million men in the requisite age group, Germany had 10 million, allowing it to mobilize vast numbers of reserves. There was also the issue of quality: German reserves were better trained, as were its 112,000 NCOs (compared to France's 48,000). With France's GNP running at only 55 per cent of Germany's in 1913 and its share of world manufacturing production around 40 per cent of Germany's, France struggled to fund the military effort. At the outbreak of war a French report catalogued Germany's superiority of *matériel*: '4,500 machine guns to 2,500 in France, 6,000 77 millimetre cannon to 3,800 French 75s, and an almost total monopoly in heavy artillery.'[8] Belief in a short war, calculations based on the number of divisions that could be instantly mobilized, rather than the war potential of German steel and chemical industries, plus the military support France expected from Russia, and rather optimistically from Britain, added to the general atmosphere of wishful thinking that suffused French defence policy on the eve of the First World War.

The course of the war taught the French army lessons about the new kind of warfare, particularly on the Western Front, where firepower and not the spirit of the infantry was the key to success in land warfare, particularly after the French offensive had ground to a halt in Lorraine with the loss of over 600,000 men. The French lost 1.5 million men in total. Arguably the French navy's chief contribution to the war effort was to provide safe passage for colonial troops to fight on the Western Front and in major peripheral theatres such as Gallipoli and Salonika. This *Force noire*, as it was termed by General Charles Mangin, a leading commander of overseas troops, provided 569,000 North African and colonial troops, which were vital in filling the gaps left by French casualties in 1914–15. France also learnt how difficult it was to coordinate military strategy with its Russian ally on the other side of Europe, despite the combined superiority in army strengths at the outbreak of the conflict. As the war quickly proved not to be over by Christmas, so the importance of stamina not speed was crucial, as the proportion of national income devoted to armaments rose from 4 per cent on average in 1914 to 25 or 33 per cent in the new 'total war'.[9] Consequently, the financial, industrial and diplomatic power of France's British ally became essential in raising loans, supplying ammunition to all of the Allies and arguably in bringing in Italy and ensuring the benevolence of the USA, let alone the direct support of the Dominions and India. Even though the French and Russians did the brunt of the work in checking the German armies for the first two years of the conflict, until in 1916 Haig's army rose to more than a million, it is clear that France and Russia alone would not have been able to defeat the Central Powers in what had become a long drawn-out 'total' war. As Europe's armies were stalemated, so the defensive came to dominate military thought, particularly after 1917–18 showed it to be the most effective mode of combat. But the German attempts to bleed the French to death by repeated assaults on the Verdun redoubt in 1916 and the reckless assaults by General Nivelle in 1917 pushed the French to their limits, as the widespread mutinies of that year demonstrated. This was to mould the thinking of the High Command and shape the new verities behind military strategy in the 1920s and 1930s. It would be reinforced by the key presence in those years of Marshal Philippe Pétain, the 'saviour of Verdun', the enlightened queller of the 1917 French infantry mutinies and author of the potent aphorism that 'firepower kills'.

France emerged from the war a victor, but only as part of a vital coalition with the USA and Britain, which would soon disintegrate. Feeling that its security was still vulnerable to Germany from 1919 to 1925, its defence strategy remained fixed to the execution of the Versailles Peace Treaty. Here it was not supported by the powerful 'Anglo-Saxons'. Moreover, its moral position was undermined by the international climate of pacifism and desire for collective solutions for international peace typified by the newly established League of Nations. Its defence policy was more fundamentally constrained (like Britain's) by two other factors: first, it was clearly a declining great power on to whom was cast the role of world policeman following the American withdrawal into isolation in the inter-war years; second, it remained the second largest colonial power at a time when empire was becoming increasingly difficult to maintain. Over the longer term it would be confronted by the inability to coordinate strategy with the modern exigencies of war, culminating in defeat in 1940 and the loss of its independent strategic ability for four years.

The importance of Versailles

France emerged from the First World War still firmly impaled on the horns of its age-old dilemma of a continental versus an overseas strategy. But the European dimension dominated from 1919 to 1926. The Versailles strategy appeared the only credible guarantee of French security. Occupation of the left bank of the Rhine was perceived as vital to French security by providing the means for a rapid strike at the heart of Germany to meet any German threat. This 'forward defence'[10] was seen in military terms as the best way of avoiding another long war with its eastern neighbour, when it eventually recovered, by denying it the possibility of mobilizing its massive war potential. Without it, as Marshal Foch, Allied Supreme Commander, famously predicted after Versailles, the peace would be 'but a 20-year truce'. Occupation of the Rhineland also provided France with the ability quickly to come to the military aid of its new eastern European allies Poland, Czechoslovakia, Romania and Yugoslavia. They were envisaged as a substitute counterweight to Germany now that its traditional ally Russia had become communist and an international pariah. That this superficially impressive corset around eastern Germany was made up of militarily weak and divided lesser powers that were a potential liability did not seem to occur to the diplomats who negotiated the treaties. They appeared to have largely ignored the military, who had grave doubts about how strategy could be coordinated with them.

Post-1918 French strategy was initially offensive. The French High Command favoured – ironically in view of 1940 – mobility and mechanization through the use of aircraft, in which France was world leader in terms of quantity and quality, and tanks, of which it possessed 2500 Renault FT's and over 100 heavy armoured ones.[11] This offensive strategy was outlined in a succession of military plans 'each one ordered to offensive requirements, if not to that of the alphabet – Plan T in 1920, Plan P in 1921, Plans A and A bis in 1924 and 1926 respectively'.[12] In this way France hoped to overcome the weakness resulting from a lower population and inferior industrial strength.

But concentrating on Europe did not get France off the other horn of the strategical dilemma – the Empire. It was clear that France was overextended, and with a much smaller navy since the 1921–22 Washington conference had imposed new international fleet parities in capital ships: Britain 5; USA 5; Japan 3; France 1.75; Italy 1.75. Its Empire had even grown at the end of the war by additions from the German and Ottoman empires, most notably Syria and the Lebanon, all of which needed defending. This 'penchant for ubiquity', as Maurice Vaïsse has remarked, meant that France still had 900,000 men under arms on 1 July 1920 and 850,000 a year later. This weakened France diplomatically, as such a large army evoked fears of renewed French preponderance on the European continent, and financially, given France's massive war debts to reimburse. There were 100,000 troops stationed in Germany alone and 57,000 were used to intervene in the Ruhr in January 1923. In 1925 over 70,000 troops had to be taken from metropolitan France to support action in Morocco and Syria. Marshal

Lyautey's remark in September 1920 smacked of understatement: 'We have taken on more commitments than it is materially possible for this country to shoulder.'[13]

Defensive strategy again

For as long as the Versailles clauses continued to be upheld and France remained on the Rhine, its security was reasonably secure. But during the 1920s that position was eroded through an unfortunate combination of external and internal factors. The Versailles settlement progressively lost its power to constrain and Germany began to recover. As if living on a war footing in Europe was not enough, France was drawn into overseas conflicts, often instigated by otherwise bright junior officers in search of action, in Syria in 1925–26, Morocco in the same year (where Pétain led a 300,000-strong army) as well as Indochina. Added to this, France was confronted by severe financial problems that obliged it to reduce its defence expenditure, cut its military service from 18 months to one year and reduce its peacetime infantry divisions from 32 to 27. Furthermore, Locarno and Geneva filled the air, as French diplomatic strategy became one of conciliation of Germany. It was slowly cajoled into allowing its material guarantees to slip behind a mirage of collective security, notably by agreeing to evacuate the Rhineland, which was complete by 30 June 1930. From an offensive position, France was progressively pushed into a defensive strategy, eventually reflected in its mobilization plans. By 1927 earlier plans for an immediate offensive strike on German territory had been abandoned. The 1927 military law clearly stated: 'The objective of our military organization is to ensure the protection of our frontiers and the defence of our overseas territories.'[14] This would culminate in the ultimate in defensiveness: the Maginot Line. The material had dictated the psychological; soon the psychological would condition the rest.

Construction of a line of fortresses down France's eastern border, 'The Great Wall of France', to the 'uncrossable' Ardennes hills, begun in 1929, was completed in 1932. Intended principally to protect the industrially rich region of Alsace-Lorraine and to block a traditional invasion route, it was also designed to allow a mobile thrust into Belgium to block a German attack. But the unintended impact that these static defences had on French mobile warfare and on the collective psyche was more far-reaching.[15] Named after the then War Minister, André Maginot, these defences epitomized the defeat of the Foch strategy and the victory of that of Pétain, commander of the French army, vice-president of the Superior War Council and from 1922 inspector general of the army. Foch's strategy was for France to maintain occupation of the Rhineland at all costs. Pétain's strategy was motivated by more practical problems: diplomatic pressures and France's vain search for solid allies; eventual evacuation of the Rhineland; progressive reduction of French military service, which by 1928 was down to one year. Pétain also believed that the lessons of the First World War needed to be taken on board in strategic planning: a war of attrition, of trenches and hence not a mobile war, in which defence was superior to attack and in which firepower was determinant. Most important of all, there should be no repeat of the terrible massacres that had decimated French society. In many ways France was still fighting the last war. Faith was now placed in the Guibert idea (1743–90) that the best wars were those that do not have to be fought because the enemy is deterred. The Maginot philosophy undermined the geo-strategic importance of the Rhine and accommodated the financial, diplomatic and psychological constraints that France could not ignore. More seriously, Maginot conditioned the collective mentality of the military and civilians.

This complacency was the more catastrophic because the French armed forces badly needed reorganizing, despite the cosmetic reforms of 1927–28. They lacked coordination between the three autonomous service ministries and the Colonial Ministry. By 1930 the territorial army's strength in Europe was illusory, owing to an inefficient High Command, unfocused strategy, poor equipment, too many officers, too few men and very low morale. And yet , because of general disorganization, the military budget continued to rise from 1927 to 1931, with only 12 per cent going on new equipment from 1919 to 1934 and much of that being for fortifications in the latter years. Added to this was the trough of the lost war generation, whose impact would halve the number of recruits available for military service from 1935. Obsessed with conserving men, military chiefs were further drawn to the defensive strategy, to the point of using tanks merely to escort infantry and avoid troop losses.

The French navy emerged very weak at the end of the war. Paradoxically, its renewal dated from the Washington conference in 1921–22, when it was officially relegated to the second rank. Unhappy at the humiliation of parity with Italy and, at a more practical level, deeply worried about defence and communications with the Empire rather than fighting battles on the high seas, the French Ministry of the Marine pushed for fleet expansion. In 1922, given the impossibility of matching the Royal Navy's capital ships, the French went for submarines. The naval strategy recalled that of the 1880s *guerre de course* in which smaller vessels were intended to harry the British. Thus initially the navy was organized with a view to potential difficulties with Britain, although more as a means of pressing its reluctant friend into signing a defence alliance and of showing that it was not merely a second-rank power. The navy, like the French nuclear weapon 30 years later, was as much a *force de persuasion* as it was of *dissuasion*. But its principal deterrent role was targeted from 1924 at a putative Italo-German coalition. The navy was favoured by continuity at government level. Georges Leygues was Navy

Minister in 10 governments from 1925–30 and 1932–33, while navy chiefs such as Admiral François Darlan ensured that the navy obtained funding second only to the army. New pocket battleships designed to assure Mediterranean sea control over Italy (also rearming navally by 1935) followed Mussolini's ambitions in North and East Africa, which the French regarded as in their sphere of influence. By 1939 France had the largest navy of the continental powers.

From a position of considerable strength in 1919, French military aviation declined rapidly. Two-thirds of squadrons were demobilized from 1919 to 1920 and the aeronautical industry's workforce reduced from 200,000 to a mere 10,000. The French quickly lost a technical advance and with it a string of world records, which went to Americans and Germans, pushing it into third place by 1927. The problem was that the airforce was controlled by the ministries of Commerce, War, Navy and Colonies, who neglected it. Only in September 1928 was an Air Ministry established. But it was not until 1933 that a French airforce, distinguished more by quantity than by quality, was created.[16]

With a poorly organized army unable to go on the offensive before the second month of mobilization, a navy more attuned to maritime protection and an airforce in a subsidiary role, a reactive and defensive philosophy permeated the French armed forces. France placed its confidence in the chimera of collective security represented by the League of Nations (itself denied a military force) and the fashionable thinking of the day – disarmament, promoted by the 'Anglo-Saxons'. These, together with financial constraints and German demands for equality, coalesced in the Geneva disarmament conference of February 1932. But disarmament meant abandoning the security of French military superiority over Germany, as the military repeatedly pointed out. With the centre-left coalition's victory in the May 1932 elections, the military's influence declined and relations with the politicians deteriorated. At the Lausanne conference Germany succeeded in not having to pay any more reparations. At the Geneva conference it obtained equality of treatment and a few months later slammed the door on the disarmament conference and the League of Nations.

Despite the clear German threat of the early 1930s, the French army remained fixated on maintaining its basic structures and numerical establishment while continuing to neglect its weaponry, munitions and equipment. France's absence of modernization, as Robert Frank has shown, was demonstrated in the last years of peace by the fact that France was spending four to five times more on fodder for horses than on fuel for motorized vehicles.[17] Responsibility lay with the military, the politicians and also the interplay of the two in that age-old problem of French civil–military relations. France's defence chief from the beginning of 1935, General Gamelin, also discovered outdated thinking as 'strategic and tactical concepts remained rooted in the positional warfare of 1915–18'. His predecessors from 1921–34, Pétain and Weygand, had emphasized manpower in battles of attrition, derived directly from their war experience.[18] Once again quantity not quality characterized the 15 March 1935 decision to increase military service to two years. But when Hitler remilitarized the Rhineland the following year and the government asked the military whether a riposte could be mounted, the army command prevaricated, eventually claiming that mobilization was the only solution but that that would be unacceptable. Without a rapid intervention force France did not have the instrument of its foreign policy. The fait accompli was preferable to military action. Gamelin might struggle to overcome inter-service rivalry and find support for modernization, mechanization and re-equipment right down to the defeat of 1940, but it did not stop him being branded as 'the man who lost the Battle of France'.[19] When war seemed probable after 1936, French foreign policy fumbled around on a vain quest for alliances quite uncoordinated with the military. When military expenditure did increase in 1936, and especially 1938, it was too little too late and poorly targeted – a situation worsened by the weaknesses of France's industrial infrastructure, productivity and labour relations in the wake of the 1936 Popular Front reforms. It was not surprising that Gamelin should seek to delay the onset of any conflict and gain time until French rearming was complete, and that he should plan strategically for a long war of attrition with Germany in which France and Britain's industrial and military potential would be fully realized.

From 1936 the threat to France was not just from its north-eastern frontiers, but also from its eastern borders, the Mediterranean and Africa in the shape of an expansionist Italy, and from its southern borders with the Spanish Civil War and Italo-German intervention. Overwhelmed by this concatenation of security threats, France was numbed into even greater passivity and defensiveness. Worse still, in March 1936 Belgium renounced the 1920 Franco-Belgian defence pact, declaring itself neutral and denying any French strike through Belgium at an advancing German army. There was no time to extend the Maginot Line. Munich was the measure of the passivity. Gamelin was justified in remarking on 19 December 1938: 'The whole question is to know whether France wishes to renounce being a European great power.'[20] The answer would be delivered very starkly in the next 18 months.

The military situation at the beginning of 1939 made passivity a virtue out of necessity. The Axis powers were able to mobilize 203 divisions and 13 million men against France and Britain's (if an alliance could be sealed with London) 106 divisions and six million men. Although rearmament was well under way by 1939, according to Maurice Vaïsse, France would be ready only by 1941.[21] When the French declared war on 3 September 1939, they waited in the expectation that German forces would impale themselves on the

Maginot defences. But at the end of the 'phoney war' (September 1939–May 1940) German mechanized divisions swept through the Ardennes gap from Maubeuge to Sedan along virtually undefended roads. Again France had miscalculated the direction and nature of the attack. The idea of professional mobile mechanized tank divisions expounded by a little-known colonel in the secretariat of the Conseil Supérieur de Défense Nationale, Charles de Gaulle, first published in *The Edge of the Sword* in 1932 and *Towards the Professional Army*, had gone unheeded. The French were no match for the German panzer divisions. As in 1870 France was defeated within six weeks. The surprise was that much greater for France supposedly having one of the best armies in the world: 'We will win, because we are the strongest' went the refrain. Once again the French had fallen prey to an irrational sense of superiority, because to believe anything else would have demanded supreme efforts and sacrifices throughout the inter-war years, which they were not willing to make. If an army is the expression of the nation, its economy and its morale, then the political powers must shoulder much of the responsibility. But the reasons for the defeat were above all military: the failure of military doctrine, and inadequate preparation and equipment, added to which was 'the refusal of the officers, and especially the generals, to stay shoulder-to-shoulder with the regime in France's hour of supreme crisis'.[22] Loyal to France they may have been, but not to the Republic. Thus, when the question of what to do next emerged with the option of an evacuation of the state authorities to North Africa or an armistice, senior officers were ready to jettison the Republic for the solution proposed by Marshal Pétain in June 1940 and to which prominent officers from the navy and airforce quickly rallied. The defeat of France also signalled that of the Third Republic.

Defeat was not inevitable for the French in 1939–40. But 20 years of hesitation and internal divisions had left France again vulnerable to a German knock-out blow – this time not deflected or diminished by any eastern counterweight (Hitler having secured his flank by the August 1939 Non-Aggression Pact with Stalin). Few ordinary French people welcomed another war with Germany in 1939, given the 1.5 million dead of 1914–18. But indecisive national leadership, and public rows between government members and between ministers and the High Command deepened the uncertain mood of the French during the eight months of 'phoney war'. Unclear whether to shed further blood by fighting again, or to make terms with Hitler's Germany, France was once again adrift and felt friendless. Though the British were engaged at France's side, their military effort was modest (less than one-tenth the size of France's army). The USA remained resolutely neutral (with an ambassador staying accredited to the collaborationist Vichy regime until 1942). The Soviet Union was neutralized by the Nazi–Soviet Pact; most small French allies, such as Poland, were rapidly engulfed by Germany. This sense of betrayal to the German terror was deftly exploited after the collapse in June 1940 by a poster depicting a German soldier cradling an infant child, over the slogan, 'Abandoned peoples, trust the German soldier!'

Even if the misnamed 'Fall of France' was actually the disintegration of a flimsy Western alliance, France's military performance came as a shocking disappointment to its allies and its people. The humiliation was not perceived passively by its people; it conditioned the very nature of French foreign and defence policy in the post-war world as well as exacerbating still further civil–military relations.

The Third Republic voted itself out of existence at the spa town of Vichy on 10 July 1940, vesting plenipotentiary powers in the 84-year-old saviour of Verdun, Philippe Pétain. The new French leader demanded scapegoats, blaming defeat on 'Too few arms, too few allies, too few children'. Making the best terms possible with Germany's armistice delegation, Pétain retained two-fifths of metropolitan territory, the powerful French navy and the colonies. With an infamous handshake with Hitler in October 1940 at Montoire, he 'entered onto the path of collaboration' with the Nazi Reich.

After the armistice France ceased to have an independent defence policy. Germany did not share Vichy's goal of a privileged place for France in Hitler's New European Order. The wholly unequal power relationship that underlay the putative partnership was irreversible, given that the French army was reduced by the terms of the armistice to a security force of only 100,000 men, and that 1,850,000 men were prisoners of war, 250,000 were wounded and 120,000 dead, even if Vichy still had the navy. A large majority of the rest of the French army pledged their loyalty to the head of state, France's highest-ranking officer, Marshal Pétain, whose government contained the highest number of military personnel since that of Marshal Soult in 1832. Many remained in post in the Empire, largely loyal to Vichy. A few chose military collaboration with Germany through the Légion des volontaires contre le bolchévisme, the *Milice* or the *Waffen SS*, but these never totalled more than 11,000. By November 1942, following German occupation of the southern zone, the armistice army was disbanded and 'there was no more French army in France'.[23] This marked the nadir of French strategy and defence.

It was only by the development of a 'parallel France' with another military apparatus that France would slowly claw itself back into the great power league. General de Gaulle might claim from London on 18 June 1940 that 'France has lost a battle, it has not lost the war' in an attempt to rally the French to his Resistance, but few heard his call and even fewer responded (7000). By July 1942 the Fighting French numbered only 70,000. But they were swelled by troops initially stationed in Chad and French Congo who formed the crux of the new French army, which by 1 September 1944 numbered 560,000, even if 300,000 were native colonial troops. By May

1945 the French army totalled 1,300,000. If de Gaulle's organization had anything so grand as a defence policy, it was totally dependent on the Allies. But its strategy was clear: to ensure participation of French forces, at however symbolic a level, in the Allied struggle to earn France a place at the top table at the war's end. The new French army did this by providing the French corps that served in Italy in 1943–44, and the Free French 1st Army, which helped liberate France in 1944–45 and eventually helped conquer Germany on the Rhine and Danube. After the Liberation, for the first time for many years French military strategy and diplomacy were in complete harmony. They were geared to participating in Allied victory, even if French forces were of lesser military value given their diminutive size (Soviets 22 million, Americans 12 million and British 5 million) and dependence on the Allies for materiel. But they were crucial to Gaullist myth making internally and externally in restoring France to the 'front rank' in the world. The conjuring trick that de Gaulle performed ensured that France was considered a victor at the end of the war. France was handed the mantle of great power status, from permanent member of the new United Nations Security Council to an occupation zone in Germany, even if those clothes were 'tailored too large for it'.[24]

Gaullist strategy

Defeat conditioned Gaullist post-war strategic priorities: to maintain French colonial possessions as a symbol of great power status, to keep in check the German threat and to develop French strategic capability to ensure national independence. Development of a nuclear capability, whose power was clearly demonstrated at Hiroshima in 1945, motivated General de Gaulle's establishment of the Commissariat à l'énergie atomique on 31 October 1945.

The problems facing the French armed forces were enormous. The whole military machine had to be rebuilt with meagre financial resources. General de Gaulle attempted to remedy their dispersed, competing and cumbersome nature by reforms designed to coordinate defence. On 4 January 1946 the Comité de défense nationale chaired by the head of government was created. True to ideas expressed in *Towards the Professional Army*, he set up a rapid reaction force composed of professional soldiers to overcome the inflexibility of the 1930s. This did not survive de Gaulle's resignation in January 1946 following disagreements with his left-wing coalition on the nature of the Fourth Republic's constitution. The centralized and collegial system he put in place did survive him, but became a liability in the hands of unstable coalition governments of the Fourth Republic, which preferred immobilism to action in defence matters. From 1946 to 1958 to preserve political balances the upper echelons of the defence organization were tinkered with

15 times, diluting responsibilities and undermining the cornerstone of the centralized Gaullian system, the National Defence Staff.

Other problems remained. The first was French opinion's broadening disaffection for the armed forces, increasingly held responsible for the 1940 defeat. This facilitated budgetary cuts, which drove the military's share of public spending between 1946 and 1949 from 25 per cent to 18.7 per cent. The second was the seed of insubordination that had been planted in the army by General de Gaulle himself when he had called on French officers and men to rebel against the politicians of Vichy and join him. In September 1944 a 'purge commission' was established to deal with those officers who had continued to obey the Vichy authorities. This resulted in 650 retirements and 6630 officers cashiered, the High Court judging senior officers. Traditional military discipline was turned on its head when refusal to obey a legally constituted political authority became a virtue and obedience a crime; the lesson would not be forgotten. The purges and the difficulty in integrating the irregular resistance forces (Forces françaises de l'intérieur) into the army produced a crisis of morale, a surfeit of officers and eventually a recruitment problem. The army was characterized by an incestuous recruitment pattern. From 1954 to 1958 44 per cent of all officers graduating from the elite Saint Cyr academy were themselves sons of military personnel compared with 30 per cent in 1937–39.[25] Demoralized and disenchanted, the military were cutting themselves off from the nation and becoming 'a state within a state'. This undermined the French armed forces under the Fourth Republic and made them a serious liability for the political authorities.

The more France's power declined, the more was asked of its armed forces. The old dilemma of competing continental and imperial strategies grew more striking than ever. In June 1946 of 460,000 troops only 110,000 were stationed in France, isolating the army physically from the nation. French troops occupied Germany and still had to defend the Empire with uprisings in Algeria from May 1945, then the Levant and Madagascar from 1947. With too few troops, a navy in desperate need of modernization and an airforce totally dependent on Allied equipment (despite attempts to rebuild it through the nationalization of four-fifths of the aeronautical industry), France was clearly overstretched.

Imperial strategy

France was willing to cut back on its armed services, but not on the commitments. It hung on to its colonies for more than they were worth. Circumstances forced Paris to expand the armed forces. By 1957 they had risen to 1.2 million men. The Indochina War from 1946 to 1954 cost France more than it received in Marshall Aid and swallowed up an entire

class of Saint Cyr officers every three years. France's problem was that
politicians and the army would not accept another defeat after 1940. For
this reason no friendly hand was extended to the Vietnamese independence
leader Ho Chi Minh, with whom a compromise could probably have been
worked out in the initial stages. Winning at all costs made the Indochina
War being fought in jungles and paddy fields against new guerrilla tactics
a 'dirty war' in more ways than one. Such a 'revolutionary war', it was
claimed by new philosopher/soldiers, demanded similar revolutionary
responses – subversion, ideology, propaganda and psychological warfare.
Calls came from important generals, such as Lionel-Martin Chassin writing
in 1954, for the army to shed its post-Dreyfus stance of being 'la grande
muette' and to involve itself in politics. Following other revolutionary
nations' model, such as Mao's China, he maintained that proper indoctri-
nation was as vital for the French nation as it was for colonial populations
if the Empire was to be maintained. Recalling the decay of the Eastern
Roman Empire, he wrote:

> Whatever the extent of disorder and internal anarchy, all can be saved
> so long as one disposes of a solid and sufficiently national army capable
> of fulfilling two historical functions in a period of disintegration;
> defend the empire without and place in power within a leader capable
> of effecting the necessary rectification in re-establishing order and
> authority.'[26]

To legitimize the war effort it was presented as a conflict of Western
civilization against communism. But the war's cost and casualties (even if
only professional soldiers were waging it) made it unpopular with the French
public. A May 1953 poll showed 65 per cent in favour of ending the war, as
French politicians knew. Thus, as General de Gaulle remarked, 'the determination to win the war alternated with the desire to make peace without
anyone being able to decide between the two'.[27] Despite the USA financing
80 per cent of the Indochina War and France deploying 204,000 troops in
the region, France was defeated by the Vietminh's guerrilla warfare following
a 56-day siege of the Verdun-like position of Dien Bien Phu in May 1954.
France conceded independence in Geneva the following month. Apart from
the financial and human cost of the war (some 20,000 French soldiers lost
their lives), France emerged with its international credibility in tatters. For
the French army it was a stab in the back by the politicians. More broadly, it
was confirmation of French decline from great power status. It underlined
the degree to which France was dependent on Washington in terms of
foreign and defence policy. This in turn bred resentment and a yearning for
greater independence from the USA.

France enjoyed a mere three months and four days' peace before a similar
scenario was played out over Algeria. North Africa had long been considered

the French army's traditional sphere of influence since its 'pacifying mission' from the early nineteenth century. North Africa was also considered the cornerstone of the Union française and in particular France's Euro-African strategy. Still smarting from the defeat at Dien Bien Phu and believing that the 1954 peace treaty was a sell-out by the civilian authorities, the military were not prepared to accept a similar humiliation in their own 'backyard'. This was a war the army had to win at all costs and the 'dirty war' they fought was a measure of their desperation. By 1958 there were half a million troops in Algeria posing a serious threat to civil–military relations.

In the first two years of the war neither side looked like winning. The National Liberation Front (FLN) was ill-equipped and France had insufficient troops to control the world's tenth largest nation by area. But the FLN, borrowing tactics from de Gaulle's wartime resistance, made the war a political struggle, enlisting international Third World support for its cause. The French army's frustration grew despite socialist Premier Guy Mollet's dispatch of half a million conscripts to Algeria in 1956. That autumn the army, independently of the government, engaged in a strike of dubious legality intercepting in mid-air the entire external leadership of the FLN and its leader Ben Bella. By 1957 France was beginning to win the military struggle just as it started to lose the political battle. In 1957 parachutists led by General Massu won the so-called Battle of Algiers, breaking up the whole FLN network in the city. But, just as the army believed victory on the ground was in sight, growing domestic and international opposition was draining the politicians' will to prosecute the war. In April 1958 another French government fell, this time with no replacement. The army had had enough.

The Algerian struggle must be set against a backdrop of declining attractiveness of soldiering in France. This contributed to low morale and the soldier's sense of being unloved and unappreciated. In terms of comparative national salaries, between 1945 and 1960 that of a colonel plummeted from third to thirteenth place. As prestige declined, so a sense of alienation from the nation increased. Pay was better when fighting abroad than in garrisons in France.[28] Resentment at the perceived pusillanimity of ephemeral Fourth Republic governments boiled over in May 1958 when it became clear that the political authorities were willing to countenance independence for Algeria to escape the extremely unpopular conscript war being fought there. The army staged a putsch in Algeria on 13 May 1958, setting up a Committee of Public Safety under the leadership of the Commander-in-Chief, General Raoul Salan. In an extraordinary turn for a modern democratic state, the army threatened to seize Paris in 'Operation Resurrection' if General de Gaulle was not recalled. They tightened the screw on 24 May by seizing Corsica. The navy was reluctant to participate in any attempt to retake the island, the police, gendarmerie and majority of sub-prefects having gone over to the parachutists. As Philip Williams noted: 'The Corsican collapse completed the withering away of the French state.'[29] The whole edifice of the Fourth Republic would soon follow.

The army was up to its neck in Third World-style politics. It agreed to withdraw only after General de Gaulle accepted to return to power on condition that he be allowed to draft a new constitution. The army had gained a taste for politics. Some of France's most senior military leaders would not be embarrassed about attempting military coups again in 1960 and 1961 in response to the perceived betrayal by de Gaulle in wishing to grant independence to Algeria. In 1960, following de Gaulle's sacking of the popular General Massu, Algiers was reignited as the *Pieds noirs* erected barricades, egged on by fraternizing parachutist units. On 21 April 1961 four senior generals seized power in Algiers in the *putsch des généraux* in the name of Algeria remaining French. But the revolt was ill-prepared and lasted a mere four days. Some 14,000 officers and men were implicated in the revolt, splitting the French army. Conscripts heeded de Gaulle's calls to turn against their rebel officers. Many officers realized the divorce between army and nation and turned away from the prospect of civil war. Senior French officers were arrested and imprisoned, others had their careers broken, and some such as General Salan went underground to continue the struggle. The underground 'resistance' movement of senior rebel officers and civilians opposed to de Gaulle's aim of divesting France of its cumbersome empire became the Secret Army Organization (OAS), led by Salan. A terror campaign was conducted in France and Algeria punctuated by assassination attempts on de Gaulle himself. It would take that model of military insubordination, General de Gaulle, to remove the army from politics and modernize it. The primary defender of the Republic would no longer be the army, but the atom bomb.

France performed an active defence role in its decolonization wars and dutifully carried out its occupation of Germany. But in the cold war that was underway from 1947 its contribution to protecting France from possible Soviet expansionism was slight. Budgetary and military constraints ensured that its defence was based on alliance not armaments.

Continental strategy

Threat of European war resulting from Soviet expansionism westwards, epitomized by the communist takeover of Czechoslovakia in February 1948 and the Berlin blockade in June, seriously preoccupied French defence planners. Domestic unrest provoked by communist-led strikes paralysing much of the country in the autumn of 1947 was a further threat. The army was asked to respond to both security threats and quickly confessed its inability to prepare mobilization plans for such eventualities. In an eerie rerun of 1940, there was much discussion in June 1948 of transferring French resources to North Africa in the event of invasion or insurrection. This option was not retained. France was forced to seek alliances for its security that its own military could not provide. In March 1947 the Dunkirk Treaty was signed with Britain against Germany and extended to the Benelux countries by the Brussels Pact of March 1948. This embryonic European security system, with its international planning committees, was undermined by Franco-British differences on everything from personalities to strategy. The Brussels Pact would become the organization at the heart of the Western European Union where Franco-British differences would endure. But the need for US protection and hardware to counter the Soviet threat explains French cajoling of the Americans to join a broader defence system, which in April 1949 became NATO.

International tension increased with the explosion in the summer of 1949 of the first Soviet bomb, the victory of the communist forces of Mao Zedong in China and the following year the onset of the Korean War. The French High Command reported that France would have no chance in the event of a Soviet invasion westwards given the latter's enormous military superiority of 25 divisions in East Germany and another 75 ready for action against NATO's mere 14. Again it was the French who in August 1950 called for a reinforcement of NATO military structures and appealed to the Americans for a greater commitment. On 15 September 1950 a meeting of the Atlantic Council in New York established an integrated Anglo-American force. On 18 December in Brussels a Supreme Allied Command Europe (SACEUR) was created under American General Eisenhower with a General Staff based at Supreme Headquarters Allied Powers Europe just outside Paris. The French obtained a place on the all-important military Standing Group in Washington and they pushed for Western European defence to be concentrated between the Rhine and Elbe rivers as far east as possible. They also encouraged an increased US commitment to Europe. NATO divisions rose to 50 and US troops rose to 3 million, of whom 400,000 were stationed in Germany and 50,000 largely in bases in north-east France. With Washington supplying and financing much of French rearmament through the Mutual Defence Assistance Act and the 1951 Mutual Security Act, France reversed its retrenchment policy modernizing and increasing its armed forces substantially. Military service rose to 18 months; defence expenditure increased to one-third of public spending by 1954. This encouraged the development of France's indigenous arms industries such as aircraft and aero-engine manufacturers Marcel-Dassault and SNECMA. Whereas the French territorial army and airforce were given priority in the integrated allied strategy, the navy remained the Cinderella service. France's continental security was largely financed and provided through an integrated Atlantic defence strategy.

However, dependence on the USA began to be seen in a different light following the acrimonious debates over the issue of a European Defence Community (EDC) from 1951 to 1954 (see Chapter 5 on Germany) in which Washington pushed for German rearmament against French wishes. The EDC debate also brought to a head the strategical dilemma of a continental versus an overseas strategy. Most military chiefs opposed the EDC not so much because it meant rearming Germany, so long as sufficient guarantees were in place, but because it reduced French defence autonomy. They calculated that concentrating France's defence efforts in Europe would mean sacrificing defence of the French Union. For de Gaulle, still in the political wilderness, collective defence, whether of the NATO or the EDC variety, could not fully guarantee French security. Nuclear weapons appeared to offer a means of securing national independence and grandeur.

The French bomb

After the early post-war honeymoon, French disenchantment with the USA increased from 1954. Differences with Washington grew over German rearmament, the EDC, Indochina, the Arab states and the Algerian War. They were exacerbated by the 'Anglo-Saxon' domination of NATO at the level of doctrine and command. Nevertheless, French attitudes to the USA remained ambivalent. The apparent decline of the Soviet threat following the Korean War and Stalin's death in 1953 suggested a reduced need to rely so heavily on the USA. Conversely, when in December 1954 Washington appeared to impose on NATO the US strategy of massive retaliation, some in France believed that this was a prelude to an American troop withdrawal from Europe and a reduced commitment to European defence. The new NATO strategy highlighted the gap between nuclear states (which since 3 October 1952 included Britain) and non-nuclear ones. French prestige was undermined. In November 1956 Britain and France mounted a large military expedition to retake the Suez Canal recently nationalized by the Egyptian leader Colonel Nasser. Washington refused to provide support scuttling the whole exercise by putting financial pressure on Britain to withdraw. Some French politicians and defence planners concluded that it was foolhardy to rely on US protection over issues not of vital interest to its ally and suggested regaining some of France's diplomatic and military independence. Development of a French nuclear weapon offered a solution.

The dropping of US atomic bombs on Hiroshima and Nagasaki in August 1945 demonstrated to the world the power of nuclear weapons: 66,000 people were killed on impact in Hiroshima and 80 per cent of the city's structure was destroyed; 40,000 were killed in Nagasaki. Japanese surrender followed immediately. The message was not lost on the French.

French scientists had participated in the US, British and Canadian wartime effort to develop nuclear energy for military purposes, even though the French had only tenuous official links with the programme. In the immediate post-war period it had been thought that France, like Canada, would concentrate on the peaceful uses of nuclear technology. But in setting up the Commissariat à l'energie atomique, responsible for civil and military programmes, on 31 October 1945 and placing it directly under his control, General de Gaulle demonstrated his intention to give France its own nuclear weapon. Following de Gaulle's resignation in January 1946 the military aspects of French nuclear research seemed to wane. But a series of incidents, from the vain French request to Washington to use nuclear weapons to aid their encircled troops at Dien Bien Phu, to the rearming of Germany and Britain's acquisition of the nuclear bomb, gave France new impetus. On 26 December 1954, Premier Mendès France informed the Cabinet that a programme for the development of a French nuclear weapon would be accelerated. He justified it on the grounds of the international leverage France would gain, as well as the superiority it would have over Germany, to whom such weapons were denied.

From the mid-1950s the prospect of European integration accelerated the French nuclear weapon programme. Signing the EURATOM treaty to create a European atomic programme risked denying France nuclear independence. By bringing its nuclear programme forward it could confront its partners with a fait accompli. Added to this was the successful launch into orbit of the Soviet satellite *Sputnik* in 1957. This demonstrated to the Americans and the world that the Soviet Union had the capability to deploy intercontinental missiles with nuclear warheads that could directly threaten US cities. American defence of Europe appeared vulnerable. The possibility emerged of an American president refusing to sanction the use of nuclear weapons, in the event of a Soviet invasion of Western Europe, for fear that American cities would be attacked. The French needed their own weapon to ensure ultimate defence of their territory.

The French were undaunted by the costs involved in developing the second generation of nuclear weapons, the thermonuclear bomb. The Americans exploded theirs on 31 October 1952, the Soviets on 12 August 1953 and the British on 15 May 1957. Socialist Premier Guy Mollet's government switched the French programme to thermonuclear weapons and sanctioned the development of a French strategic bomber capable of delivering a French warhead. Thus France did not, as is sometimes believed, wait until de Gaulle's return in 1958 to launch its nuclear weapons programme. Even before his return a date had been set for France's first nuclear test, which took place in the Sahara desert at Reggane on 13 February 1960.

French nuclear strategy

Despite nuclear weapons development in the 1950s, France did not have clear views on their relationship to defence and foreign policy, or a strategy for their use. Some historians have suggested that the rationale for a French nuclear weapon had less to do with adopting a military posture in relation to a potential enemy and more about credibility with its principal allies. Wolf Mendl has argued that it was a force more of persuasion than dissuasion.[30] Others have suggested that France developed an independent nuclear weapon because the USA would not share with it the nuclear know-how and fissile material shared with Britain, or that dependence on US fissile material eroded French independence should the USA suddenly stop supplying it.

In French military circles under the Fourth Republic a nuclear strategy for France was beginning to evolve. As early as 1950 Colonel Ailleret in his lectures at the army staff college, the Ecole de guerre, had spoken of atomic weapons as the cornerstone of all future military strategy. In November 1951 he was put in charge of a special unit on the General Staff to investigate nuclear matters. With the 1956 Suez Crisis, Ailleret took charge of a pro-gramme to accelerate production of a French nuclear weapon. In April 1956 Colonel Gallois had begun to develop French nuclear strategy around the idea of a massive riposte by a smaller power wishing to deter a larger one. However, thus far no clear idea existed for an independent nuclear force integrated into national strategy. The French weapon was for the moment conceived of more as a trump card for use in European and Atlantic councils than against a potential enemy. But from 1958 General de Gaulle made nuclear strategy a primary instrument of French foreign and defence policy. At no point in France's recent history would strategy, foreign and defence policy be so in tune. But to achieve that unity of purpose it was necessary for de Gaulle to adopt a radically different foreign and defence policy – national independence. This meant overhauling relations with the USA.

Just as France's nuclear weapons programme began before de Gaulle returned to power, so France's relations with the USA began their deterio-ration under the Fourth Republic. As the economy expanded and recon-struction advanced, so France's capacity to assume its own defence increased, especially as the nuclear option, as Ailleret had pointed out, was recognized as being a cheap form of defence. Hence France's increasing demands for a greater say, even equality, in NATO policy making. When de Gaulle returned to power in 1958, he took on board the many 'humiliations' administered to himself and France by the USA since the war, as well as the strategic value of a French nuclear weapon outlined by Colonel Gallois.

French relations with the USA declined after 1958. In September 1958 de Gaulle's request to London and Washington for a three-power directorate in

NATO to deal with questions of international security and strategy was rejected, as de Gaulle probably expected. In March 1959 France withdrew its Mediterranean fleet from NATO command following the failure of the USA to supply submarines to France. In the same year it refused the installation of Intermediate Range Ballistic Missiles (IRBMs) on French territory so long as the warheads remained under US control. In 1960 it refused to allow the USA to stockpile tactical nuclear weapons on French soil, obliging the Americans to move their fighter-bombers to Britain and Germany. De Gaulle's strategy, which had been maturing in the wilderness years, was clearly set out on 3 November 1959 in a speech to the Institut des hautes études de défense nationale (IHEDN) in Paris:

> The defence of France must be in French hands. This is a necessity with which we have not always been familiar in the course of the past years. I know it. It is essential that it becomes so again. If it should happen that a country like France has to make war, its effort must be its own effort . . . Naturally, French defence will be coordinated with that of other countries if need be. That is in the nature of things. But it is indispensable that it be a French defence and that France defends itself, by itself, for itself and in its own manner.[31]

This established the premiss for an independent defence strategy, the nature of which was quickly defined. On 23 November 1961 de Gaulle told a meeting of French officers: 'France must keep control of its will, its image and its future. That demands that our military power should include atomic weapons. A great state that does not possess them, while others do, is not master of its destiny.'[32] This justified the setting-up of a strategic nuclear strike force, a *force de frappe*. General Gallois tailored the doctrine for its use to French needs in 1961. The so-called doctrine of 'the weak to the strong' ('faible au fort') postulated that, no matter how powerful the adversary, with a nuclear weapon it is possible to inflict such damage as to make anyone unwilling to risk the consequences. But for that to happen the response had to be immediate and with all possible means. Gallois's doctrine of deterrence was further refined by General Ailleret's notion that for the deterrent effect to be credible France's nuclear weapon must have no specific target, it must be directed at all points of the compass ('tous azimuts'). In this he was elaborating on de Gaulle's 3 November 1959 statement: 'As it is possible to destroy France, in the event, from all points of the world, it is necessary that our force be so organized as to be operational anywhere on earth.'.[33] Growing French military self-confidence was reflected in the evolution of French strategic objectives, which moved from the quasi-defeatist 1958 triptych of 'Strike, intervene, survive' to the more reassuring 1963 version of 'Deter, intervene, defend'.[34]

De Gaulle's holistic approach to the notions of 'grandeur' and 'national independence' included economic expansion, as well as industrial and scientific regeneration, to fund and realize his grand design for enhancing France's world status. On 18 June 1961, the anniversary of his call for the French to join him in the Resistance, he intoned: 'We French must rise to the rank of a great industrial power or resign ourselves to decline.'[35] This was vital to fund France's nuclear weapon, which in the first five-year military programme law of 1960 gave an absolute priority to nuclear weapons, at a time when the Algerian War was draining resources. That war led de Gaulle to conclude that France should be freed from the burden of empire. On 11 April 1961 he explained in a press conference: 'It seems to me contrary to the present interest and new ambition of France to remain bound by obligations and burdens that no longer fit its power and influence . . . It is a fact . . . [that] decolonization is our interest and is therefore our policy.'.[36]

Even the constitution figured in his matrix of plans for achieving his grand strategy of French independence and grandeur. The Fifth Republic's constitution was tailored to his needs. It gave the President of the Republic considerable executive power, especially in foreign and defence policy. De Gaulle took this a step further after France's first nuclear test by giving the President absolute control over detonation of the bomb (see Chapter 2 on policy making). This also contributed to the 'demilitarization' of French defence.[37] It was vital at a time of military insurrections to ensure that France's nuclear weapon should depend essentially on political command. In this he was creating 'a nuclear monarchy', in which the head of state was responsible for the ultimate defence of national territory. It was not surprising, therefore, that on the announcement of the first French nuclear test on 13 February 1960 de Gaulle should exclaim: 'Hourra for France! From this morning it is stronger and prouder.'.[38]

With de Gaulle in power the USA grew more worried about the French nuclear programme. The American Congress was hostile to the USA sharing atomic secrets. Washington favoured non-proliferation to maintain the exclusivity of the three-power nuclear club. Even when in May 1961 President John Kennedy visited Paris, he refused to lift the ban on US companies supplying high-technology equipment to France for the manufacture of IRBMs (range 2400 to 6400 kilometres). This refusal delayed French IRBM production for three to five years, contributing further to the deterioration in relations between Paris and Washington. It buttressed de Gaulle's belief that a truly independent defence policy necessitated a powerful indigenous arms industry, and eventually a thriving arms export industry to minimize production costs. This helps explain subsequent French enthusiasm for the European Space Agency and development of the ARIANE space rocket with its launch site in French Guiana. This offset development costs for France's own missile development and gave it access to sophisticated European rocket and space technology.

Franco-American differences spilled over into NATO. Western European nations were worried at the American change of position on nuclear strategy prompted by Soviet weapons development after *Sputnik* in 1957 and production of an intercontinental ballistic missile (ICBM). Now that the Soviets appeared to have the delivery systems to strike American cities directly, the USA retreated from its strategy of 'massive retaliation' by which it would unleash the whole of its nuclear arsenal against an aggressor. This deterrent strategy was fine for so long as the USA maintained nuclear superiority. The Europeans believed it would best deter the Soviets from using their massive superiority in conventional forces to mount an invasion westward. It also relieved them of the huge cost of having to expand their conventional forces, as well as making a new war in the heart of Europe less likely. But Washington sought to withdraw its commitment to automatic nuclear retaliation in favour of a graduated response allowing for escalation and greater flexibility. They attempted to convince the reluctant Europeans that NATO should adopt this strategy of 'Flexible response'. For de Gaulle, here was further proof that France could not rely on American–dominated NATO, which, in the event of war, would control French forces through the integrated command structure. France must 'defend itself, by itself, for itself and in its own manner'.

An autonomous foreign and defence policy based on an independent nuclear weapon had as its logical consequence withdrawal of French forces from NATO's command. This had been taking place piecemeal since 1958. But on 5 September 1965 de Gaulle notified the allies that France would withdraw all its forces from NATO command by 1969. The withdrawal, when it came in 1966, was not therefore the surprise it has sometimes been claimed to be. On 21 February 1966 the French President gave his reasons: the Soviet threat had diminished since the anguished days of the 1962 Cuban Missile Crisis; American nuclear protection had been reduced; France had developed its nuclear weapon; national independence was incompatible with a system of integrated defence. On 7 March he instructed his principal allies to withdraw all 26,000 troops stationed in France by 1 July 1967 together with all NATO military organizations and commands. However, France remained a party to the NATO treaty and its obligations, including that of mutual military assistance. Collaboration was to continue between the inter-allied command and the French High Command and France was to participate in the Atlantic Council.[39]

Development of the nuclear strike force

A successful nuclear test in 1960 by no means provided France with a nuclear weapon to defend itself. De Gaulle was pleased that he had beaten the international test ban treaty of 5 August 1963 signed in Moscow, which

outlawed underwater and atmospheric nuclear tests, though France would
still not sign up to it. It still had an enormous amount of development to do
on its bomb. For the moment it was still an 'A' bomb rather than the new
generation 'H' bomb, with its greater power/size ratio. The 'H' bomb would
only be tested at Muroroa in France's overseas Pacific territory of Tahiti in
1968. Equally important was the question of delivering the bomb to enemy
territory. France needed a strike force (*force de frappe*). But it did not possess
the necessary ballistic missile technology for such a force. It did have a
technologically advanced aircraft industry and resorted to aircraft for its
delivery system. The idea was for a low-flying supersonic bomber with a
range of 3000 kilometres, which would not be easily detected. In 1959 the
prototype of the Dassault-built Mirage IV had its maiden flight. It was to
constitute a strike force of some 50 bombers armed with 60 kiloton 'A'
bombs operational from 1964 and organized into the Strategic Air Force
(Forces aeriennes stratégiques) command.

From 1960 a land-based strategic ballistic missile went into construction.
The long-term plan was for submarine-launched missiles. During the 1960s
nuclear weapons absorbed the largest part of the defence budget. But de
Gaulle did not live to see either France's land-based nuclear missiles on the
Plateau d'Albion in Provence from 1971 or the first nuclear-powered and
armed submarine, the *Redoutable*, which entered full service the same year.
Redoutable had been launched four years earlier without its full complement
of nuclear weapons, demonstrating how symbols of French power often
preceded reality. Nevertheless, a nuclear submarine was vital. Largely free
from geographical constraints, virtually undetectable and invulnerable, it also
allowed for a counter-attack even if the national territory was destroyed. This
reinforced the credibility of the *faible au fort* deterrence doctrine. Without
the nuclear submarine, most defence analysts were extremely sceptical about
the credibility of France's nuclear strike force, mischievously nicknamed the
'bombinette'. Because Mirage IV bombers had a limited operational range
and needed to be refuelled in flight, it was believed that France's Strategic
Air Force would be unable to penetrate Soviet air defences, while the land-
based missiles were likely to be taken out in a first strike. Only after de
Gaulle's death in 1970 did France complete the elements of a superpower-
in-minature's strategic triad: land-based medium-range missiles on the
Plateau d'Albion, and a ballistic-missile-armed nuclear-submarine flotilla,
complementing the Mirage force. This, even more than its permanent
membership of the UN Security Council, restored France to the great power
'club', arguably a status it had not enjoyed since 1914.

Since de Gaulle's death in 1970 all Presidents of the Republic have maintained the strategy of an independent nuclear weapon, even though in opposition up to 1978 Socialist leader François Mitterrand and his party had
opposed the nuclear strike force. Since then a fairly broad consensus,

unknown in other European countries, has existed among political parties, public opinion and even the Catholic Church on the need to maintain the nuclear weapon. Indeed, the dogged critic of Gaullist military policy, Mitterrand, was able to declare in Gaullist vein as President on 16 November 1983: 'The centrepiece of the deterrent strategy in France is the head of state, it is me.'[40] Bitter memories of three invasions and the humiliation of defeat and collaboration in 1940 allowed such a consensus to form. As the ultimate defence of French territory, the nuclear bomb has reconciled nationalists, who believe in its capacity to threaten, and pacifists, who, according to Maurice Vaïsse, 'see above all in the nuclear an instrument of non-war'.[41] Consequently, France was not affected in the early 1980s by the anti-nuclear protests that swept through Europe. But this consensus has been at a price. Defence has not been a subject of much political or public debate and consequently military thinking and planning has become somewhat stultified.

The nuclear weapon absorbed around 30 per cent of the military budget, despite initially being considered a cheap option. Fortunately, the remarkable expansion of the French economy during the 1960s actually reduced military spending as a proportion of public sector spending. It fell from 28.5 per cent in 1960 to 17.9 per cent in 1969, while military spending as a share of GDP fell during the same period from 6.34 to 4.17 per cent, settling at around 3.8 per cent until the end of the 1980s. This compared favourably with Britain's 4.1 per cent (USA 5.9 per cent). France's nuclear weapon did enhance the country's autonomy and security, and had benefits of a non-military nature. It allowed the French to rediscover their self-confidence after the war and a messy decolonization. It helped build national sentiment and cohesion through the defence consensus. It projected the image of an advanced technological state, not to mention the industrial spin-offs from the nuclear programme. By the 1980s with its four squadrons of Mirage IV bombers, its 18 medium-range missiles and its six nuclear submarines, France had become the third nuclear power in the world ahead of Britain and China – the only non-superpower to maintain the full panoply of nuclear elements, air, land, sea. This restored France to a degree of foreign and military predominance unknown since 1870.

However, there is much that smacks of the 'emperor's new clothes' in France's nuclear policy. But , as nobody dared assume the role of the child and ask the question, indeed as no French person wanted to know the answer, the myth of a powerful and independent French nuclear policy continued as a potent force. But then Gaullian symbolism had always been a powerful weapon in itself. There was, however, some suggestion, particularly in the 1960s, that the French nuclear weapon was an expensive anachronism in an era when defence cooperation was really what mattered. In reality the so-called independent nuclear weapon was never as independent as French politicians and the military would have us believe. During this period France's nuclear strike force relied on the NATO early warning system (NADGE) for the detection of incoming missiles. Soviet progress in missile precision, anti-ballistic missile technology and submarine detection systems maintained doubts about the true effectiveness of France's nuclear capability. But then it could be argued that that mattered little, because, for all their diplomatic bravado and anti-Americanism, the French continued to live under the protection of the American nuclear umbrella as the ultimate guarantee. Even the famed Gaullian single-minded strategy of the 'weak to the strong', founded on the notion of immediate and massive retaliation by France's strategic nuclear armoury, was eroded during the 1980s. French planners had always rejected a strategy of graduated response, but, by developing their own tactical nuclear weapons to be used in the early stages of an attack, they now adopted it, camouflaging the new weapon as 'pre-strategic' in 1984. This introduced an element of ambiguity into French strategy, undermining the strength of the deterrence doctrine of an assured massive response.

By allowing the nuclear weapon to absorb a disproportionate share of the defence budget, France relegated conventional forces to Cinderella status in terms of military planning and modernization, the consequences of which were harshly felt in the 1991 Gulf War. France's armed forces had been drastically cut from one million in the years 1957–62 to 657,000 in 1964 and 500,000 in 1969–70. Its land army fell from 830,000 to 228,000 in 1990, with conscription being reduced from 18 to 12 months in 1970. These reductions were largely the consequence of events such as the ending of the Algerian War and the reduction of the Soviet threat, but they were an opportunity to modernize France's armed forces. An attempt was made to increase the mobility of the French army, whose mission was to ensure the security of the French people and the integrity of French territory. This was to be achieved by fighting alongside the allies in the European theatre and by a capacity to intervene abroad to protect French possessions and come to the aid of the numerous governments with whom it had military agreements. The latter was to be achieved by stationing some 30,000 troops abroad, but also by the creation in 1983 of a rapid reaction force of some 47,000 men for intervention overseas, the Force d'action rapide (FAR). However, one-third of the FAR were conscripts, making it a weighty political decision to engage them in battle, given the implications for public opinion back home. This limited the FAR's operational effectiveness and signalled the problems that France confronted on a grand scale over the dispatch of forces to the Gulf in 1991. Because military planners focused so much on the *force de frappe* and because of the absence of any wide and serious discussion of defence matters, France's conscript army was not modernized to suit modern warfare's demands for professionalism, flexibility, rapid reaction forces, heavy lift or intelligence sharing agreements. Absence of these elements handicapped France's contribution to the Gulf War and signalled the need to rethink radically French defence and strategy in the post–cold war era.[42]

Other French defence priorities also needed rethinking, notably that of a predominantly national arms industry. The fact that by the 1980s some 40 per cent of French arms production was going to export to offset the development and production costs of maintaining a national arms industry had drawbacks. It often led France to sacrifice its diplomatic moral standards to the need to secure particular defence, or defence-related, contracts, often with widely recognized disreputable regimes. The tail was wagging the dog. By the 1990s it had become increasingly difficult for France to hang on to its dubious status as the world's third largest arms exporter in the era of the 'peace dividend'. France's indigenous arms industry, protected by national preference purchasing, and reliant on increasingly impecunious Third World governments, eschewed restructuring until the 1990s. Defence needs also dictated diplomacy over the question of nuclear testing and the refusal to sign the 1968 Nuclear Non-Proliferation Treaty (NPT). Because, unlike Britain, France did not rely on US technology for its nuclear weapon, it was obliged to continue nuclear testing to upgrade its bomb. By 1995 it had carried out 192 tests, second only to the two superpowers. In so doing it attracted opprobrium from countries close to its test site such as Australia and New Zealand from 1966 and world opinion generally in 1995 when President Jacques Chirac restarted testing in the Pacific. In 1995 world opinion forced Chirac to abandon testing altogether and France finally signed up to the NPT treaty. With the fall of the Berlin Wall and the eclipse of the Soviet threat in the short term, the French nuclear strike force's doctrine of immediate strategic retaliation became obsolescent. The 1991 Gulf War demonstrated how a small Third World country could ignore the so-called deterrent effect of Western nuclear weapons. That war also demonstrated that a strategic threat to France was now more likely from regional hegemons in the 'south' along the southern Mediterranean rim. French planners took time to accept this fact and the need to modify France's 'all-nuclear' strategy. French strategy and defence have struggled to break out of the old Gaullian mould suited to the cold war and based on primacy of the nation state, independence, national sanctuary, conscription and the predominance of nuclear strategy. There is still a long way for France to go to complete the adjustment to the 'New World Order', where the name of the game is rapid reaction forces, peacekeeping and international cooperation.

Notes

1 Quoted in Alistair Horne, *The French Army and Politics 1870-1970* (London, Macmillan, 1984), p. 1.

2 Jean-Baptiste Duroselle, preface to Jean Doise and Maurice Vaïsse, *Politique étrangère de la France: Diplomatie et outil militaire 1871–1991* (Paris, Seuil, paperback edn, 1992), p. 6.

3 Tombs, *France*, pp. 193–9.

4 Tombs, *France*, pp. 40–1.

5 Kennedy, *Rise and Fall*, pp. 219–20.

6 Doise and Vaïsse, *Diplomatie et outil militaire*, pp. 24–6.

7 Martin Alexander, 'The French Experience 1919–62: French Military Doctrine and British Observations, from World War One to the Algerian War', in J. Gooch (ed.), *The Origins of Contemporary Doctrine* (Camberley, SCSI, no. 30, 1997), p. 32.

8 Douglas Porch, *The March to the Marne: The French Army 1871–1914* (Cambridge: Cambridge University Press, 1981, p. 97, quoted in Kennedy, *Rise and Fall*, p. 223.

9 Kennedy, *Rise and Fall*, pp. 260–3.

10 R. J. Young, *France and the Origins of the Second World War* (London, Macmillan, 1996), p. 19.

11 Doise and Vaïsse, *Diplomatie et outil militaire*, pp. 328–9, 340.

12 Young, *France and the Origins*, p. 19.

13 Quoted in Doise and Vaïsse, *Diplomatie et outil militaire*, p. 3.

14 Quoted in Doise and Vaïsse, *Diplomatie et outil militaire*, p. 341.

15 Young, *France and the Origins*, p. 20.

16 Doise and Vaïsse, *Diplomatie et outil militaire*, pp. 360–2.

17 Robert Frankenstein, *Le Prix de réarmement français, 1935–39* (Paris, Publications de la Sorbonne, 1982).

18 Alexander, *Gamelin*, pp. 34–6.

19 Alexander, *Gamelin*, p. 378.

20 Quoted in Doise and Vaïsse, *Diplomatie et outil militaire*, p. 394.

21 Doise and Vaïsse, *Diplomatie et outil militaire*, p. 404.

22 Alexander, *Gamelin*, p. 399.

23 Doise and Vaïsse, *Diplomatie et outil militaire,* p. 453.

24 Jean-Pierre Rioux, *La IVe République*, vol. 1, *L'Ardeur et la necessité*, p. 125, quoted in Doise and Vaïsse, *Diplomatie et outil militaire*, p. 480.

25 Figures quoted in Doise and Vaïsse, *Diplomatie et outil militaire*, p. 499.

26 Quoted in Horne, *French Army*, p. 76.

27 Quoted in Horne, *French Army*, p. 74.

28 Horne, *French Army*, p. 79.

29 Philip Williams, 'The Fourth Republic: Murder or Suicide?' in Philip Williams, *Wars, Plots and Scandals in Post-War France* (Cambridge, Cambridge University Press, 1970), p. 151.

30 See W. Mendl, *Deterrence and Persuasion: French Nuclear Armament in the Context of National Policy, 1945–1969* (London, Faber, 1970).

31 Quoted in de Carmoy, *Les Politiques étrangères*, pp. 335–6.

32 Quoted in de Carmoy, *Les Politiques étrangères*, p. 340.

33 Quoted in de Carmoy, *Les Politiques étrangères*, p. 338.

34 Quoted in *La Défense: La Politique militaire française et ses réalisations*, Notes et Etudes Documentaires, no. 3343, 6 Dec. 1966 (Paris, La Documentation Française), produced by the Ministry for Armed Forces Information Service.

35 Quoted in Jean-Baptiste Duroselle, 'Changes in French Foreign Policy since 1945', in Stanley Hoffmann *et al.*, *In Search of France*, p. 351.

36 Quoted in Duroselle, 'Changes in French Policy' in Stanley Hoffmann *et al.*, *In Search of France*, p. 351.

37 Doise and Vaïsse, *Diplomatie et outil militaire*, p. 609.

38 Quoted in Doise and Vaïsse, *Diplomatie et outil militaire*, p. 608.

39 Doise and Vaïsse, *Diplomatie et outil militaire*, pp. 602–7.

40 Quoted in Doise and Vaïsse, *Diplomatie et outil militaire*, p. 626.

41 Doise and Vaïsse, *Diplomatie et outil militaire*, p. 626.

42 For a full account of French defence reforms, see Shaun Gregory, *French Defence Policy into the Twenty-First Century* (London, Macmillan, 2000).

4
French intelligence

For a state with such a long tradition of spying on its enemies (abroad and within) remarkably little serious study has been devoted to the French intelligence services. This is all the more true of the role of intelligence in the formulation and execution of foreign and defence policy and generally in maintaining and projecting France as a world power. The French intelligence services have been at the crossroads of how the French see themselves as well as how they regard the rest of the world. The intense turmoil and political fragmentation produced by four revolutions, two coups d'état, three foreign invasions resulting in 16 different constitutions in just over two centuries has led the French to mistrust themselves as much as the wider world. Among democratic states rarely has this provided such justification for spying on one's own citizens as much as on foreign powers. Indeed, the two were often synonymous given the French predilection for what Raoul Girardet has called conspiracy myths.[1] A strong belief in democratic values has tempered this, making the traditional ambivalence that all democracies entertain with their secret services particularly potent in France. Intelligence officers' loyalty to the state rather than to a particular regime, or to the preservation of order rather than political orthodoxy, has been a problem. Suspicion of politicians and political groups has led to democratic values being sacrificed to stability.[2] Consequently, French leaders mistrustful of their official intelligence services have often preferred to set up their own informal intelligence-gathering agencies to operate at home or abroad in order to provide the kind of information they wanted to hear. This distanced them further from democratic scrutiny, as well as committing the heinous intelligence error of failing to ensure the separation of intelligence gathering from its analysis and exploitation. This has led to the multiplication of intelligence agencies amongst whom, at best, coordination is poor, and, at worst, rivalry is merciless. The temptation to outmanœuvre or steal a march on rivals has led to blunders and scandal that have further discredited the intelligence services in the eyes of their political masters and public opinion. Poor civil–intelligence relations help explain why intelligence has often been excluded from the policy-making process. A French preoccupation with internal subversion, potentially supported by foreign powers, has blurred the lines between domestic surveillance and counter-intelligence to a degree not witnessed in the Anglo-Saxon world, where the former has theoretically been perceived as the prerogative of the police and the latter that of the intelligence services.

This culture and absence of an 'intelligence community' (said to characterize the Anglo-Saxon model) explain the chequered history of modern French intelligence. If the role of intelligence is to 'reduce uncertainty', then it could be suggested that the French services have not always performed well over the last century and a quarter. A primary function of the state has been undermined: that of knowing one's enemies and one's friends. However, this has not always been the fault of the intelligence services. A perennial problem has been the reluctance of policy-makers to take the intelligence agencies seriously and build intelligence assessments into the decision-making process. Much of this is attributable to the dishonourable performance of French counter-intelligence at the time of the Dreyfus Affair.

Birth of the modern intelligence service and the stigma of Dreyfus

A modern French intelligence service was put in place following France's defeat in the Franco-Prussian War. Until 1871 France had no organization devoted solely to intelligence gathering or counter-intelligence. Since the seventeenth century it did have the notorious 'cabinet noir', whose mission was to intercept and read mail in the interests of state security. A special border police concerned from 1811 with state security had by 1855 seen its mission extended inland to maintain surveillance on the railways under the responsibility of the prefects. These surveillance activities were supplemented in Paris by a special force in charge of the surveillance of embassies and foreigners resident in the capital. The humiliating defeat of 1870 brought home to the military the need to have a foreign intelligence service capable of providing systematic intelligence on potential enemies.

According to the man called upon by General de Gaulle to create from scratch an intelligence service for the Free French in 1940, Colonel Passy (*nom de guerre* of André Dewavrin), the role of a Deuxième bureau is to prepare a summary of all information likely to help the General Staff plan military operations. The mission of a Service de renseignement (SR) is to gather information by any means, which it then passes on to the Deuxième bureau to exploit.[3] In June 1871 the Ministry of War created a service intended to 'inform about the plans and operations of the enemy'. Attached to the Deuxième bureau of the Etat-Major général in 1876 it was given the name of 'Statistical and Military Reconnaissance Section'. Staffed with only five officers and four auxiliaries at the time of the Dreyfus Affair in 1894, it was given the massive task of intelligence gathering and counter-intelligence, even if at the time the distinction was not clear. But counter-intelligence quickly gained the upper hand, with General Lewal, its head, commenting in 1883:'Though it is useful to know an adversary's plans, it is more important to stop him learning ours.'[4] Despite working in collaboration with the 'special commissaires' of the Interior Ministry's Sûreté, the military maintained full operational command. From 1886 counter-intelligence was boosted following the appointment of the nationalist General Boulanger as War Minister and Colonel Sandherr as head of the Statistical Section. Having recently promoted a parliamentary bill to repress espionage, Boulanger set about tightening up internal military security. His circular of 25 July 1887 ordered all local military authorities to keep two lists: *Carnet A*, to record all foreign residents of military age; *Carnet B* to provide details of French nationals suspected of spying,

In October 1894 the Dreyfus Affair emerged from this repressive climate, heightened by renewed tension with Germany and growing anti-Semitism. The French Statistical Section discovered a docket (*bordereau*) containing sensitive military secrets in the Prussian military attaché's waste-paper basket and rashly attributed authorship to Captain Alfred Dreyfus, a staff-officer of Jewish origins. So began a series of errors that quickly mutated into conspiracy, fabrication of evidence and perversion of justice, which culminated in the greatest political scandal of modern French history. Revelations about the role of the French intelligence services stigmatized them to this day in the eyes of politicians and the public, as well as damaging civil–military relations. The episode also laid bare the problems arising from the absence of a clear distinction between foreign intelligence gathering and counter-intelligence. On 1 May 1899 Waldeck-Rousseau's left-of-centre Republican government closed the Statistical Section. All counter-espionage activities were transferred from the Etat-Major to the Sûreté générale at the Interior Ministry. The latter became responsible for everything from counter-espionage to border surveillance. The Deuxième bureau merely retained control of the research section. From 15 September 1899 counter-espionage was 'exclusively' the prerogative of the Sûreté générale. Bitter rivalry between the two services ensued. Counter-espionage was now carried out by the 'special commissaires' of the Sûreté, whose numbers rose from 122 in 1899 to 387 in 1914. In theory at least, until the Second World War counter-espionage was carried out by non-specialized civil servants from the Interior Ministry. They comprised 'special commissaires' operating in border areas, section 5 of the Renseignements généraux for surveillance of foreigners and the *service officiel* of the Sûreté devoted to mail interception. This was an embryonic version of the modern Direction de la surveillance du territoire (DST) created officially in November 1944.[5]

Despite losing most of its domestic surveillance activities, the SR of the Etat-Major continued to exist as an intelligence-gathering organization, albeit in diminished form. Indeed, from 1913 it recovered some of its former powers after the War Minister decided to give the military a 'foreign counter-espionage' mission. The First World War accelerated this process allowing the SR to claw back some control over domestic counter-espionage. In May 1915 much of the domestic and foreign intelligence services were centralized in the Section de centralisation du renseignement (SCR), attached to the Deuxième bureau at the War Ministry. By the end of 1915 the War Ministry's Cinquième bureau had control of the SR, SCR, propaganda, post and telegraph, the economic section and the inter-allied office. It was placed in the hands of Major Ladoux, best remembered for the arrest of the alleged spy Mata-Hari. After Ladoux's dismissal in April 1917 the SCR was placed under direct control of the SR and by the end of the war counter-espionage was centralized under a Commissariat à la sûreté nationale under the direct authority of the Président du conseil.

Assessment of Germany before the war

What then was the record of the French intelligence services from the Franco-Prussian to the First World wars? One measure of their record might be how successful France was in assessing its most persistent potential enemy Germany. If the stated objective of the French intelligence services was to 'inform about the plans and operations of the enemy', then the ultimate test must be to evaluate their performance at the outbreak of war. It is well known that the French High Command misjudged both the strength and the direction of the German attack in 1914 and quite wrongly based French strategy on an early victory. These serious errors of judgement, according to Christopher Andrew, arose from weakness in three areas: intelligence collection, intelligence analysis and in France's self-assessment.[6]

Poor intelligence gathering was not the main reason for the miscalculations of government and High Command in 1914. On the eve of war the author of a Senate report on France's armed forces was able to document, mainly from public sources, what he called the 'flagrant inferiority of our military equipment compared to that of Germany'. Even Chief of the General Staff General Joffre confessed in his memoirs that German military writers had publicly discussed the possibility of a German attack through Belgium. Nevertheless, the weakness of France's highly fragmented intelligence collection was in part to blame for the almost devastating German sweep into northern France halted only *in extremis* on the Marne some 30 miles from Paris.

Even when France had clear superiority over Germany in certain areas of intelligence, the advantages were scandalously wasted. France's long tradition of intercepting diplomatic messages had enabled it to develop the science of cryptography and cryptanalysis, so that by the 1880s it had a clear superiority over Germany in this field. Superiority in interception and deciphering meant that in communications intelligence France had a substantial lead over the other great powers. By the turn of the century it had broken most of their codes, even if their degree of sophistication was occasionally limited, with the US State Department referring to the Secretaries of the Army and Navy respectively as 'Mars' and 'Neptune'.[7] By 1909 an Inter-ministerial Commission on Cryptography had been established, which brought together the ministries of the Interior, War, Navy, Post Office and Colonies, but not, significantly, Foreign Affairs, which chose to remain aloof. Rivalry between the Interior and Foreign Affairs ministries, both of which had possessed *cabinets noirs* interception services since 1905, was fierce. Both were intercepting the same traffic and were willing to use the evidence to discredit ministers whose policies they disliked. So it was with Prime Minister Joseph Caillaux's secret negotiations with Germany at the height of the 1911 Agadir Crisis. But even Caillaux recklessly threatened to reveal, at the murder trial of his wife in July 1914, the existence of the inter-cepts if there was no acquittal. She was gallantly acquitted. But rumours of the existence of the intercepts led Germany to change its diplomatic codes on the eve of the First World War. Thus irresponsible ministers, inter-departmental rivalry between code-breakers and delay in extending the art to the War Ministry ensured that on the eve of war the French cryptographic advance was squandered.

French 'human-intelligence' gathering suffered from a similarly frag-mented organization as well as from a lack of funds. Even these monies were often misused, with a sizeable sum of the War Ministry's secret fund being allocated until 1911 to a large Bastille Day lunch. The reorganization of French intelligence after its debacle in the Dreyfus Affair did not reap benefits. Apart from the inter-service rivalry that dogged the intelligence services and hindered their mission, the truncated SR remained largely ineffective. At the time of the 1905 First Moroccan Crisis it had a mere five officers at headquarters and seven at frontier posts along France's eastern border from Nancy to Nice collecting German, Italian and Austrian intelli-gence. But no field officer was stationed north of Nancy and none was responsible for Belgian or Dutch intelligence. Not until 1913 was an intelli-gence post created for the first time at Mézières on the Belgian border. This was too late to provide anything but negligible information on German preparations for the attack on Belgium.

If the collection of intelligence about France's main potential enemy was inadequate, the use to which it was put was even worse. To be fair, this was partly to do with the broader incoherence of French foreign and defence policy making in the decade before the First World War. Before the 1911

Agadir Crisis the Foreign and War ministries lived in a state of almost mutual ignorance. Apart from failing to inform military planners of the 1902 secret Franco-Italian non-aggression convention, the Quai d'Orsay never gave the War Ministry an official diplomatic appraisal of Anglo-French relations after the 1904 Entente Cordiale. Such poor coordination improved slightly after 1911, but was not absent during the July Crisis.[8]

The role of assessing Germany as a potential enemy devolved mainly on the Ministry of War, but the Ministry was not up to the task. The legendary instability of governments under the Third Republic was partly compensated by the stability of ministers, who often retained the same portfolio in successive government. This was not the case with the War Ministry. Not only did the Ministry of War change hands more than any other in the Third Republic, but most of the office-holders were of modest ability. On rare occasions when the Ministry was fortunate enough to attract a capable minister, it was quite impossible for him, as one of the members of the Senate Army Commission explained in February 1914, to master its 14 separate departments as well as the 11 standing committees and the hundred or so *ad hoc* committees of the High Command. The combining of the posts of Commander-in-Chief and Chief of the General Staff in July 1911 (until 1916) in the person of General Joffre improved coordination over the French army, but nothing at all was done to improve the use made of intelligence within the General Staff. In August 1914 the Deuxième and Troisième bureaux (Operations) were still operating as 'watertight compartments' and the rivalry between the two was a serious handicap in assessing Germany. In the final years of peace, as Christopher Andrew suggests, 'intelligence assessments were accepted by Operations and by Joffre only when they re-inforced their "preconceived ideas"'.[9] This classic intelligence error was repeated over the Schlieffen Plan and over France's grossly misjudged and nearly catastrophic assessment of Germany's use of reserves and heavy artillery.

The third area that contributed to France's miscalculations about Germany as a potential enemy was how France assessed itself. The legendary strategist Sun Tzu taught long ago that it is as important to know yourself as to know your enemies. This the French failed to do. Their attitude on the eve of war can only be described as overconfident. Less than a month before the outbreak of war the author of a Senate report, Charles Humbert, caused parliamentary uproar when he gave a devastating account of France's inferiority in armaments to Germany, most notably its almost complete deficiency in heavy artillery. Yet, although the Senate debate was widely publicized, it had no visible effect on morale. When the French government and people went to war three weeks later, albeit without enthusiasm, it was with a greater confidence in victory than at any time since the Franco-Prussian War. Such confidence had been on the increase since 1905. During the First

Moroccan Crisis the vast majority of the Cabinet and High Command believed that a war with Germany would lead to defeat on a similar scale to 1870. By the time of the Second Moroccan Crisis of 1911, Germany was considered to be much less formidable. Although the idea of going to war with it was declined, it was no longer because France believed in inevitable defeat, but rather because it did not yet believe it had a 70 per cent chance of victory. French confidence continued its exponential growth, helped in 1912 by a General Staff report forecasting a Triple Entente victory over the Triple Alliance in the event of an Austrian offensive in the Balkans. French intelligence reports highlighting French inferiority to Germany were often seen as defeatist. Consequently, the French High Command was not encouraged to tailor strategy to French means, leading Joffre to take risks beyond the capabilities of his armies. During the July Crisis, Joffre was utterly confident that victory would be swift and certain. In the event, France was saved from rapid defeat only by the 'Miracle of the Marne'.

What was striking about this transformation of French confidence in less than a decade was that it did not reflect any belief in German military decline. Indeed, Germany in 1914 was even more of a formidable opponent than in 1905. France's growing confidence in victory, according to Christopher Andrew, reflected less a changing assessment of its enemy than a changing assessment of itself. It found its ultimate expression in the new strategic doctrine of the offensive adopted by the French High Command at Joffre's behest after Agadir. That doctrine placed the greatest emphasis on the élan of the French army, with the enemy's intentions relegated to a very poor second.

Of course, some of France's confidence derived from its improved diplomatic position after 1905. Even so it could not expect substantial military support from Russia and Britain in the early stages of the war. The sheer scale of the Russian army might have impressed on paper, but, as the General Staff calculated in July 1913, Russian troops would not make contact with the Germans until 15 days after mobilisztion and could not launch a general offensive until the twenty-third day. Russia would therefore be of no direct assistance for two to three weeks during the crucial early battles of what was expected to be a short war. With Britain the opposite was true. The British Expeditionary Force could intervene quickly but with little might. Though the Anglo-French military conversations were overall more regular and more fruitful in terms of potential cooperation should Britain decide to fight alongside France, their execution remained hypothetical until the night of 3 August 1914. This strengthened the case for France to know its enemy and its friend. The importance of good intelligence in assessing German plans and potential was arguably all the more important because France would be militarily alone in the initial stages of the conflict. Again France appeared to reason purely in terms of confidence. It believed that on its own it could gain a substantial advantage over Germany on the Western Front that would allow it to win the war, despite having no numerical superiority over the German army and inferior armaments. Christopher Andrew concludes: 'Her confidence had a psychological rather than a material origin.'[10] It rested on the traditional belief that France, all said and done, was superior to Germany. Just as French public opinion in 1914 held to the irrational belief that war would be short because they wanted it to be short, so the French government and High Command's assessment of Germany as a potential enemy was based less on concrete evidence than on wishful thinking. This was something that intelligence was unable, or not allowed, to dispel.

The golden age of French military intelligence

The performance of French intelligence and the use to which it was put improved once war had begun. Intelligence may have been partly to blame for the military reverses of August 1914, but deserved some credit for the Miracle of the Marne a month later. The explanation was twofold: Joffre had learned his lesson and now accepted that intelligence should be integrated more fully into strategy; the Deuxième bureau's capacity for intelligence gathering improved dramatically, as aerial surveillance, radio intercepts and cryptography began to be used more effectively. Though the Germans had changed their codes on the eve of war, by 1 October the French had broken the German primary Ubchi code and were able to do so repeatedly. Though they were at first deluged by the volume of enemy traffic, it was possible to draw up a picture of German troop movements by an elementary form of traffic analysis. By guessing at direction from the strength of signal, and aided by German organizations systematically applying certain call signs to particular geographical locations, the French were soon relying on this and German intercepts as a principal intelligence source on German movements. The use of signals intelligence in September 1914 during the Marne and the following month in the Race to the Sea dramatically improved the standing of French cryptography and intelligence among the High Command. The French were helped by Germany having no cryptographic service before the war and taking two years to develop one. French intelligence successes attracted more finance and better coordination. This bred further success. The War Ministry's Bureau du Chiffre and GHQ's Service du Chiffre were able to build up the stability and tradition necessary to crack the particularly complex submarine codes and the immensely sophisticated German ciphers of 1918. After 1916 better use of direction-finding equipment (notably from the navy's coastal listening posts) and German radio traffic analysis allowed the French to chart the enemy's order of battle in what one historian of French intelligence has referred to as 'perhaps the single most important source of operational intelligence on the Western Front'.[11]

Despite the intelligence revolution that affected all major powers during the war, French intelligence, perhaps more than any other, continued to be dogged by the user's natural tendency towards scepticism when intelligence did not confirm preconceived ideas. Problems of how to catalogue, analyse and interpret masses of data and put then to use before they had perished were common to all the powers, as was overcoming greater secrecy, camouflage and deception measures. French intelligence was particularly proficient at prisoner-of-war interrogation, an art they subsequently lost, which goes some way to explaining the shameful torture of the Indochina and Algerian conflicts.

French intelligence's weakest arm was the domestic security service, which ironically had become the senior intelligence service after the Dreyfus Affair. The number of French people spying for Germany in the war is one measure of its failure. German documents reveal that from the beginning of the war a number of French deputies, some former ministers, were in contact with the head of the German legation in Bern (the hub of German international propaganda) about undermining France's commitment to the war. French counter-intelligence had greater success with the alleged spy Mata-Hari, even if the head of French counter-espionage in 1917, who secured her arrest, Captain Victor Ladoux, was himself arrested four days later for spying. In 1919 a court martial acquitted him, but he never returned to the service. A Ministry of the Interior report of 8 June 1918 criticized 'the inactivity of our [counter-espionage] services, and especially of Captain Ladoux'.[12] Nevertheless, with the French pioneering many sophisticated intelligence techniques and its code-breakers surpassing even the wizards of the British Admiralty's Room 40, the First World War was the golden age of French military intelligence, when its influence was greatest. This ensured the domination of military intelligence during the inter-war years.

The inter-war years

Military intelligence that had made a name for itself in the war had no distinct name after it. The military intelligence and counter-espionage service continued as an independent section of the General Staff of the War Ministry, but with no official title other than 'Deuxième bureau SR–SCR'. The Deuxième bureau was the principal centre for the collection, analysis and dissemination of intelligence on foreign powers. During the inter-war years military intelligence – still located logically at 75 rue de l'Université, near the German embassy, where it had been since the creation of the Statistical Service after the Franco-Prussian War – focused on both foreign intelligence and counter-espionage. Despite its 1932 relocation to 2 bis Avenue de Tourville, earning it the nickname of '2 bis', military intelligence still saw Germany as its greatest potential enemy. The service, which now had 120 staff including those stationed at the six frontier posts, was divided into two. The first was the secret intelligence service known as the Service de renseignement (SR), or more popularly as the Services spéciaux, which gathered intelligence on potential adversaries, forwarding the data for analysis and use to the Deuxième bureau of the General Staff. The SR also possessed a small cryptanalysis unit (Section D), which in conjunction with the Foreign Ministry's Cabinet Noir and the General Staff's code section intercepted foreign encyphered communications. The second was the Section de centralisation du renseignement (SCR), charged with counter-espionage abroad. A further task was the protection of SR operations and agents abroad as well as the recruitment and control of agents who had penetrated foreign services. Towards the end of the 1930s some 1500 agents were said to be operating in Germany alone. SCR kept in contact with the Sûreté Nationale and the Préfecture de Police of the Interior Ministry. SCR, like SR, was organized geographically in the 1930s according to main poten-tial enemies with a German, Italian and then Russian section supported by sections devoted to archives and revolutionary propaganda. Largely as a result of its wartime successes, military intelligence had again taken the lead in counter-espionage activities, with internal security largely subservient to it.[13] The Quai d'Orsay, unlike the British Foreign Office, had no intelligence service of its own and no role in the supervision of the intelligence process, though ambassadors usually had modest *fonds secrets* with which to reward informants.

Since the war, domestic intelligence, run from the Interior Ministry, had been augmented by the creation of a special brigade in the Sûreté générale along the lines of the British Special Branch. It remained diminutive with a mere 10 inspectors, aided by the long-standing special police of the 5th section of the Paris Renseignements généraux, whose duties were not restricted to counter-espionage matters alone. Internal security had a monumental task, as France was a primary target of not just German, but Soviet espionage and subversion. This privilege derived from Paris being the headquarters of a two-million-strong Tsarist international émigré community, and France the friend and ally of the anti-Soviet Polish and Romanian governments, let alone a source of military technology vital to the modern-ization of the Soviet armed forces. The Soviets were aided in their task by the creation in 1920 of the French Communist Party (Parti communiste français or PCF). Soviet subversion was in evidence amongst regiments during the French occupation of the Ruhr in 1923. With the continued bolshevization and Stalinization of the PCF, Soviet intelligence thrived in France. Jean Cremet, a member of the PCF's central committee from 1926, coordinated espionage with Soviet intelligence agents. They operated from the new Soviet embassy in Paris and used trade-union contacts in French armaments industries to supply information. The hundred-strong spy network controlled by the PCF and the Soviet embassy was eventually revealed in 1927. However, although a trial convicted eight people of espionage, Cremet and other senior figures fled to Moscow. This was by no means the end of PCF service to Soviet intelligence, with household communist names such as Jacques Duclos and André Martel continuing the link.[14]

These revelations, and French inter-war society's political and social divisions, fuelled the belief among French intelligence officers that foreign and domestic subversion was widespread and united. Politicization was one of the major problems of French domestic intelligence during these years, encouraged by the contemporary development of French spy fiction with its emphasis on conspiratorial theories of history. Fact imitated fiction, reaching its zenith in 1932 with the *Fantomas* trial of 1932, named after the fictional detective thriller novels of the period. Leading communists were tried for co-ordinating French 'worker-correspondents', on the Stalinist model, to produce information on local affairs for the PCF official newspaper *L'Humanité* and Party officials. The information was passed on to the Soviet embassy. Although five were convicted, Jacques Duclos escaped to Moscow. Charges against him were dropped following the left's election victory in November 1932, when Communist Party support was needed to bolster a parliamentary majority. Duclos's connection with Soviet espionage appears not to have ended there. It is generally believed that by 1937 he was the impresario of Soviet intelligence (NKVD) in France, having been re-elected to parliament, become second-in-command of the PCF and vice-president of the Chamber of Deputies. In 1969 he was even a candidate in the presidential elections. The fact that successive French governments preferred to overlook aspects of Soviet espionage was partly a result of France's desire not to alienate the USSR as a potential ally after Hitler's coming to power in 1933. It was also a consequence of not wishing to antagonize the Communist Party after 1936, and to avoid the embarrassment of having state secrets revealed. But this sent out the wrong signals to the public and to the guardians of those secrets, blurring the lines of loyalty to the state. It also prepared the ground for the French establishment's penetration by Soviet moles or 'agents of influence', revealed after the Second World War. From 1948 the US Army Security Agency was able to crack Soviet intelligence ciphers (code-named VENONA) to reveal several inter-war Soviet agents or sympathizers in senior positions in France. These ran from the Air Minister of the 1930s, Pierre Cot, to Edouard Pfeiffer, principal secretary to Edouard Daladier, War Minister from January 1936 to May 1940 and Premier from April 1938 to March 1940. This may also have laid the foundations for an extensive Soviet espionage network in France after the Second World War.[15]

Many intelligence officers were severely critical of politicians' lack of purpose in tackling the general 'decadence' of the period. Communist and fascist threats provided legitimacy for the blurring of intelligence and police lines of demarcation, so that the former increasingly assumed a domestic role. Frustration increased as their legitimate and well-founded warnings about

Germany's military build-up were ignored by the High Command from 1930 to 1939. In 1935 the head of the Deuxième bureau, Colonel Koeltz, warned Britain's military attaché that Germany would probably be in a position to make war by the following year. By 1936–37 army intelligence and the Deuxième bureau of the Air Ministry were warning of *Luftwaffe* training in tactical ground support and tank/Stuka combinations to break an opponent's organized defence. A mixture of cryptography – automated since the end of the war – informants, spies, listening posts, industrial intelligence and military attachés gave the French such precise assessment of German circumvention of the Versailles Treaty as to disqualify the poor image of French intelligence analysis in the 1930s painted by some historians. The problem was also poor integration into diplomatic decision making. Poor coordination between the Foreign Ministry, which tended to sneer at secret intelligence gathering, and the War Ministry, was not new. But this was not the fault of the intelligence services. From 1935 to 1938 liaison depended on a solitary officer, Colonel Paul de Villelume. Not until May 1938 were Quai d'Orsay and senior defence officials brought together in a weekly liaison committee, established under one of the deputy chiefs of the army staff, General Henri Dentz, an intelligence specialist. Even then coordination between Quai and War Ministry was never as bad as has often been assumed.[16]

Hitler's coming to power in 1933 and the reconstitution of German intelligence, proscribed by the Versailles Treaty, demanded French counter-measures. The French were up against a better-funded German military counter-intelligence (the Abwehr). A series of decrees in 1934, 1935 and 1937 reorganized the Sûreté générale to make it more responsive to national security issues by creating the Direction centrale de la sûreté nationale and the post of 'Contrôleur général de la surveillance du territoire' to tackle counter-espionage. For the first time since 1899 national security had its own independent police service and resources. By basing it on military regions, the government hoped to facilitate liaison with the military and encourage the unity of counter-espionage services in the event of war.

In 1937 military intelligence took a step in the same direction with the creation of a counter-espionage section in each military region (Bureau de centralisation militaire) and the creation in the SCR of a new section devoted to 'preventive defence'. According to Colonel Paillole of the German section of the Deuxième bureau – subsequently deputy director of counter-espionage – at this time spying was transformed in legal terms from being a political act to a crime against the state encapsulated in the notorious term *secret de défense*. As before the First World War, spy-mania gripped the country. The number of arrests for spying jumped from 40 in 1936 to 153 in 1937; Paillole's superior, Colonel Schlesser, put the numbers for 1939 at 400 and 1940 at 1000. The February 1939 decree set down clearly the respective roles of domestic and foreign intelligence in counter-espionage matters in peace and war. In peacetime, domestic counter-espionage was placed under the exclusive control of the Interior Ministry, while beyond French frontiers was the responsibility of the War Ministry. However, as with the First World War, in wartime the War Ministry, through the Army General Staff's SCR, assumed responsibility for gathering domestic and foreign counter-intelligence. The military centralized counter-intelligence information and then passed it to the Interior Ministry for assessment. War and Interior ministry liaison fell to the SCR and the Contrôle général de la surveillance du territoire (CGST). For the first time since the Dreyfus Affair, counter-intelligence was unified and centralized in the hands of the military.[17]

In the inter-war years the French were particularly successful in signals intelligence. At the end of 1936 the Popular Front's War Minister, Edouard Daladier, secretly authorized domestic listening posts at the headquarters of the Deuxième bureau to intercept foreign embassies' diplomatic traffic. Deciphering German codes was facilitated by the Deuxième bureau's penetration since 1931 of the heart of the German war machine, including the Abwehr. It controlled an agent by the name of 'Asché' (pseudonym for Hans-Thilo Schmidt), now working for Goering's Forschungsamt (security and intelligence service). He handed to French intelligence the intercepts and decrypts of the Stuttgart post listening in to France. Thanks to Asché, who had previously worked for the Chiffrierstelle, the German War Ministry's cipher section, the French were able to read most German intercepts. Thanks again to Asché, French cryptologists, according to Paillole, were on the point of reconstructing the infamous German Enigma cipher machine. In July 1939 French, Polish and British military collaboration on cracking the Enigma codes was rewarded when two Polish reconstructions of the Enigma machine arrived in Paris complete with the initial results of Polish code-breakers. After Poland's defeat, Polish cryptologists were eventually transferred to Paris, where they teamed up with their French counterparts under the leadership of Colonel Bertrand of the Deuxième bureau. Together they worked at the top-secret 'PC Bruno' in the Chateau de Vignolles, 50 kilometres north-east of Paris, in the 'French Bletchley Park'. In January 1940 PC Bruno and Britain's Bletchley Park made the breakthrough with the Enigma codes. Collaboration between French and British intelligence increased following a meeting in early January 1940 between the head of the Deuxième bureau, Colonel Louis Rivet and the head of British secret intelligence, Major-General Sir Stewart Menzies ('C'). It was agreed that the French should be given exclusive responsibility for use of Enigma intelligence on the Western Front. By March 1940 what the French referred to as 'Source Z' and the British as 'Ultra' could be decoded rapidly enough to make it operationally exploitable.[18]

Military intelligence's success in penetrating the German war machine went even further. Anti-Nazis were a particularly fruitful source of secret intelligence. The most informative was Colonel Hans Oster, deputy to Admiral Canaris, head of the Abwehr. His friendship with the Dutch military attaché in Berlin produced highly sensitive information, which was relayed through the French SR outstation in the Netherlands and through Belgian military attachés. French intelligence gained reasonably accurate warnings of the many alerts about a German attack from November 1939 to May 1940.[19] Assessments of the degree and type of German rearmament, the likely nature of its warfare, even the accurate prediction of a German remilitarization of the Rhineland in 1936, demonstrated the efficacy of French military intelligence. Some of it was used to determine when the German offensive in the West would begin, even if in the end it did little to stave off French defeat.

Many historians of France used to start with defeat and then work backwards, imagining how every aspect of the French war machine was 'decadent', including intelligence. Recent analyses have concluded that pre-war French intelligence services generally performed well compared to the agencies of other powers.[20] The problem had less to do with poor intelligence, and more to do with how intelligence was used by the French High Command, confused foreign policy-makers and a hesitant political class, as well as poor coordination between all three. Lack of coordination and centralization of intelligence meant that intelligence warnings about Nazi Germany were not always given due consideration, as French ministers preferred the less pessimistic views of the French ambassador in Berlin, François-Poncet, when they chimed in with their own wishful thinking.[21]

At the outbreak of war the SR and the Service de contre-espionage (CE) were fused together in the Cinquième bureau (secret services) under the experienced Colonel Rivet. Headquarters were at 2 bis Avenue de Tourville, near the Invalides. SR was ordered to concentrate its military intelligence activities almost completely on Germany, whereas CE was directed to widen its brief from counter-intelligence to diplomatic intelligence, internal security and postal and telephone censorship. For the first, and perhaps last, time in its history French intelligence possessed a relatively coordinated and unitary organization akin to the Anglo-Saxon model of an intelligence community. Ironically, this centralized system would presage the most radical divisions in French intelligence history. Collaboration and Resistance, which followed defeat nine months later, split French intelligence physically and ideologically.

War and division

During the Phoney War counter-espionage worked overtime to counter the perceived threat of Fifth Columnists. SR turned its attention to gathering intelligence on when Hitler would begin his westwards offensive and the German order of battle. They were blessed with an over-abundance of inconclusive intelligence reflecting German confusion over when to mount the Western offensive. This fuelled fears of imminent invasion in October and November 1939, with another 10 or so alerts right down to the real thing on 10 May 1940, all sapping morale and undermining combat readiness. Because Gamelin and the High Command were so focused on French weaknesses, notably lack of war preparation, they tended to believe that Germany would attack soon after finishing with Poland. French intelligence with its privileged access to high-grade informants such as Schmidt more accurately predicted an extended delay before the offensive. But Gamelin preferred to trust his assumption that Hitler would not rest rather than hard intelligence from his intelligence chiefs. On 14 November he modified his strategy to adopt the so-called Dyle Plan. Believing that the Germans were on the verge of a surprise attack against The Netherlands or Belgium, Gamelin shaped a new pre-emptive strategy, which committed Allied forces on the left flank to a cross-country dash to buttress the Belgians on the Dyle river east of Brussels in the event of a German violation of Belgium. By this strategic modification, like Joffre at the outset of the First World War (under whom he had served his apprenticeship), Gamelin ignored intelligence assessments and miscalculated the timing and direction of the German offensive. French intelligence was right and Gamelin wrong. A mixture of bureaucratic inertia, rivalry between armed services and personalities made change difficult, so that intelligence on the combined use of aeroplane and tank forces that had so effectively defeated the Poles was noted but not applied.

Defeat and the armistice were not the end of France's official intelligence services. At the beginning of the summer the head of French intelligence Colonel Rivet had transferred his services from Paris to the so-called Free Zone in the south. A note of 27 June 1940 disbanded much of the Cinquième bureau, reconstituted it in 'camouflaged' form and split the SR from counter-espionage, ending the short-lived period of unity. General Weygand, Minister of National Defence in the first Vichy government, agreed to a double-headed structure for counter-espionage. The first, created by the decree of 8 September 1940, comprised the eerily named Bureaux des menées antinationales (BMA). It was charged with protecting national defence secrets and the armistice army against 'anti-national activity', such as de Gaulle's Resistance, which Vichy viewed as treasonable. But anti-national activities also involved the more sordid side of Vichy ideology, such as anti-Semitism and political police activities. They were encouraged by the heavy presence of extreme right elements in the Vichy intelligence services, notably from the fascistic Cagoule organization. Some of this work was carried out by parallel Vichy intelligence services such as the sinister Centre d'information et d'études (CIE), which worked with the BMA.[22] The eight BMA were located in the armistice army's main garrison towns from Bourg-en-Bresse in the east to Toulouse in the west, with an additional three bureaux in

Algiers, Rabat and Tunisia. Their role involved both counter-espionage and foreign intelligence gathering. Britain and the Soviet Union were the official targets, but unofficially they targeted the German occupying forces.[23] However, it is difficult to tell from the many self-justificatory post-war accounts what proportion of time was spent spying on the Allies or what damage they caused. British signals intelligence at Bletchley Park continued to maintain close links with the head of French signals intelligence Colonel Bertrand after Vichy began collaboration in July 1940. Bertrand transferred his cryptanalysis section, with the connivance of the deputy head of the first Vichy government General Maxime Weygand, to the Chateau des Fouzes (code-named *Cadix*) just north of Nimes in the southern zone. He continued to help the British in cracking the Enigma codes until German occupation of the southern zone in November 1942.[24]

Nevertheless, questions remain as to what Vichy intelligence organizations did with their information. For some three decades after the war Vichy's excesses were minimized and the Resistance's role maximized. It seems that most of the French intelligence services' disreputable activities in support of the Vichy regime have been overlooked in favour of the more 'patriotic' role of the unofficial branch of the French services dedicated to organizing against the invader. Focusing on the clandestine role of the Vichy intelligence services (pseudonym 'Entreprise des travaux ruraux' (TR)), has been due in no small part to the organization's best propagandist, its former head, Paul Paillole, in a series of books and memoirs, which he continued to publish long after the war. The TR engaged in offensive counter-espionage directed against the occupying forces through its centres in the main towns of the southern zone, masquerading as outposts of the corps of agricultural engineers. It is claimed that by October 1942, with the connivance of the still surviving Surveillance du territoire (domestic security service now controlled in the southern zone by Vichy's police), over a thousand Abwehr and Axis agents were arrested, of whom 16 were transferred to North Africa for execution. However, one must wonder what the German authorities thought of this and why they did so little to stop it. Apparently, on 14 September 1941, following pressure from the Germans, a decree was issued by Premier Admiral Darlan and his Interior Minister Pucheu transferring counter-espionage to the civil authorities. A month previously a new intelligence organization had been created, the Centre d'information gouvernemental (CIG), designed to bring together the three SR services, War, Navy and Air ministries, and to limit their semi-clandestine activities. From 1941 Darlan and Pucheu ordered Vichy police and security services to hunt out the embryonic Resistance movement in France. By March 1942 the BMA had been abolished. In August 1942 a new military intelligence service was created, the Service de sécurité militaire (SSM), under the direction of the ubiquitous Major Paillole, though with limited means and now under tight Vichy control.[25]

The extension of German occupation to the whole of France in November 1942 following the Anglo-American landings in North Africa ended the official existence of French counter-espionage services in metropolitan France, including the Surveillance du territoire units, which the German authorities abolished. The intelligence services in the southern zone decamped to Algiers. However, they left behind them a dual structure of clandestine intelligence services: the TR, now run by Major Roger Lafont, known as Verneuil, the future head of the post-war counter-espionage organization, the Service de documentation extérieure et de contre espionage (SDECE); and a branch of the SSM intended to prepare the setting-up of military intelligence once France was liberated.

The ambivalence that had characterized these intelligence services was not present in the intelligence service of the 'other' France, that of the Resistance. From the outset General de Gaulle had wished the Resistance, which he personified, to be much more than just a fighting force. That demanded sound intelligence. He chose one of his earliest collaborators in London, Major Dewavrin (pseudonym Passy), to set up a Deuxième bureau of the Free French General Staff. After a series of name changes, on 4 August 1942 this eventually became the Bureau central de renseignement et d'action (BCRA). It contained six sections: political action, intelligence, military action, counter-espionage, a technical section and a command section. Counter-espionage was run by Lieutenant Roger Warin (pseudonym Wybot), following his arrival in London in November 1941 after leaving the CIE and BMA. Authoritarian and inherently mistrustful, he was replaced at the end of 1942. After the war he went on to run France's security service, the DST, until 1959.[26] The BCRA's mission was to supply the British with intelligence about France (principally as a form of currency exchange for other services) and to ensure that the developing Resistance remained united behind General de Gaulle. It was much better at the latter than the former, which is probably what de Gaulle would have preferred anyway. British intelligence believed that there was at best a lack of security-consciousness amongst the Free French (as the ill-fated Anglo-Free French Dakar expedition in autumn 1940 suggested), at worst penetration of French intelligence. The British Secret Intelligence Service was regularly intercepting Free French diplomatic and BCRA traffic and producing reports for Churchill on their content.[27] As for de Gaulle, he bitterly resented British intelligence's restrictions on his own services and their ability to run operations themselves in France.[28] Overall, Resistance intelligence, like the Resistance itself, was valued more by de Gaulle for its political rather than its military contribution.

With the occupation of the whole of France in November 1942, the heads of the various intelligence services (among them Paillole, Rivet and Ronin) in the southern zone moved to Algiers. Under the orders of General Giraud, de Gaulle's American-sponsored rival for leadership of the Resistance, they joined a newly created Direction des services de renseignement et de la sécurité militaire (DSR-SM). The head was Colonel Rivet. Paillole was placed in charge of military security with control over the clandestine TR and SM networks that had remained in metropolitan France and to which were now added the Surveillance du Territoire and interception services. These services (largely those of the former '2 bis') underwent a series of reorganizations during which de Gaulle's own network was finally integrated into a unified Direction générale des services spéciaux (DGSS) in November 1943 under the control of the Gaullist anthropology professor, Jacques Soustelle. Such was the dominance of the military in intelligence affairs that Giraud protested at the appointment of a civilian to such an important post. De Gaulle replied: 'If that bothers you, we will dress him up as a general.'[29] De Gaulle outmanœuvred Giraud for control of the National Liberation Committee and reasserted control over the intelligence services. On 6 November 1944 the DGSS became the Direction générale des études et recherches (DGER), well known for the excellent restaurant in the base-ment of its Paris headquarters open to anyone with a secret agent card. On 19 April 1945 the Gaullist Passy resumed control of France's secret services.[30] Passy's mission was to bring order out of the chaos of factions jostling for position in France's post-Resistance secret services. In April 1944 Paillole successfully negotiated with the Allies for French intelligence to have the right to operate in France after the Liberation. De Gaulle's aim of ensuring that full French sovereignty was restored by the French for the French was accomplished.

Fourth Republic

Although Paillole was successful in ensuring that French counter-espionage kept its autonomy after the Liberation, he was unable to maintain its unity. A passionate believer in intelligence as an 'indissociable whole', in November 1944 Paillole was unable to stop de Gaulle from splitting the foreign intelli-gence service from military intelligence, and resigned. The architecture of French intelligence for the rest of the twentieth century was established. By January 1946 Passy had created the Service de documentation et de contre espionage (SDECE), responsible to the head of government and isolated from the new military security service, the Service de renseignement militaire (SRM), responsible to the defence ministry. The SDECE, which replaced the DGER, was led by Colonel Chrétien, then Colonel Lafont (Verneuil), and the SRM by Colonel Labadie.

Domestic security became the prerogative of the new and powerful DST under its creator Roger Wybot, responsible to the Interior Minister. The DST consciously broke with the French idea that only the military were capable of intelligence gathering, centralizing analysis and the manipulation of agents. More importantly, Wybot separated the operational side of intelligence gathering from its analysis. The DST was able to capitalize on France's strong tradition of internal security, justifying its existence in the short term by the need to hunt-out collaborators and from 1947 to seek out communists. Whereas the foreign intelligence and military security services continued as rivals, Wybot's DST largely controlled the operational side of French counter-intelligence in similar fashion to J. Edgar Hoover's FBI. Nevertheless, it still competed with lesser rivals such as the Renseignements généraux (RG), also of the Interior Ministry, and the Paris Prefecture of Police, which ran its own RG – the RGPP. The SDECE, which became the Direction générale de la sécurité extérieure (DGSE) in 1982, was left with foreign intelligence gathering and attempting to protect its own services from foreign penetration.

The rivalry, fragmentation and zig-zagging responsibility between civil and military intelligence that characterized the French services after the Dreyfus Affair continued after the war. The Interior Ministry had gained control of counter-espionage from the military after 1899. The military regained pre-eminence from 1913 until the end of the First World War on the back of Franco-German tension and conflict. The inter-war years saw a shared responsibility on paper, but which shifted towards the military as tension with Germany increased. After the war predominance shifted again to the Interior Ministry, helped by the splitting in 1944 of the military branch of counter-intelligence between the Defence Ministry and the head of government.[31]

On emerging from the war at an international level, France was no longer an intelligence power. It had missed out on the enormous growth in wartime electronic and scientific intelligence. Although dwarfed by the American and Soviet intelligence machines, unlike British intelligence France failed to carve out niche areas and use them to strike up partnership agreements with the Americans or British (notwithstanding their reluctance to share secrets with a government that contained communist ministers until May 1947). Poor civil–intelligence relations fuelled by political turmoil, personality and bureaucratic problems worsened the position. Certainly up to 1958 the SDECE was the Cinderella intelligence agency. Few heads of government put its services to serious use. In 1947 its personnel was reduced to a mere 1500 from some 10,000 at the Liberation. The SDECE was forced to rely increasingly on inferior-quality personnel on short-service secondment from the armed services. The quality of recruit declined and the military ethos increased, leading to further decline in the perceived utility of the SDECE by the civilian authorities. Until the 1960s the military represented some 40 per cent of the SDECE's personnel, from which time de Gaulle raised it to 60 per cent. This was very different from Britain, where a high standard of civilian recruit, often from the elite universities of Oxford and Cambridge (albeit with problems such as the Cambridge Five), was attracted to an intelligence career in the Foreign Service and Secret Intelligence Service (SIS). This ensured that intelligence was taken seriously and integrated into policy making. France's engagement in a number of imperial 'hot wars', as opposed to fighting the cold war, meant a concentration on military intelligence in which the military were largely the end-users. The SDECE's resources were targeted on the Far East and North Africa as a result of the Indochina and Algerian wars. Almost all intelligence stations in Europe, especially in Germany, were ordered to devote some of their resources to monitoring the activities of the Algerian independence movement, the FLN. This reinforced the SDECE's image as of more immediate use and proximity to the military than to its responsible authority the head of government.

The mission that French intelligence assigned itself during this period was very much a reflection of how France saw itself in the world: vulnerable on all fronts. Domestic subversion was a concern, first from former Collaborators and, as the cold war got underway, from communists. The German menace lived on into the early 1950s and foreign intelligence spent much time gathering material in Germany on the possibility of political or economic German resurgence. Conscious of France having missed out for at least four years on weapons technology development, French intelligence services in Germany were given the brief of bringing home the fruits of German wartime scientific, technological and military developments, notably nuclear and rocket science, like all the Allied Powers. Consequently, French intelligence kept a close watch on the Anglo-Saxons. Anxiety also grew over London and Washington's clear intention to ensure Germany's redevelopment.[32] The DST had desks devoted to spying on the Americans and British. This welter of missions dispersed French intelligence efforts at a time when, ironically, France's belief in a world role was strongest and least attainable.

Post-war French intelligence was weighed down by other handicaps. Inter-agency rivalry was as virulent as internecine squabbling within the same agency, between soldiers and civilians, alumni of London and Vichy, between Gaullist and socialist. Despite the purges of the Liberation, the pro-Giraudist camp of the Deuxième bureau regained influence to represent a third of SDECE personnel. Turf wars led to serious blunders and a culture of plots and intrigue. Because the French services shared no single political affiliation other than blanket anti-communism and pro-colonialism, political parties sought to place their own men in the services, undermining effectiveness, credibility and neutrality. Politics contributed to French intelligence's unclear focus. The Soviet Union should have been a primary target for the intelligence services. But the French Communist Party's quarter of the electorate and pre-eminent position in coalition governments up to 1947 made it difficult for the SDECE and DST to single out communists or the USSR. Both the SDECE and its predecessor the DGER were attacked by the Communist Party for being 'a secret police at the service of capitalist corporations'. The DGER earned the precious title of Direction générale des ennemis de la république.[33]

A further handicap was the Resistance legacy of intelligence as action. Failure to insulate intelligence gathering from action missions endures to this day. As Douglas Porch notes,

> the temptation for a minister or ambitious service chief to court media attention through some brilliant coup by his personal special service or by a newly created action branch of a traditional service could prove overwhelming, and often would end in scandal.[34]

The French intelligence services laboured under a final handicap: the 'spectre of communist infiltration'. Given the powerful role of communists in immediate post-war France, they were able to demand important positions for themselves in government and bureaucracy. There had been Soviet penetration of the wartime Resistance, as the KGB defector Vasili Mitrokhin revealed. At the Liberation Soviet intelligence instructed its newly established Paris residency to profit from the 'current favourable position' to renew contacts with the pre-war agent network and recruit new agents. The Foreign Ministry, intelligence agencies and political parties were targeted, but particular attention was paid to scientific and technological institutes. Soviet penetration was remarkably successful, as the Mitrokhin Archive demonstrates. Three years of Communist Party control of the Air, Labour and Industry ministries provided an opportunity to place communists in strategic positions. In 1949 the chief of the Air Ministry's security section, Major André Teulery, appointed by communist Air Minister Charles Tillon, was arrested for selling secrets to the Yugoslav military attaché. The communist science professor, Frédéric Joliot-Curie, was appointed Director of Scientific Research, giving him responsibility for France's atomic agency and the scientific section of the foreign intelligence agency. He assured Moscow that French scientists would always be at the USSR's disposal.

Although the PCF lost its powerful government position from 1947, communist sympathizers ready to do favours for the Soviet Union were already in place. In 1964 intercepts of the Soviet Security Service, the NKGB (which from 1941 to 1946 had infiltrated communist sections of the French Resistance), revealed Soviet penetration of the West. Code-named VENONA, these intercepts exposed communist infiltration of de Gaulle's inner circle, André Labarthe, director of civilian affairs, and Admiral Muselier. The decrypts showed that Labarthe and the 1930s Air Minister, Pierre Cot, had passed on intelligence to the Soviets. Though France was not alone in having spies within its intelligence services, as the Cambridge Five proved, even French intelligence specialists suggest that the discoveries were merely the tip of the iceberg and that many agents and contacts went undetected.

Soviet defectors in the 1960s, notably Major Anatoly Golitsin, claimed that the French services were penetrated. The KGB's most important cold war agents in the French Foreign Ministry were cipher personnel rather than diplomats. Nevertheless, some diplomats continued to provide information to the Soviets up to the 1970s and 1980s, including the future French ambassador in Beijing (1969–75), Etienne Manac'h. A cipher officer code-named JOUR enabled much of the cipher traffic between Paris and embassies abroad to be decrypted. He remained active for nearly a quarter of a century and was secretly decorated in 1957 and 1982 with the Order of the Red Star.[35]

The KGB's most remarkable achievement during the Fourth Republic was to penetrate every service in France's intelligence community. For most of the cold war the Paris residency ran more agents – 50 or so – than any other KGB station in Western Europe. KGB files for 1953 give as its particularly 'valuable agents' four officials in the SDECE, and a further one each in the domestic security services (the DST), the RG, the Foreign Ministry, the Defence Ministry and the Naval Ministry. KGB penetration of the French intelligence community continued through the 1960s and 1970s. At least four French intelligence officers and one former head of department in the Sûreté générale were active KGB agents during the period 1963-66. In the 1970s the quality, though not the quantity, of Soviet agents declined. The Paris residency was running 55 agents in 1974, although the Mitrokhin archive does not reveal whether they included senior civil servants or intelligence officers. However, between 1978 and 1982 no fewer than six cipher personnel at the Quai d'Orsay were under active KGB cultivation. Although it is hard to assess overall Soviet penetration of the French services, the mere perception of it by other states prejudiced France's ability to be taken seriously in intelligence liaison. Although probably unaware of the identities of the Soviet agents in France, the British and American intelligence communities were cautious about exchanging classified information with the SDECE and DST. [36] The DST was able to retrieve some of its reputation in the early 1980s through its high-level agent in the KGB Science and Technology Directorate. In July 1981, newly elected President Mitterrand personally informed Ronald Reagan of the documents being received from the KGB officer code-named FAREWELL.

This was not sufficient to overcome the enduringly poor image of French intelligence. It had been not helped by the involvement of politicians and the squabbling intelligence agencies in the two farcically investigated scandals of the Fourth Republic, the 'Generals Affair' and the *affaire des fuites*, both of which involved the dissemination of top-secret defence information.[37] Distrust from France's allies and disdain from government and public opinion undermined French intelligence services beyond the Fourth Republic. Calculating that attack was the best means of defence, in 1964 de Gaulle ordered the SDECE to break off relations with the CIA as Franco–American tension increased. This denied the Americans access to interceptions of Soviet radio traffic from French monitoring stations. However, the French lost most given their reliance on the CIA for much of their electronic surveillance. More importantly, this break with the CIA, which lasted for three years, increased the isolation and Cinderella status of the SDECE, for which de Gaulle only ever had scant regard.

Disdain for the French intelligence services reached its zenith at the end of the Fourth Republic. French intelligence performed well during the Indochina War, certainly in terms of intelligence about the growing strength of the Vietminh, their intentions and capabilities. They even knew the date of the fateful attack on Dien Bien Phu in May 1954. What they were less successful in predicting was the degree of Chinese assistance to the Vietminh around Dien Bien Phu. But Alexander Zervoudakis has shown that responsibility here had more to do with the French government than intelligence. Without consulting the Commander-in-Chief, General Navarre, it had decided at the Berlin conference of 25 February 1954 that when the major world powers met the following May Indochina would be on the agenda. This changed the strategic basis of operations in Indochina by encouraging the Vietminh to push for one great victory that would shock the French and the other powers in time for the Geneva Conference in May. The Vietminh diverted all expenditure and forces against the French garrison at Dien Bien Phu to achieve overall victory in the war.[38]

Like the army, which made up most of its personnel, French intelligence agencies felt handicapped by a lack of political support during the Algerian War. Like the army, they stuck to a strategy of total victory, underplaying and even undermining the chances of a moderate political solution. Like the army, they did their image and credibility an immense disservice by engaging in dubious moral actions. The Resistance legacy of action manifested itself in assassinations, bombings, torture and lynching, alienating not only French and world opinion, but, more importantly, moderate Arabs. Frustration turned to disloyalty and conspiracy contributing to the Fourth Republic's collapse. By 1958, the intelligence services, like the army, were a virtual law unto themselves committed to nothing less than *Algérie française*.

Fifth Republic

Like the army, the intelligence services faired no better under General de Gaulle. The General allegedly referred to their activities with patronizing disdain as 'low-life police activities'. The problem was the complicity of the terrorist OAS with the DST, RG and SDECE. French security services were involved on both sides of the struggle mirroring, ironically, French intelligence's wartime support for de Gaulle while nominally serving Vichy. De

Gaulle attempted to rectify this by cashiering the DST's head Roger Wybot in 1959 and by purging the internal and foreign intelligence agencies of their *Algérie française* mentality. Unable to trust in the loyalty of his official intelligence services, de Gaulle led the way in developing parallel intelligence organizations that subsequently became a way of life in the French intelligence world. De Gaulle used the services of his loyal lieutenant Jacques Foccart, 'the man of the shadows', to lead the struggle against the OAS and to orchestrate delicate intelligence missions in Africa. Throughout his presidency de Gaulle made little room for intelligence in foreign policy formulation, referring to the SDECE as 'le Guignol' (Mr Punch the puppet). In October 1965 the SDECE's Arab service was implicated in the reckless kidnapping of the Moroccan opposition leader Ben Barka. De Gaulle saw this as an attempt to undermine his policy of convincing the non-aligned states to fall in behind French leadership in a third bloc intended to rival the superpowers. He downgraded the service by removing it from prime ministerial responsibility and passed it to the Defence Minister, under whose tutelage it has since remained.

The lack of seriousness with which the SDECE was treated carried over to subsequent presidents. Although President Georges Pompidou (1969–74) had confidence in the newly appointed director general of the SDECE, the aristocratic Alexandre de Marenches, intelligence was not rehabilitated, nor allowed to participate seriously in policy formulation or defining the country's strategic national interests. Pompidou continued to refer to it as the 'thingamajig', claiming that bankers like himself were better informed than France's intelligence chiefs. Under Giscard d'Estaing and Mitterrand the SDECE continued to be undermined by the Quai d'Orsay and top civil servants' disdain for it. In opposition Mitterrand had pledged to abolish the SDECE, referring to the intelligence services as a 'costly farce'.[39]

The French intelligence community has been at a particular disadvantage to powers such as Britain and the USA in not possessing a popular French spy fiction. The British secret services have generally been well served by spy novels, often written by former intelligence officers, such as Ian Fleming, John Le Carré or even Graham Greene, thereby affording them an apparent realism. A sense that intelligence agencies mirror the state and national characteristics has helped British intelligence. Though detached from the reality of the intelligence world, in very different ways James Bond and *Smiley's People* enhanced the image of the British intelligence services in the popular mind. French intelligence had no such popular champion 'licensed to thrill' during the cold war.[40] The only popular French spy literature was that of the 1930s. It exalted the heroic achievements of France's pre-First World War and 1930s secret services and was immortalized in the writings of Robert-Charles Dumas, Pierre Nord and Pierre Benoît. Contemporary French cinema also contributed to making the Deuxième bureau an internationally known agency synonymous with 'espionage à la française'. For the cold war, however, no such French heroic spy adventure literature mythologized and promoted the SDECE. The best-selling spy fiction series of the 1960s and 1970s written by Gérard de Villiers entitled 'SAS' did not glorify the French post-war intelligence services. Its eponymous hero, an Austrian prince, was a CIA operative rather than an agent of the French Republic.

Having battled for years against its poor image, even with conservative governments, the French intelligence community braced itself for a shock with the victory of the Left in 1981. However, not only did the new socialist President Mitterrand, backed by a socialist government with a large parliamentary majority, not disband the SDECE; he used the intelligence services more than his predecessors. This was partly prompted by the wave of terrorism that hit France in 1985–86. Mitterrand's suspicion of the official services led him initially to create his own intelligence service at the Elysée, exacerbating rivalries and provoking further scandals such as that of the 'Vincennes Irish'. Under Mitterrand, and the Fifth Republic in general, the worst features of French intelligence culture were exacerbated. Parallel services funded by the infamous Elysée 'secret funds' developed with a penchant for action safe from democratic accountability. Fragmentation undermined any hope of developing an intelligence community working towards collectively conceived national goals along the Anglo-Saxon model. Although an organization to coordinate and centralize French intelligence, the Comité interministériel de renseignement (CIR), was set up in 1962, it failed to meet for 27 years. After 1989 it met merely twice a year. Questions remain as to its ability to harmonize views into coherent recommendations along the lines of the British Joint Intelligence Committee.

Myriad intelligence agencies have blurred the distinction between domestic counter-intelligence and foreign intelligence, making spying on one's own nationals easier, especially given the intelligence services' absence of public accountability. No report on the services is prepared for parliament and their budget comes via other ministries and the Presidency's secret funds. The RG alone employs 3800 personnel to provide what *Le Monde* in 1997 called 'political information' on domestic matters in a manner that was a 'typical French incongruity'. This figure does not include personnel from the other domestic security services, the DST and the RGPP. The overall poor esteem and suspicion in which intelligence continues to be held in France by everyone from the political establishment to the public has not stopped the authorities from calling for its expansion. The 1997–2002 *loi de programmation militaire* scheduled an increase in the DGSE's size from its 1997 level of 4000 personnel to 5700, and for the Direction du renseignement militaire (DRM) from 1600 to 1900. Of comparable size and world role, Britain employed just under 2000 personnel in the Security Service MI5 and probably around 3000 in the foreign intelligence service MI6, though a further 5000 were employed at the Government Communication Headquarters (GCHQ) and 4800 in the Defence Intelligence Staff.[41]

The call to expand the French intelligence community came during the 1990–91 Gulf War, when the French felt handicapped by their reliance on American intelligence. Defence Minister Pierre Joxe confessed that 'Without Allied intelligence, we were almost blind'.[42] At that time the French were relegated to indulging their predilection for covert operations rather than analysis using commando teams travelling under the unfortunate acronym of CRAP. Since then the 1994 defence White Paper called for greater resources for intelligence. The aim was to catch up with other Western intelligence agencies, particularly in the high-technology areas of Comint, Elint and Imint (Communications, Electronic and Imaging intelligence). France sought to eradicate the deficiency in satellite and communications intelligence by launching more spy satellites under the HELIOS programme, joint funded with Spain and Italy and possibly Germany. An effort was made to unify military intelligence by the creation in 1992 of the DRM. Economic intelligence had always had a high priority in France. Former head of the SDECE/DGSE, Pierre Marion, revealed in his memoirs how Air France first-class cabins were bugged to gain intelligence on France's commercial competitors, not least the Americans. Economic espionage on US companies led to a diplomatic row at the end of the 1980s. Unabashed, in 1995 France set up an Interministerial Committee on Economic Security following the publication two years previously of the Martre Report on economic intelligence.[43] French intelligence, like that of other powers, is beginning to focus on potential security threats from international organized crime, money laundering, drug trafficking, terrorism and weapons of mass destruction. Yet, despite a 70 per cent increase in the DGSE's budget from 1989 to 1993 and its new expensive headquarters in the Paris suburbs, French intelligence can no longer afford the luxury of national independence. Even the head of the DGSE from 1989, Claude Silberzahn, admitted the impossibility of France catching up with US satellite intelligence or the large capability of Britain's GCHQ or even with the German services.[44] This explains France's insistence on the development of a European intelligence agency that would allow it to bridge the gap more effectively.

French intelligence's expansion was also due to Mitterrand's changed attitude to intelligence during his second term from 1988. The DGSE chief appointed by Mitterrand in 1989, Claude Silberzahn, explained in his memoirs how Mitterrand had privately requested him to do two things. First, to work more closely with the President and his office in order 'to put the DGSE back into the apparatus of the French State'; second, to 'civilianize' the DGSE. The latter was already underway: two-thirds of the DGSE's personnel were civilians, although command posts were largely held by the military. However, attempts to release the military's grip on the DGSE did not go unchallenged. The DGSE remained dependent on the military for training, equipment and access to HELIOS satellite intelligence, and lost out to the powerful new DRM. Another of Silberzahn's priorities was to improve the long-standing bad relations with the Quai d'Orsay by creating a strategy directorate chaired by a career diplomat.

The French have attempted to address the problem of inter-agency rivalry by swapping chiefs across the intelligence services. In 1992 General Heinrich from the DGSE became head of the DRM, while the former head of the DST, Philippe Parant, was from the DGSE. In 1996 the former Director of Intelligence at the DGSE became head of the DST. Apart from rivalry, French intelligence services have been characterized by a lack of continuity in their leadership. Between the departure of the long-serving Roger Wybot in 1959 and 1973 the DST had five different directors. But the DGSE holds the instability record, with seven different chiefs from 1981 to 1996. Much still needs to be done to overcome the culture of mutual antipathy between political leaders and the intelligence services exacerbated by the former's ignorance of the nature and role of intelligence. Whereas in Anglo–Saxon countries 'intelligence studies' are now a recognized serious academic subject, in France this is far from being the case. Even in the programmes of the exclusive nursery of top French bureaucrats and ministers, the ENA, there is no mention of intelligence matters. In 1986 the Chairman of the Parliamentary Commission on Defence, François Fillon, confessed to a journalist that he had never met the intelligence chiefs, despite having to account to parliament for part of their budgets. Mutual ignorance and disdain have led the intelligence services often to act as a loose cannon, as the *Rainbow Warrior* Affair showed. On 10 July 1985 the DGSE sunk environmentalist group Greenpeace's flagship *Rainbow Warrior* in Auckland harbour in a desperate attempt to stop it disrupting French nuclear testing in the South Pacific. The incident killed a foreign journalist and ended farcically in a blaze of publicity with the French agents' capture by the New Zealand police. Defence Minister Charles Hernu and the head of the DGSE, Admiral Pierre Lacoste, took the blame and resigned. Although President Mitterrand denied all knowledge of the mission, most specialists believe the operation could not have been carried out without the Elysée's consent. The multiple irony was, of course, that such an incident should happen under a socialist President and government that in opposition had been so critical of the intelligence services and even committed to their abolition, let alone professing green credentials and pledging to halt French nuclear testing. There was a brief attempt to bring some scrutiny to bear on the intelligence services. The socialist Prime Minister, Laurent Fabius, appeared on television to order the Defence and Interior ministers to present an annual report on their intelligence services to the Speakers of both houses of parliament. No report appeared. The opportunity was missed to bring the French services under parliamentary scrutiny in similar fashion to the 'big bang' of the early 1990s that opened up the British services in the aftermath of the *Spycatcher* revelations.

Despite some improvement in civil–intelligence relations, the French services remain dogged by a legacy of disdain and cynicism dating back to the Dreyfus Affair. French policy-makers have reacted to intelligence with inconsistency and ambivalence, occasionally treating it seriously, more often refusing to integrate it into the policy-making process. This may have suited their purposes. However, this *ad hoc* use of what most other powers consider a precious resource cannot be justified in the unpredictable post-cold war era. In 1995 intelligence chief Claude Silberzahn explained that, for intelligence to be systematically integrated into the policy-making process, a coordinated structure was needed at the highest political level chaired by the President and comprising the Prime Minister, the ministers of Foreign Affairs, Interior and Defence, the Chief of the General Staff and all the intelligence agency chiefs. However, a commission summoned to report on the desirability of such a National Security Council rejected this.[45] Until that step is taken, French intelligence will continue to be undermined by inter-service rivalry and a perceived lack of seriousness by its political masters, the French establishment, public opinion and other states. The French need to know themselves and the value of an intelligence community before they can realistically and effectively assess their place in the world. The abiding French belief that what France does or says is a permanent source of admiration or jealousy for the rest of the world is the kind of national complex that the intelligence services have tended to feed rather than overcome. In the twentieth century the French intelligence services have mirrored the state they claim to serve.

Notes

1 Raoul Girardet, *Mythes et mythologies politiques* (Paris, Seuil, 1986).
2 Douglas Porch, *The French Secret Services: A History of French Intelligence from the Dreyfus Affair to the Gulf War* (New York, Farrar Strauss Giroux, 1995), p. 18.
3 Colonel Passy, *Souvenirs I: Deuxième bureau Londres* (Monte Carlo, Raoul Solar, 1947), pp. 53–4.
4 All quoted in Bertrand Warusfel, 'Le Contre-espionnage français', in *Cahiers du Centre d'etudes d'histoire de la défense*, no. 1, *Histoire du renseignement* (Paris, Cahiers du Centre d'études d'histoire de la défense, 1996), p. 14.
5 Warusfel, 'Le Contre-espionnage', pp. 15–16.
6 Christopher Andrew, 'France and the German Menace', in Ernest May (ed.), *Knowing one's Enemies: Intelligence Assessment before the Two World Wars* (Princeton, Princeton University Press, 1984).
7 Porch, *French Secret Services*, pp. 33, 38.

8 Samuel Williamson, 'Joffre Reshapes French Strategy, 1911–1913', in Paul Kennedy (ed.), *The War Plans of the Great Powers, 1880-1914* (London, Unwin Hyman, 1979), pp. 136–7.
9 Andrew, 'France and the German Menace', p. 141.
10 Andrew, 'France and the German Menace', p. 141.
11 Porch, *French Secret Services*, p. 82 and generally pp. 78–82.
12 Quoted in Porch, *French Secret Services*, p. 100.
13 Warufsel, 'Le Contre-espionage', pp. 19–20.
14 Porch, *French Secret Services*, pp. 118–25.
15 Porch, *French Secret Services*, pp. 126–35.
16 Alexander, *Gamelin*, pp. 46–50, 159–60.
17 Warusfel, 'Le Contre-espionage', pp. 20–2.
18 Paul Paillole, *Services spéciaux (1935–1945)* (Paris, Robert Lafont, 1975), pp. 63–4, 68, 76; Alexander, *Gamelin*, pp. 324–6.
19 Alexander, *Gamelin*, pp. 324–5.
20 Peter Jackson, 'French Intelligence and Hitler's Rise to Power', *Historical Journal*, 41/3 (1998).
21 Walter Laqueur, *A World of Secrets: The Uses and Limits of Intelligence* (New York, Basic Books, 1985), p. 11; Martin Alexander, 'Did the Deuxième Bureau Work? The Role of Intelligence in French Defence and Strategy 1919–1939', *Intelligence and National Security*, 6/2 (1991), 293–333.
22 Pierre Péan, *Le Mystérieux Docteur Martin (1895–1969)* (Paris, Livre de Poche, 1993), pp. 222–30.
23 Warusfel, 'Le Contre-espionage', pp. 22–4.
24 Martin Thomas, 'France in British Signals Intelligence, 1939–1945', *French History*, 14/1 (2000), pp. 55–7.
25 Warufsel, 'Le Contre-espionage', pp. 24–5.
26 Warufsel, 'Le Contre-espionage', pp. 25–6.
27 Thomas, 'France in British Signals', pp. 64–5.
28 Christopher Andrew, *Secret Service: The Making of the British Intelligence Community*, London, Sceptre, paperback edn, 1992), pp. 648–50.
29 Quoted in Porch, *French Secret Services*, p. 220.
30 Roger Faligot and Pascal Krop, *La Piscine: Les Services secrets français 1944–1984* (Paris, Seuil, 1985), p. 23.
31 Warufsel, 'Le Contre-espionage', pp. 27–33.
32 Pierre Jardin, 'Le Renseignement français en Allemagne au lendemain de la Seconde Guerre Mondiale (1940–55)', in *Cahiers du Centre d'études d'histoire de la défense*, no.1, *Histoire du Renseignement*, pp. 62–7.
33 Faligot and Krop, *La Piscine*, p. 36.
34 Porch, *French Secret Services*, p. 278.
35 Porch, *French Secret Services*, pp. 279–92; Christopher Andrew and Vasili Mitrokhin, *The Mitrokhin Archive: The KGB in Europe and the West* (London, Allen Lane/Penguin, 1999), pp. 196–202.
36 Andrew and Mitrokhin, *Mitrokhin Archive*, pp. 600–1, 608–9.
37 Philip M. Williams, *Wars, Plots and Scandals in Post-War France* (Cambridge, Cambridge University Press, 1970), pp. 37–73.
38 Alexander Zervoudakis, 'Nihil mirare, nihil contemptare, omnia intelligere:

Franco-Vietnamese Intellignce in Indochina, 1950–1954', in Martin Alexander (ed.), *Knowing your Friends: Intelligence inside Alliances and Coalitions from 1924 to the Cold War* (London, Frank Cass, 1998), pp. 195–225.

39 Porch, *French Secret Services*, pp. 396–405.

40 See Wesley K. Wark (ed.), *Spy Fiction, Spy Films and Real Intelligence* (London, Frank Cass, 1991).

41 J. F. V. Keiger, 'Une perception britannique du renseignement français', in Pierre Lacoste, *Le Renseignement à la française* (Paris, Economica, 1998), pp. 601–5; Jean-Marc Pennetier, 'The Spring-Time of French Intelligence', *Intelligence and National Security*, 11/4 (Oct. 1996), p. 798 n. 57; figures on British intelligence personnel calculated according to conflation of *MI5: The Security Service* (2nd edn, London, HMSO, 1996), p. 10, and Michael Herrman, *Intelligence Power in Peace and War* (Cambridge, Cambridge University Press, 1996).

42 Quoted in Porch, *French Secret Services*, p. 493.

43 Pennetier, 'Spring-Time of French Intelligence', p. 782.

44 Pennetier, 'Spring-Time of French Intelligence', pp. 790–4.

45 Pennetier, 'Spring-Time of French Intelligence', p. 795.

5

Germany

Geography and material power have determined that for the last century and a quarter Germany has been at the heart of France's relations with the world. As veteran diplomatist Harold Nicolson put it in 1939: 'French policy has, for the last sixty years, been governed almost exclusively by fear of her eastern neighbour.'[1] The seasoned observer of international affairs and future editor of *Le Monde* newspaper, André Fontaine, wrote in 1952: 'France has a German policy; she has no other.'[2] Three wars with Germany since 1870 resulting in over two million French deaths, economic and financial devastation, and on two occasions international humiliation and political collapse have conditioned France to ensure that its eastern neighbour remained either an emasculated foe or a tame friend. How best to deal with the German 'threat', 'problem' or 'question' has been contingent on both domestic and international politics and has manifested itself at different moments as a desire to crush, contain, conciliate or even collaborate with Germany.

The German problem

Historically the hereditary enmity between the French and German peoples can be taken back to the division of Charlemagne's empire in 843 and the struggles between the successors of Louis the German and Charles the Bald. Venom was added by Louis XIV's seizure of Strasbourg, the German uprising against Napoleon and finally the wars with modern Germany from 1870.[3] Henceforth the German threat was measured by comparative indicators of power. In 1815 France's might in Europe was still great. Napoleon's bid for mastery of Europe had failed, but many believed France could and would renew the attempt. France had no serious continental rival. Compared to Prussia, who would progressively become its potential enemy, France was far superior in demographic, economic and military terms. However, 1871 marked the intersection of the might and fortunes of the two powers in demographic and industrial terms. The newly formed German Empire now had a population of 41 million compared to France's 36 million. Iron and steel production – a measure of a country's war potential – were roughly equal, but German coal production was 2.5 times France's, while the latter's manufacturing was still double that of Germany. In A. J. P. Taylor's view, the Franco-Prussian War was in power terms a war of equals. France lost and the French bid for European mastery ended. Henceforth Germany's power would increasingly overshadow France's.[4]

By 1910 the strength and fortunes of the two states were the reverse of a century before. German had established supremacy over the European continent, having overtaken France according to every important indicator. Germany's population was 65 million, France's 39; German iron production was three times France's, steel four times, coal seven times, while German defence estimates were twice France's.[5] The German 'question' was the principal issue in French foreign and defence policy. Yet, despite German power's inexorable progression, France's response to it was a good deal less linear.

The Franco-Prussian War may have been started by Napoleon III, but Bismarck welcomed it. France emerged from the war militarily destroyed, territorially mutilated, in a state of political anarchy and occupied. The devastating defeat of the French army at Sedan on 1 September 1870 also toppled the regime that was responsible for it – the Second Empire. The Third Republic declared on 4 September 1870 was born of a humiliating defeat at the hands of Germany, just as it would die by one at the hands of the same foe 70 years later. France's loss was Germany's gain and the balance of power in Europe was completely altered. 'Europe had lost a mistress and gained a master,' said one diplomat. Bismarck did all he could to impose a victor's peace according to the Napoleonic model. On the back of French defeat he completed the unification of Germany to form the German Empire, the Second German Reich. He rubbed salt into French wounds by proclaiming the new German State in the Hall of Mirrors in the Palace of Versailles, which for two centuries had been the symbol of French greatness and power. (This would be the beginning of the tit-for-tat battle of symbols between France and Germany: the railway carriage at Rethondes where Germany signed its surrender in 1918 was used by Germany for the French surrender in 1940; the 100,000-strong police force France was granted in 1940 France was exactly what Germany was granted by the Versailles Treaty; 11 November was chosen by Germany in 1942 for the total occupation of France.)

The annexation of Alsace and Lorraine sealed the Empire and scarred France. The payment of a huge indemnity (exactly proportional to the one that Napoleon had imposed on Prussia in 1807) and a temporary German army of occupation were enshrined in the Treaty of Frankfurt on 10 May 1871. Bismarck knew that annexation would delay reconciliation and set about isolating France diplomatically by creating an anti-French network of alliances. He was successful in keeping France in quarantine for 20 years. But he also laid the seeds of a profound mistrust and fear of Germany that was to be at the heart of another two European wars. The posture France adopted towards Germany fluctuated broadly according to domestic politics: the left preferred conciliation, the right increased defence expenditure.

Evolution of the German threat

The Treaty of Frankfurt had no more moral authority for Frenchmen than the Treaty of Versailles for Germans. It gave birth to the idea of *revanche* – the reconquest of the lost provinces. However, the myth of *revanche* was greater than the reality. French politicians were generally more sanguine about the return of the lost provinces. But Berlin shaped an intimidatory foreign policy to provide for the eventuality of a French war of revenge. On 20 May 1882 Bismarck signed the Triple Alliance, bringing together Germany, Austria, Hungary and Italy. It would be continually renewed over the next three decades, becoming one of the major axes of the European diplomatic system. Russia was neutralized as a potential French ally by the Reinsurance Treaty (1887) with Germany, while few expected Britain to abandon its policy of splendid isolation. France was isolated by Germany, but also by itself. As a Republic born of revolution it was a pariah for autocratic monarchies such as Russia. Meanwhile, Britain was not unhappy to see France's might in Europe diminished so long as a European balance of power was maintained.

France profited from its forced introspection to pay off the German war indemnity (aided by 14 German banks) by 1873, six months before the stipulated date. Excess capital was devoted to military reconstruction. The ability to acquit itself so quickly of the war debt demonstrated the size of the French middle classes' purse and foreshadowed its use as a diplomatic asset and weapon. From 1872 credits were voted to introduce a five-year military service. By 1875 France and Germany were almost equal in terms of arms and men. Germany had not expected such a rapid revival in France's military fortunes. Bismarck set about intimidating France by giving the impression that it could be the subject of a preventive war. But the *War in sight* crisis of spring 1875 soon passed when France alerted other powers to this unwelcome possibility. Franco-German relations now took a new direction.

Franco-German détente 1878–1885

The international socialist movement fostered détente – German socialists had condemned the annexation of Alsace-Lorraine. Détente was also encouraged by French intellectuals' admiration for German thinkers, writers and musicians. A rapprochement was developing in finance, trade and commerce. By 1887 Germany was France's third biggest supplier and France's fourth biggest client. As in the 1920s and 1950s, peace by economics was sought via a Common Market. A Franco-German customs union was discussed. In 1888 the former French parliamentarian, Count Paul de Leusse, wrote a pamphlet entitled *Peace by a Franco-German Customs Union*. Though Bismarck was said to favour it, the German press was opposed. Bismarck wished to profit from this détente to encourage French colonialism, which he calculated might lead it into conflict with Britain or Italy (in Tunisia) and would in any case distract it from *revanche*. France did not need much encouraging. It was anxious to seek abroad the glory it was denied in Europe. By 1900 the French Empire was the second largest in the world, its 'expansive urge' largely motivated by psychological and material compensation for the loss of Alsace-Lorraine.

By the 1880s Franco-German relations were relatively good. One observer remarked in 1881: 'One would say that a century has elapsed since 1871.'[6] Republican political leaders from Léon Gambetta to Jules Ferry, whose governments dominated this period, recommended that Alsace-Lorraine be put on the back burner and that overtures from Germany be welcomed. From 1883 to 1885 Bismarck's support for France on colonial issues began to transform détente into rapprochement. There was even talk of alliance. In 1884 the French War Minister, General Campenon, told the head of a German mission of officers that he was always telling his colleagues to recognize the Frankfurt Treaty and to make an alliance with Germany: 'With such an alliance France would at one blow regain her standing. France and Germany united would rule the world.'[7]

The initiative for a Franco-German alliance came to nought. Nevertheless, Bismarck could see the advantages of such an agreement with France looking to the wider world and Germany to Europe (in similar fashion to the 1957 European Community). As the German Chancellor told Jules Ferry: 'I hope to reach the point when you will forgive Sedan as you have forgiven Waterloo. Renounce the Rhine, and I will help you to secure everywhere else the satisfactions you desire.'[8] Although Bismarck backed French intervention in Tunisia in 1881, encouraged and supported it in Morocco in the 1880s and the West African coast in 1884 and in Egypt, Madagascar and Tonkin, Ferry was suspicious of Bismarck's motives and unwilling to go any further for fear of upsetting nationalist public opinion.

The fall of the Ferry government over colonial policy in 1885 put an end to the Franco-German honeymoon by discrediting imperial expansion. It ushered in more robust foreign and defence policies for the next decade, most notably at the beginning of 1886 with the ultra-nationalist and revanchist War Minister, General Boulanger. Franco-German relations reached their nadir in April 1887 during the Schnaebelé Affair, when

German police seized a senior French police official on the German border for alleged spying. Pandering to nationalist opinion, Boulanger called for military action. But the war scare was ended by negotiation in April 1886 and the bellicose Boulanger was excluded from the next government. However, the damage had been done. France and Germany reverted to reinforcing military capabilities rather than reducing differences.

Bismarck's fall from power in March 1890 opened the way for France to break out of its diplomatic isolation with an entente and military alliance with Russia between 1891 and 1894. New-found security allowed France's Foreign Minister, Gabriel Hanotaux, who occupied the Quai d'Orsay for all but six months of the period from 1894 to 1898, to develop a two-prong strategy in which imperial expansion ran alongside a conciliatory policy in Europe. Though this brought France closer to Germany, it brought it to the brink of war with Britain in Africa.

Franco-German détente in the 1890s

Improvement in Franco-German relations was encouraged by the decline in sensitivity of the Alsace-Lorraine question. A new generation had emerged in the 'lost provinces', which had been educated by German schoolmasters, done its military service in old Germany and had no first-hand experience of France. Meanwhile the old German population was increasing rapidly from 70,000 in 1875 to 300,000 in 1910 (15.7 per cent of the total population). In cities such as Strasbourg, the administrative capital, and Metz the percentage of Germans was 40 and 50 per cent respectively. By 1909 the number of mixed marriages had increased by 16.4 per cent. For many Alsace-Lorrainers the attraction of returning to the French fold receded as German prosperity increased, abetted by French anti-clericalism from 1901 and especially after the 1905 French separation of church and state, which repulsed the pious inhabitants. In the 1898 Reichstag elections 12 of the 15 deputies from the Reichsland of Alsace-Lorraine declared their allegiance to the Empire.[9] In France also, sentimental attraction was replaced by resignation, encouraged by the development of the largely pacifist and anti-militarist French socialist movement committed to détente with Germany. Closer economic and financial ties with Germany further contributed to the sharp decline of *revanche* amongst all but the most extreme elements in France, even if many wished for their eventual return by peaceful means. In 1898 the German ambassador in Paris reported that most Frenchmen were beginning 'to forget Alsace-Lorraine'.[10]

Attitudes in French governing circles were also more conciliatory. Hanotaux, who had worked with Jules Ferry, recognized the need for collaboration with Germany to ensure peace and give France greater freedom. In Hanotaux's words, this meant leaving the Alsace-Lorraine question 'out of practical politics'. Although neither he nor any other French politician was willing to recognize officially the clauses of the Frankfurt Treaty, the question of a compromise, perhaps involving some colonial compensation for Germany, was countenanced. Tangible signs of détente were Kaiser Wilhelm's invitation for French warships to attend the official opening of the Kiel Canal in 1895 and Germany's participation in the 1900 Exposition Universelle de Paris (last attended in 1867), with German visitors being the most numerous. By spring 1894 Franco-German colonial agreements in Africa were under negotiation and four years later the Fashoda showdown with Britain provided stimulus for a Franco-German rapprochement.

France's problem arose from the contradiction in its international position of being both a continental and a colonial power. Though it might have Germany as an adversary on the European continent and Britain as a rival in the colonies, as a continental power it needed British support against Germany, and as a colonial power German support against Britain. The worst case scenario for France was an Anglo-German entente, which seemed possible between 1899 and 1901.

Fashoda pushed *revanche* further into the background. In 1898 the new Foreign Minister, Théophile Delcassé, was hopeful for a peaceful settlement of the Alsace-Lorraine question. In December 1898 the German envoy von Huhn was greeted in Paris with talk of 'forgetting the past' and of 'substituting for the policy of sentiment a new policy which responds to real interests'. Delcassé insisted to him that France was ready 'to support German colonial aspirations everywhere, particularly in China'. The French press backed this policy but the Germans did not respond to the overtures.[11]

Seeking rapprochement with Germany did not mean France dropping its guard, particularly when Berlin did not follow up Paris's advances. The Franco-Russian Alliance was reshaped in 1899 to cover preservation of the European balance of power. Given Delcassé's vision of France as a Mediterranean power with an African empire stretching from Morocco and Tunisia in the north to the French Congo in the south meant restricting German access to the Mediterranean. Delcassé's Mediterranean strategy involved bringing Morocco under French rule, which in turn demanded that Italy, Spain, and Germany be enlisted to overcome British reticence. Envoys were sent to Berlin in the summer of 1901 to offer colonial compensation for German acquiescence over a changed status for Morocco. Again Germany proved reluctant. So ended Delcassé's overtures to Germany. Henceforth he sought to draw closer to Britain, as the 1904 Entente Cordiale proved.[12]

The triangular power play between France, Britain and Germany tended to mean that a French understanding with one led to a deterioration of relations with the other. Contrary to German expectations, Delcassé managed to maintain both the entente with Britain and the alliance with Russia, despite London and Saint Petersburg's rivalry in central Asia and the Far East. Germany was beginning to feel encircled. Its reaction was to seek to destabilize France's diplomatic links by attempting to lure the Tsar into a new Russo-German alliance at Bjorko in July 1905.

Franco-German tension in 1905

Delcassé had first sought to gain control of Morocco with German support against Britain; he now tried with British support against Germany. Having secured Italian, British and Spanish consent for French ambitions in Morocco, he believed that Germany could be confronted with a fait accompli, despite its being a signatory to the 1880 Madrid Convention, which guaranteed Moroccan independence. This simply presented Berlin with an opportunity to disrupt France's diplomatic ties at a time when France was at its weakest since signing the Russian Alliance. At the beginning of 1905 Russia was on the brink of a devastating defeat in the Far East by Japan, which would reduce its effectiveness as an ally in Europe. In France the War Minister had embarked on a republican crusade to rid the High Command of its monarchical and clerical elements, thereby demoralizing and disorganizing the army. Meanwhile the 1900 naval building programme was nowhere near completion. France was unprepared for war and Germany knew it. Chancellor von Bülow and the *eminence grise* of the German Foreign Office, von Holstein, seized on the occasion to force France into a confrontation over Morocco in the belief that Britain would refuse, and Russia would be unable, to support France. In one fell swoop, Germany calculated, the Entente Cordiale would be destroyed, the Dual Alliance exposed as ineffectual and France would be drawn into the German orbit.

At the end of March 1905 the Kaiser called at Tangiers during his annual Mediterranean cruise. He asserted Germany's demand for free trade and equal rights in Morocco and confirmed the Sultan's status as ruler of an independent country. By April Delcassé was making half-hearted attempts to appease Germany and settle the international dispute. Though he had indications of British support, which he hoped would force Germany to back down, he was not supported in Cabinet. Prime Minister Rouvier feared a German surprise attack would lead France 'to defeat and to the Commune' and after unofficial soundings from Germany agreed to force Delcassé's resignation. On 6 June Rouvier won Cabinet support for Delcassé's resignation. But Germany was not appeased and called for an international conference to settle the Moroccan question. Here it went too far. Instead of destroying the Entente Cordiale and pulling France into dependence on Germany, it produced the opposite effect. London and Paris drew closer together and French public opinion drew away from Germany. The 13-nation Algéçiras conference from 16 January to 7 April 1906 was a diplomatic defeat for Germany, with France supported principally by Russia and Britain. It paved the way for the Anglo-Russian agreement of 31 August 1907, which completed the Triple Entente and signalled the shift of great power rivalry from empire to continental Europe. Germany now protested at its own encirclement. Paradoxically, Franco-German relations began to improve.

Franco-German détente 1907–1911

After Algéçiras Franco-German financial and commercial relations witnessed another period of expansion. French and German banks collaborated in the Ottoman Empire, the Balkans and Latin America. German firms increased their investment in France by creating subsidiaries or by taking shareholdings in French firms. In the area of electricity German AEG expanded its subsidiary and reinforced its entente with French Thomson-Houston. Similar arrangements took place in the area of machine tools, while German subsidiaries were opened up in France in textiles, maritime and life insurance and the hotel industry. German iron ore production covered only three-quarters of its needs, so between 1906 and 1910 exports to Germany of French Lorraine ore from Meurthe-et-Moselle tripled. German steel-makers Krupp and Thyssen went even further by buying up large swathes of Lorraine and Normandy ore mines and companies. The complementarity of French and German steel-makers needs, which would be at the heart of Franco-German rapprochement in the 1920s and 1950s, was amply demonstrated by French producers having a surfeit of ore, but a lack of coal and coke. In 1905 French coke covered only two thirds of France's needs and by 1910 only a half. French steel-makers, such as Schneider and Saint-Gobain, looked to the coal mines of German Lorraine and the Ruhr. In partnership with German industry they created the Internationale Kohlen Bergwerks-Gesellschaft to ensure supply from 37 coal mines in Alsace-Lorraine. French firms took controlling interests in, or bought out, German coal producers or set up with them companies whereby Germany got French ore and France got German coking coal. French industrialists were less adventurous than steel-makers in investing in Germany, though Michelin and Renault set up German subsidiaries in 1906 and 1907 respectively, while companies such as Air Liquide preferred joint ventures with their German counterparts. This interpenetration of interests between 1906 and 1910 was reflected in the growth of Franco-German trade, even if Germany's dominance led to cries in some French circles of a 'German invasion'.[13]

Financiers, industrialists, diplomats and politicians in both countries believed that this was an opportunity for a more permanent economic, even political, rapprochement between France and Germany. But from 1905 in France a nationalist revival was underway whose protagonists were hostile to French capital propping up foreign economies, especially Germany's. Ignoring this, Paris was able to secure a Franco-German agreement over Morocco on 9 February 1909. It recognized economic equality in exchange for German recognition of France's 'special political interests' in Morocco. Despite some nationalist opposition, the agreement was well received by the French public and supporters of Franco-German collaboration, who saw in this détente reason to press for more agreements in the Congo and the Ottoman Empire. Despite government support, other colonial agreements under negotiation were held up, although Franco-German financial relations continued to strengthen. Part of the problem lay with nationalist permanent officials in the Quai d'Orsay, the Ministry of Colonies or in post abroad, who opposed any agreement with Germany. Their obstructionist policies thwarted the efforts of their political masters and brought Franco-German relations to their next crisis at Agadir in 1911.

The slide towards war 1911–1914

By the end of 1910 economic questions began to affect Franco-German relations. A new French customs tariff provoked a trade war, while the Germans were disappointed by the failure of negotiations on joint ventures in the Congo, Ottoman Empire and Morocco. Things came to a head over economic relations in Morocco. Germany accused France, not unreasonably, of violating the Algeçiras and 1909 agreements. At the beginning of 1911 revolts in Fez against the Sultan led the French to order in troops to protect the European population. This violated the Algeçiras agreements, which did not allow France to intervene in the hinterland. At the end of April Berlin protested officially and sought a bargaining counter. On 1 July 1911 the German gunboat *Panther* entered the port of Agadir and a diplomatic stand-off began. The new Caillaux government decided to negotiate. Germany wanted the whole of the French Congo. Realizing that it did not have the Napoleonic 70 per cent chance of beating Germany, the military option was ruled out. France could not expect support from Russia, whom it had abandoned during the 1908–9 Bosnian Crisis. However, Britain was fulsome in its support, believing that German *Weltpolitik* needed a warning. Negotiations between Paris and Berlin continued into the autumn. Caillaux was determined to reach a deal, even if it meant going behind the back of his Foreign Minister. An agreement in principle over Morocco was reached on 11 October. This broadly satisfied German claims on joint economic and financial ventures and conceded to its part of the French Congo. In exchange, France was allowed to establish a protectorate over Morocco. But the 4 November 1911 treaty unleashed nationalist feeling in France and

Germany. Caillaux's secret negotiations were exposed by the Senate foreign affairs committee, which criticized him for pursuing a policy of rapprochement with Germany. His government fell on 11 January 1912. The Agadir Crisis was to weigh heavily on Franco-German relations up to 1914, making rapprochement very difficult.

But Agadir did not eliminate all attempts at rapprochement. One influential supporter was the experienced and powerful ambassador to Berlin, Jules Cambon, who since taking up his post in 1907 had worked for détente, even an entente, with Germany. He believed that Franco-German détente would give France greater continental security and a freer hand in its Empire. He would be constantly dogged by the nationalist and Germanophobe machinations of the permanent officials at the Quai d'Orsay. The Poincaré government of January 1912 had to rein in Jules Cambon's enthusiasm for détente, believing it to be a German ploy to divide the Triple Entente. But by the time Poincaré had acceded to the presidency in January 1913 Cambon's efforts were bearing fruit. In June 1913 he told his brother, Paul: 'Never have we had so many opportunities as at present, not for a *rapprochement*, but for bringing about *détente*.'[14] By 1914 this was producing tangible results. On 20 January 1914 Poincaré made a gesture unprecedented by any President since 1870 of dining at the Berlin embassy. On 15 February 1914 agreement was reached with Germany over joint financing of the Baghdad railway and spheres of influence in Asiatic Turkey. On 13 April 1914 the Secretary of State at the German foreign office told Jules Cambon that if France, Britain and Germany could agree on the exploitation of central Africa 'all chance of war would be averted for many long years'.[15] But instead of being avoided war was just three and a half months away.

The Berlin ambassador was not the only enthusiast for Franco-German détente. A certain left-wing literature extolled the virtues of Franco-German reconciliation. One of the most popular novels in that vein was Romain Rolland's *Jean Christophe*, published between 1905 and 1912. The same was true of the left-wing press. The French left, notably the socialists, believed that the obstacle to improved Franco-German relations was Alsace-Lorraine. Like Jules Cambon, who was no man of the left, they believed that a favourable settlement of the Alsace-Lorraine question could come only after an improvement in relations between Paris and Berlin. But conferences held in Bern in May of 1913 and 1914 by the French and German left to seek such an agreement foundered.

The problem was that a vociferous nationalist minority in France and Germany had moved to centre stage after Agadir. In France a new military literature took as its theme an imminent Franco-German war with books entitled *La France victorieuse dans la guerre de demain* by Colonel Boucher or *Nos frontières de l'est* by General Maitrot. A 1912 survey showed French youth (albeit Parisian and middle class) given over to nationalism and preparation for an impending struggle against Germany. Relations between French and German banks deteriorated. Newspapers such as *Le Matin* and *L'Intransigeant* kept up a campaign against the German invasion of French markets, despite growing commercial relations between the two countries. More seriously, after Agadir a Franco–German arms race had begun. Its most visible sign was the increase in land armies resulting from a series of military laws on both sides of the Rhine.

Jules Cambon believed that Franco–German animosity owed more to the irrational than to cool assessment and that the preconceived ideas of a minority made mutual hostility a self-fulfilling prophecy. However, a policy of détente with Germany demanded considerable political courage from any French leader. There was the risk that Berlin was merely seeking to draw France out of the Triple Entente's orbit or that official rapprochement might signal tacit acceptance of the status quo for Alsace-Lorraine. Franco–German rapprochement involved a risk, which in the end President Poincaré and his governments were not willing to take.[16]

War

For the second time in less than two generations, France and Germany came to blows when on 3 August 1914 Germany declared war on France. France did not go to war for Serbia, or out of blind obedience to the Franco–Russian alliance. It did so because it was unwilling to live again in Germany's shadow, which it saw as the inevitable outcome if its Russian ally was defeated by Germany. For four years the two countries were largely committed to total victory, but in France from 1915, especially in 1917, peace negotiations did take place. There remained a party in France that firmly believed that war with Germany was an error and that in the short or long term collaboration with Germany was desirable. This group, though very small, composed largely of Radical Party deputies and left-wing or anglophobe journalists, pursued defeatist policies with German subsidies channelled through the German legation in Bern. Documents captured by the Allies in 1945 from the German Foreign Ministry show that a German policy of subversion focused not on revolutionary groups but established pro-German figures capable of reversing official government policy. In France the link-man was Ernest Judet, editor of the influential Paris daily *L'Eclair*, charged in 1920 with consorting with the enemy. Another contact with Germany was Paul Bolo, the unscrupulous financier dedicated to restoring Caillaux to power. Radical deputies whose names are revealed in the German documents were René Besnard, Paul Meunier and Léon Turmel (arrested in October 1917). They were led by the Radical-Socialist deputy Léon Accambray, whom the Germans code-named 'Herr 32'. He sought to establish, through Masonic lodges (traditionally linked to the

Radicals) and parliamentary contacts, a network dedicated to undermining the Anglo-French alliance – deemed responsible for the outbreak of the war – and to seeking a separate peace with Germany.[17] Whether the individuals wished to promote a Franco-German axis once war had ended, or were merely pacifist or corrupt, is less clear. In any event their efforts failed during the First World War. Others would be more successful in the Second World War.

After 51 months of conflict the great question in peacetime was again how to deal with the German menace. A remarkable sign of how unsure France was about solving that question was the degree to which its German policy mutated during the inter-war years. It would go through three cycles moving from a desire to cripple, then to contain and finally to conciliate Germany.

From crippling to containing Germany

Despite being a victor at the end of the war, France retained a visceral fear of the loser. The idea of imposing a harsh settlement on Germany was generally popular. France was arguably the worst hit of all the powers, with almost one and a half million dead and 700,000 disabled out of a population of barely 40 million. Most of the fighting had been done in France's north-eastern departments, which were devastated. Moral anguish and suffering were widespread, with nearly every family having lost at least one of its members. Not surprisingly, the French wanted to ensure that there would be no recurrence and that the 'Boche' be not only punished, but made to pay. However, although Germany was defeated, its armies were technically unbeaten on the field of battle, having agreed to an armistice proposed by the American President Wilson. Even after territorial losses, Germany still had a population of 60 million, which was younger than France's. This gave it a ratio of men of army age in 1919 of two to France's one. German heavy industry's potential was four to one in Germany's favour. Worse still, France was now devoid of any possibility of an alliance with its traditional counterweight to Germany, Russia, still in the throes of revolution.

It is not surprising that many in France, including leaders such as Marshal Foch, Premier Clemenceau and President Poincaré, believed that a golden opportunity to eradicate the German threat should be seized. Before the war was over France's war aims included regaining Alsace-Lorraine and dismantling German territory, as Germany had done to France in 1871. More extreme elements suggested that Germany be crippled by undoing the unification of 1866 and 1871 and by returning it to a pre-Bismarckian loose federation, originally of some two dozen independent political units. They subscribed to the maxim that German unity was incompatible with French security and that peace was possible only by denying Germany the means and the temptation for revenge. In the peace negotiations opened by President Poincaré in 1919 on the symbolic date of 18 January (anniversary of the first proclamation of the German Empire at Versailles), Premier Clemenceau initially supported Foch's argument that Germany territory be pushed back to the Rhine. This idea was widely supported not just in French military and nationalist circles, but amongst eminent academics and Radical-Socialist politicians. France wanted the left bank of the Rhine as a geo-strategic springboard to keep the Reich militarily in check. It was believed that allied troops should be stationed permanently along the Rhine or for as long as it was necessary to ensure that a war of *revanche* would not take place. This would not involve French annexation, but the creation of autonomous German-speaking states possibly administered by the new League of Nations. But its 'Anglo-Saxon' allies opposed French plans. Division of Germany was perceived in Wilsonian terms as a vestige of the 'old diplomacy' with its balance-of-power doctrine. Lloyd George and President Woodrow Wilson vehemently opposed anything but temporary occupation along the Rhine with no German loss of territory. Opposition to a policy of crippling Germany pushed France into a policy of containment.

France was obliged to accept only temporary occupation of the left bank of the Rhine, with three bridgeheads to allow Allied troops to strike at the heart of Germany. A 50-kilometre strip running down the right bank was demilitarized. Seventy-five per cent of the occupation zones were occupied by 100,000 French troops. The three zones were to be evacuated over five, 10 and 15 years respectively, earlier if Germany executed the treaty before, but later in the opposite case. In exchange for the concession of temporary occupation in 1919 the USA and Britain offered France a guarantee treaty to come to its aid in the event of a German attack. Clemenceau staked much on the Anglo-American guarantee. But the US Senate, sceptical about a continued American commitment to Europe, rejected the Versailles Treaty on 19 November 1919, undoing not only the American, but also the British guarantee.

The Franco-German problem was not limited to bilateral relations. In the inter-war years it extended to the whole of Europe and notably the newly created states of Central and Eastern Europe. On every issue from the German–Polish border to Czechoslovakian independence France found itself face to face with Germany: the former representing the status quo, the latter revisionism. Europe's future was dependent on Franco-German relations. Bereft of any great power commitment, France turned to lesser powers, with a shared fear of German aggression. German invasion through Belgium in 1914 had emphasized Belgium's geo-strategic importance; on 7 September 1920 a Franco-Belgian military convention was signed. As a substitute for the traditional Russian bulwark against Germany in the east (and to avoid Germany establishing a *MittelEuropa*), France turned to Poland

and Czechoslovakia. A military convention was signed with the former on 19 February 1921 and there was an exchange of letters with the latter in January 1924. France went on building its defensive eastern arc through the 1920s by additional agreements with these two allies in 1925, supplemented by others with Romania and Yugoslavia on 10 June 1926 and 11 November 1927 respectively. France's problem was that Poland and the countries of the 'Little Entente' enjoyed poor relations, undermining concerted action against any potential German attack, but saddling France with onerous liabilities and commitments. Besides attempting to squeeze Germany into a 'Slav corset', France initially placed great faith in the new League of Nations, arguing for it to be given an international army to maintain peace. The Anglo-Saxons opposed this. Wilson preferred international disarmament, further weakening France's ability to resist potential German aggression. France was quickly disillusioned with the League as a means of containing Germany.

Containing Germany by bilateral and collective security would prove as illusory as making Germany pay. That Germany should pay reparations was generally accepted, but the question of how much and by what means remained a bone of contention between France and the Anglo-Saxons, who favoured German economic recovery. On the Inter-Allied Reparations Commission, which was supposed to set the level of German reparations by 1 May 1921, France fought to ensure that Germany strictly honoured its reparations payments. But the Anglo-Saxons favoured more and more concessions to Germany. The Versailles Treaty's economic clauses also provided France with an opportunity to contain German economic might by giving it access to German coal and iron. France obtained the coal-rich Sarre valley, not in perpetuity as it had hoped, but for 15 years, after which the population was to be plebiscited as to its affiliation. Germany was also obliged to deliver large amounts of coal to France, Belgium and Italy. Altogether this could divest Germany of up to one half of its coal output, the primary energy source, thereby strangling German industrial power. Other clauses in the treaty withdrew from Germany 80 per cent of its iron ore, as well as 40 per cent of its productive capacity in cast iron and 30 per cent in steel. The Treaty gave France the possibility of becoming the continent's biggest steel producer. According to Jacques Bariéty, French politicians rather than industrialists had this aim. The politicians saw this as an opportunity to deny Germany the economic might that had underpinned its military supremacy on the European continent.[18] Coal and steel would remain important indicators of German industrial potential, partly explaining efforts to neutralize them through the 1951 European Coal and Steel Community.

The French also sought to contain Germany militarily. There was general agreement on denying Germany heavy and offensive weaponry in terms of a high seas fleet, submarines, aviation, heavy artillery, tanks and combat gases. But on the issue of troops Marshal Foch wished Germany to have no more than a small short-service conscription army, while Lloyd George preferred a small professional army. Here again the French lost out and consent was given for a professional army of 100,000 and a small navy of 15,000 men. The Versailles Treaty's stringent restrictions on Germany were even conditional on general international arms limitation, which Germany would later use politically against the allies.

Thus the Versailles peace conference underscored a discrepancy between two attitudes to Germany. Britain and the USA believed that Germany could be morally disarmed through concessions, while France claimed that Germany would regard any concession as a weakness. The Anglo-Saxons won the argument, but not the peace. France lost on all fronts. Whatever the deficiencies of the Versailles settlement, it contained enough to make a new rise of Germany and a second world war impossible. The real problem was one of enforcement, which necessitated permanent understanding between France, Britain and the USA. The peace settlement was revised in as little as five years of its signature and the remainder undone within two decades. That the peace should turn out to be a 32-year truce, as Foch predicted, was more real for the French than the allies. Gradually, France was backed into the third phase of its relations with Germany – conciliation. Paris sought to neutralize potential German *revanche* by working more closely with it. This was epitomized in the 1925 Locarno agreements.

There was no clear demarcation between the three policies of crippling, containing and conciliating Germany. They often overlapped or even operated in parallel, according to which politician, permanent official or agency was involved. Some groups never abandoned the idea of crippling Germany, while others remained wedded to Franco-German entente. Strategies for dealing with Germany had competed since 1870. Their conflict became starkly visible in June 1940 when the issue was either continued conflict or collaboration.

From conciliation to concert

It is often thought that France's move to a policy of conciliating Germany coincided with the left's victory in the 1924 elections and Foreign Minister Aristide Briand's development of the Locarno strategy. Yet such a policy was in gestation well before. Within months of becoming Premier in 1920 the hitherto hardliner Alexandre Millerand was discussing economic collaboration with Germany, as would the presumed 'hawk' Premier Poincaré from January 1922. It is sometimes forgotten that, in March 1921 the 'dove' Briand had ordered the occupation of three Ruhr towns to force Germany into carrying out the disarmament and reparations clauses of the Treaty. But it was France's increasingly insecure international position and its overweening desire to seal an alliance with Britain that limited Paris's room for manœuvre and ushered in greater conciliation of Germany. However, German reluctance to take up offers of conciliation and its refusal to keep up reparations through 1922 made pursuit of the conciliatory policy unpopular in France. Poincaré was cornered into ordering a French occupation of the Ruhr in January 1923 to secure German coal and reparations. This was the last gasp of the hardline policy towards Germany. The Ruhr occupation was not a success and bore little fruit, even if Germany was forced to back down. In the end, domestic political considerations and fear of breaking with the 'Anglo-Saxons' led Poincaré to accept their recommendation to refer the reparations question again to two committees of experts to enquire into Germany's capacity to pay, the most important of which became known as the Dawes Committee.[19] By accepting an international solution to reparations France was letting go of the only hold it had on post-war Germany – the Versailles Treaty. As Jacques Seydoux, one of France's most far-sighted Foreign Office officials, put it on 27 December 1923, France was moving towards a 'financial reconstruction' of Europe by which it was no longer possible to deal with Germany as 'victor to vanquished'.[20] Ironically, the man most committed to upholding the Versailles system at the outset, Poincaré, was instrumental in its demise. France was now on the road to Locarno and reconciliation with Germany.

The years 1924 to 1930 contrasted with the previous four years of apparent Franco-German cold war. The new left-wing *Cartel des gauches* majority, which emerged from the 11 May 1924 elections, had no clear foreign policy towards Germany. The socialists, who supported but did not participate in the governments, were ideologically internationalist and deeply critical of the Versailles settlement, believing that a policy of concessions towards the Weimar Republic was the only means of securing democracy and peace. The Radicals were a good deal more sceptical about Germany and practical in their attitude to the Versailles Treaty. Their leader, Edouard Herriot, who formed the first government and held the foreign affairs portfolio, was committed to a policy of negotiation with Germany. Under further pressure from the Anglo-Saxons, whose goodwill he coveted, Herriot agreed at the London conference on the Dawes Plan to evacuate the Ruhr within a year and to dismantle the French administration of the left bank of the Rhine. He did so without receiving any of the concessions he had been hoping for, such as a Franco-British pact, effective checks on German disarmament or the right of the League of Nations to arbitrate and impose sanctions in the event of an international conflict. The failure of Herriot's foreign policy crystallized the debate in France over what attitude to adopt to Germany. On the left, blind acceptance of negotiation was seen as the only means of maintaining peace; while the right insisted that victory was being squandered and peace compromised.

Although by April 1925 Herriot's government had fallen on financial issues, its six *Cartel* successors did not stray from the policy of conciliating Germany. This was largely because France had no alternative and because foreign affairs stayed in the hands of the same man, Aristide Briand, until his death in 1932, making him the longest-serving Foreign Minister since Delcassé. During those seven years Franco-German relations underwent real détente. Briand's policy was helped by world economic expansion, which lessened international tensions, and the fact that his German counterpart, the nationalist but pragmatic Gustav Stresemann, remained at the Wilhemstrasse from 1924 to 1929.

Détente got underway following the agreements negotiated by Briand on 5–16 October 1925 with Stresemann, the British Prime Minister Austen Chamberlain, the Italian Premier Benito Mussolini and the Belgian Vandervelde at the Swiss resort of Locarno on Lake Maggiore. The agreements were intended to stabilize Germany's frontiers with its western neighbours. It recognized its borders with France and Belgium and accepted permanent demilitarization of the Rhineland. Most important for France was that Italy and, especially, Britain were made guarantors of these agreements with the obligation to intervene militarily in the event of their breach. In exchange Germany was to join the League of Nations, was promised a permanent seat on its Council and secured the evacuation of Allied troops from the Cologne zone of the Rhineland. France also reached agreement with Germany, Belgium, Poland and Czechoslovakia on Germany's eastern borders in deference to its East European allies. But those guarantees were far less secure than for the western frontiers. For instance, Germany refused to accept the proposal that, in the event of the League of Nations having to take military action against an aggressor in Eastern Europe, troops could be moved across German territory. This denied France the possibility of entering Germany to come to the rescue of Poland and Czechoslovakia.[21]

The Locarno agreements earned Briand the title of 'Pilgrim of Peace' on his return to Paris. But this was no starry-eyed policy, despite the lyrical rhetoric of peace. It was motivated by the need to block German *revanche*. Briand's masterful oratory presented Locarno as the beginning of the real peace process whereby Germany at last accepted, of its own volition, the Versailles peace conditions – return of Alsace-Lorraine and demilitarization of the left bank of the Rhine. The French Chamber passed the Locarno agreements with a massive majority and the following year Briand shared with Stresemann and Chamberlain the Nobel Peace prize for this collective achievement of reconciliation. Although France felt at last that it had an international guarantee of its security, Germany saw the ill-defined eastern agreements as opening the possibility of revising the eastern borders at some later date. For the moment Briand's policy created a momentum for further reconciliation. This chimed in with the underlying peace-craving mood in

France, and abroad, of ensuring that the Great War really was 'the war to end all wars'. Even when the *Cartel* governments were finally swept away by the financial crisis in July 1926, the new centrist Premier Poincaré understood that there was no going back on the policy of détente and kept Briand on at the Quai to pursue it. As Briand proclaimed in his welcoming speech on Germany's admission to the League on 26 September 1926: 'France and Germany will collaborate in the work of peace. Away with rifles, machine guns, cannon! . . . Make way for conciliation, arbitration, and peace.'[22]

Just as in 1914 Poincaré had been the first President of the Republic to dine at the German embassy in Paris since 1870, so it was Poincaré's government that for the first time welcomed a German Foreign Minister to Paris in August 1928 for the signing of the 15-nation Briand–Kellogg pact outlawing war as a means of settling international disputes.

Détente soon gave way to rapprochement. Again it was on that touch-stone of Franco-German relations, coal and steel, that the most tangible signs of improvement were realized. Between 1924 and 1926 French steel produc-tion increased dramatically, helped by flourishing export markets and by the declining value of the franc and stabilization of the mark. Encouraged by their respective governments, in September 1926 German, French, Sarre, Belgian and Luxembourg steel-makers signed a cartel agreement. The International Steel Agreement fixed production quotas, with Germany assigned almost 41 per cent and France 32 per cent. Until 1939 coal and steel would never again be a source of friction between Berlin and Paris. In 1927 a Franco-German commercial treaty removed trade as a source of disagree-ment. The improvement in Franco-German relations gradually shifted from the realm of statesmen and industrialists into the minds of the French public at large. There was general cross-party support for the Poincaré–Briand government and their German policy. Franco-German meetings of students, Catholics, intellectuals and industrialists captured the general mood, as did Franco-German journals, committees and conferences, some of which dreamed of European construction based on Franco-German reconciliation. Reconciliation and the settlement of differences continued with the June 1929 Young Plan, an international agreement to spread the rest of German reparations annualized over a period ending in 1988. In exchange the Allies agreed to withdraw all occupation troops by 1 July 1930, five years before the date in the Versailles Treaty.[23]

Despite the euphoria over rapprochement, Briand harboured doubts about the extent to which Franco-German relations could continue to improve given the remaining potential flashpoints: the German–Polish border, the 10–12 million German-speaking minorities in Central and Eastern Europe, further revision of the Versailles settlement. To maintain enthusiasm for international peace, head off German revisionism and as a device for wrapping Germany up in a supranational organization likely to diminish its sovereignty, Briand came up with a new idea that surprised many. 'In the face of the danger which threatens European peace', Briand called for a 'federal link' between the European nations 'founded on the idea of union and not unity'. This surprising speech to the League of Nations on 5 September 1929 was followed by a detailed proposal on 17 May 1930 for a European federation. This was to have a permanent political executive and many of the features of the 1957 European Economic Community, including a 'common market' with freer 'circulation of goods, capital, and persons'. Briand's memo- randum emphasized the importance of security in European integration.

> Since any possibility of progress on the way to economic union is deter- mined strictly by the question of security, and since this question is closely linked to that of progress which can be achieved on the path of political union, the constructive effort which would tend to give Europe its organic structure would have to be carried out first of all on the political level.[24]

In 1930 the three stages were to be political, security and economic, a different order from that of 1950s European integration, even if the method of dealing with the German question was the same.

In a sign of things to come, Briand's proposal for an economically inte- grated and politically interdependent common market met with British scepticism. Nor was Berlin happy with it, seeing in it an attempt to guard against revision of the Versailles settlement. While professing a commitment to Franco-German entente, Germany set about scuppering the idea. The Franco-German idyll was drawing to a close, hastened by the rise of German revisionism and its most vociferous exponent, Adolph Hitler. In 1929 he had already denounced the Young Plan as intended to 'reduce the German people to slavery for several generations'.[25] Following the German legislative elections of 14 September 1930, Nazi Party seats in the Reichstag increased from 12 to 107, making it the nation's second largest political party. A main plank of the political programme of Hitler and the Nazis was revision of the Versailles Treaty deemed responsible for all German ills, including the recent economic crisis brought on by the Wall Street Crash of 1929.

From hostility to war again

Before Briand's proposal for a united Europe had been fully debated by the League, fears of a German push eastwards were reignited. On 14 March 1931 Germany and Austria announced the setting up of a customs union. In June and July it was learnt that Germany had signed commercial treaties with Rumania then Hungary. Germany claimed that these were merely economic arrangements, but their political and strategic implications were clear to France. On 15 June 1931, as a result of the economic crisis, Berlin announced it was suspending the Young Plan payments. This effectively ended reparations. Germany had paid less than one sixth of what it was expected to pay, less than half of which had gone to France. The German tide was turning. By 7 March 1932 Briand was dead. The following year on 30 January Hitler was Chancellor of Germany.

Hitler's views on France had been clearly expressed in *Mein Kampf*. France was 'the mortal enemy of Germany' and Germans should be ready to make 'all necessary sacrifices to annihilate the hegemonic power of France'. Nevertheless, French Communists continued to denounce 'French imperialism's' exploitation of the German people through the Versailles Treaty, while the socialists led by Léon Blum viewed Hitler as merely another General Boulanger. The Radical-Socialists, though suspicious of Germany, remained wedded to the Briandist idea of Franco-German rapprochement or Europeanism, which put some on the road to Munich and appeasement. The right's reaction to Hitler was of the 'we told you so' variety, without really recognizing the specific nature of Nazism. The result was confusion, in which belief in peace continued, but without the enthusiasm of the 1920s. Wishful thinking reigned, because anything else was too awful to contemplate.[26]

France's situation was more serious than it recognized. The Versailles Treaty strictly limited Germany's army and armaments. However, the French were unaware of the collaborative agreement between the German and Soviet armies, which allowed the former to develop in secret Soviet camps the prototypes of arms prohibited under the Versailles Treaty: artillery, airforce and combat gases. The agreement, which lasted from 1922 until the end of Weimar, was supported by successive German governments, including social democratic ones, and allowed secret rearmament to take place well before Hitler came to power. By 1932 it could no longer be kept secret. The French General Staff were aware of German secret rearming. Having failed to prevent the French army's departure from the Rhine by way of compensation in 1925, the *Cartel des gauches* offered the military construction of a line of fortifications along the eastern frontier, known as the Maginot Line. A defensive strategy seemed all that was possible, given the domestic political and psychological position and the international commitment to general disarmament. But a defensive strategy was out of line with French diplomacy, which had committed it to the defence of Central and Eastern Europe.[27]

France's position became increasingly vulnerable after the Geneva Disarmament Conference's bowing from 1932 to 1934 to German calls for equality of status in armaments. Seven weeks after coming to power, Hitler ordered an acceleration of the German army programme. However, until the army was ready in 1938 his foreign policy was to be crafted so as not to excite international animosity. On 14 October 1933 Hitler announced German withdrawal from the Disarmament Conference and the League of

Nations, claiming that Germany had not in fact been given the promised equality of status in armaments. But he followed this with speeches emphasizing Germany's desire for peace. Meanwhile during the winter of 1933–34, believing in Hitler's good faith, London called for further reductions in French armaments with similar increases for Germany. Paris, and London, continued to be outmanœuvred by Hitler. His diplomacy, a mixture of forcefulness and feigned peaceableness, always left Germany with the initiative. French problems at home, such as the 1934 Stavisky scandal, the inability to grasp the true nature of Nazism and finally divisions on foreign policy between collective security and a tradition of armed alliances, disoriented French foreign policy, which oscillated bitterly between the two alternatives.

A firmer position was taken by Premier Louis Barthou, a centrist politician with a long-standing suspicion of Germany, who before the war had voted through the Three Years service law and who had presided over the Reparations Commission during French occupation of the Ruhr. He believed that the Hitlerian threat should be the driving force of French foreign and security policy. To counter it, he advocated a policy of bringing France back to its traditional alliances – Russia and Italy. He calculated that in this way potential European disputes could be settled before Hitler could use them to sow discord amongst the European powers. The problem was how to get the French right to accept an alliance with the Soviet Union and the left an alliance with Mussolini's Italy. The trick lay in doing so through the collective security offered by the League of Nations. By September 1934 Barthou had facilitated Soviet membership of the League in the hope that it would lead to a Franco-Russian alliance. Germano-Italian relations were at this time bad, despite their ideological similarities. Barthou successfully exploited differences over Austrian independence, which Rome supported and Berlin opposed, to draw Italy towards France. But on 9 October Barthou, together with the King of Yugoslavia, was assassinated in Marseilles, allegedly by a Croatian terrorist (probably backed by Italian military intelligence, the SIM)

Barthou's successor at the Quai, Pierre Laval, initially wished to carry on that policy, but French domestic political problems began to make that impracticable. The division between left and right was hardening, making alliances with Mussolini and Stalin politically impossible. Moreover, the opportunist Laval saw Franco-German détente as an easier option. After the January 1935 plebiscite in which 90 per cent of the inhabitants of the Sarre opted for a return to the German fold, Hitler declared that there was no remaining disagreement between France and Germany and that 'only a madman could envisage the eventuality of war with France'. This led many in France and elsewhere to the conclusion that perhaps French scepticism towards Germany had been misplaced. Hitler continued to exploit France's guilt complex about Versailles.[28]

On 7 January 1935 Laval signed the 'Rome agreements', a Franco-Italian alliance in all but name. Meanwhile, Germany stepped up its rearming. It created the *Luftwaffe* on 10 March, adopted compulsory military service on 16 March (a response according to Hitler to France's increase in military service to two years) and established a *Kriegsmarine* with a tonnage equivalent to 35 per cent of the Royal Navy's. At the beginning of April France, Britain and Italy met at Stresa and agreed – half-heartedly in the case of London and Paris – to oppose German expansion. France also managed to get a verbal condemnation by the League of German rearming. Fear of Germany encouraged further Franco-Italian rapprochement. Secret military staff talks began on military cooperation in the event of Germany attacking Austria or violating the demilitarized status of the Rhineland. At the same time, France drew closer to the Soviet Union signing on 2 May 1935 the Franco-Soviet mutual assistance pact.

These diplomatic precautions were useless. On 7 March 1936 the German army marched into the Rhineland in clear breach of the Versailles and Locarno agreements. Hitler justified this as self-defence against the Franco-Soviet pact, claiming that it violated the Locarno agreements and encircled Germany. Some on the French left were receptive to Hitler's argument. For them the hated Versailles settlement was at last behind Europe and genuine peace could follow. With legislative elections only six weeks away the idea of mobilizing several classes of men was anathema to the French government, even if the Radical Premier Albert Sarraut vaingloriously declared on the radio: 'We will not leave Strasbourg in range of German cannon.'[29] As Britain would not accept a military solution, still believing that appeasement could work, France let the opportunity for a riposte pass. This was a gift to Hitler, whose army could not have resisted a French counter-attack at that time. Worse still, France lost for good the buffer zone of the Rhineland and the headstart it offered in any mobilization.

A commitment to stand up to Hitler did not emerge from the French elections of April–May 1936. The new Popular Front government comprising socialist and Radical ministers supported by the French Communist Party was committed to defence cuts in its election campaign. The French left had always seen collective security as the principal means to peace, and had generally favoured conciliation of Germany. On 23 June 1936 the socialist Premier Léon Blum set out French foreign policy to the Senate:

> The parties united today in the Rassemblement populaire have always fought for Franco-German entente . . . We regret nothing of the policy we have followed for 15 years. We are determined to follow it still, for the security and honour of the two countries.[30]

Other than putting its faith in a policy of conciliation of Germany because, as Blum pointed out, Hitler too had fought in the trenches, the Popular Front supported disarmament and opposed war. Blum had never made a secret of his opposition to the Versailles Treaty and secret diplomatic alliances. Fortunately, Blum's position evolved as a result of the outbreak of the Spanish Civil War in July 1936, in which Germany supported General Franco's fascists against the Spanish Popular Front, and Hitler's decision in August to increase German military service to two years. Supported by his War Minister, Edouard Daladier, Blum embarked France on a rearmament policy, although he continued to believe that the League of Nations and negotiation with Hitler were equally valid. But Blum and his government remained prisoners of their pacifist and internationalist majority. Consequently, until the departure of the Popular Front governments' Radical Foreign Minister Yvon Delbos on 10 March 1938, foreign policy remained remarkably passive. Other than blindly wishing to follow an appeasing Britain, nothing was done to cultivate France's diplomatic allies. Franco-Soviet friendship was allowed to wither amid fears that friendship with Moscow would upset Berlin. Meanwhile Italy, outlawed because of the Abyssinian War, was quickly sliding into the German camp, which it finally joined on 1 November 1936 with the Berlin–Rome axis. Equally serious, Belgium, geo-strategically vital to France to counter a German attack, abrogated the 1920 military agreement with France on 6 March and opted for neutrality. By the end of 1936, the elaborate system of alliances, which France had constructed since the end of the last war, was in tatters. The Popular Front governments maintained a blind faith in the collective security of a now powerless League, while Hitler prepared his next move.

The year 1936 was also a defining moment for French public opinion's view of Germany. French communists had traditionally been anti-militarist and anti-imperialist and thus supportive of German revisionism regarding Versailles. But Stalin's changed perception of Hitler and Nazism led him from 1936 to 1938 to encourage policies likely to block fascism's path and to work with France. French communists followed suit and switched from their anti-militarist standpoint to voting military credits and supporting National Defence bonds. But it was the socialists who experienced the greatest difficulties in accepting a policy of firmness in relation to Nazi Germany. A small minority did, but some extreme elements turned to defeatism, others opposed rearmament and relations with the Soviet Union, while most continued to oppose war.

All of this seriously tied the government's hands and ensured that in 1938 all socialists voted for the Munich agreements. Though less ideological, the traditional peace-seeking Radicals were unconcerned about the ambiguity of the government's rearming cum negotiation stance, as they held the war and foreign affairs portfolios. On the right and extreme right, traditional anti-Germanism and admiration for fascist Italy could be synchronized, until 1936. Then, as a result of the Spanish Civil War, Germany appeared increasingly as the European bulwark against Marxism and Italy's friend.

Without becoming pro-Nazi, the French right began to lose some of its anti-Germanism and slip into its own version of temporizing.[31] Then there was a sort of magma of individuals and organizations that went along with German revisionist ideas for diverse reasons. On the left were pacifists, who made up one-quarter of socialist (SFIO) membership grouped around Paul Faure, who declared on 7 April 1939: 'Any territorial concession is preferable to the death of one wine-grower from the Maconnais.'[32] A third of the CGT trade union were pacifists, as were many in the primary school teachers' union. The leaders of the Comité de vigilance des intellectuels antifascistes were pacifists, as were best-selling authors such as Jean Giono, who wrote: 'There is no shameful peace, there are only shameful wars.'[33] From the Radicals to the classical right there were supporters of an entente even with a national-socialist Germany, largely on the grounds of anti-communism. They included former Premier Joseph Caillaux and his friends and a host of writers from Louis Bertrand to Alfred Fabre-Luce. There were writers who admired fascism, such as Robert Brasillach, Drieu La Rochelle and Paul Marion. Many would thrive during formal Franco-German collaboration after 1940. In the business world, economic considerations and anti-communism motivated closer relations with Germany for men such as Pierre Pucheu of the Comptoir sidérurgique, Paul Baudoin of the Banque d'Indochine and members of the Comité franco-allemand d'information et de documentation, founded in 1926. Closer relations with Germany were advocated by the leaders of some of the larger veterans associations, such as G. Scapini, who in 1934 met Hitler. In February 1937 work with their German counterparts culminated in the creation in Berlin of the Comité international permanent des anciens combattants. Much of the press leant towards an agreement with Germany. Other organizations were dedicated to fostering closer Franco-German relations, such as the Comité France-Allemagne and Les Cahiers franco-allemands. Leaders like Otto Abetz, Ferdinand de Brinon and Jean Luchaire would exercise considerable influence under Collaboration. Supporters of Franco-German rapprochement helped convince the French of the Reich's peaceable intentions, gradually eroding their vigilance.[34]

The wrong signals were sent to Hitler throughout this period. The French gave the impression of being willing to discuss anything, even the independence of Austria. On the night of 11 March 1938, the day after the second Popular Front government had fallen, German troops entered Austria and the *Anschluss* was proclaimed on 13 March. That day Blum formed a new Popular Front government amid severe financial and social turmoil, which distracted attention from abroad. There was no international outcry at the annexation. France discreetly demoted its legation in Vienna from diplomatic to consular status, tacit recognition of the disappearance of a state. Yet in geo-strategic terms this was an immense blow to France. A greater Germany with an extra six million population allowed the Berlin–Rome axis physically to divide the continent from the Baltic to Sicily. More than ever France was separated from its East European allies, while the German-speaking population of Czechoslovakia, France's ally since 1924, became a sitting duck for Hitler. By April 1938 the Popular Front was no longer. Its Radical-Socialist successor, in power up to the war, neither wanted to, nor probably could, stand up to Germany and continued the ambivalent policy of rearming while negotiating with Hitler.

The majority of German-speaking Sudeten Czechs had made clear their desire for an autonomous government in April 1938. Given the possibility of the Sudeten question developing into a general conflict, the French Foreign Minister, Georges Bonnet, a supporter of appeasement, consulted his Soviet counterpart. He was willing for the Soviet army to intervene in Czechoslovakia if Poland and Romania consented to Soviet troops crossing their territory. They refused. London let Paris know of its opposition to a military solution. The French, who had no stomach for war, bowed to Britain, as they continually did up to the war. Hitler increased the pressure with a violent speech in Nuremberg on 12 September calling for the martyred Sudeten people to be given the right of self-determination and hinting at German intervention. The British Prime Minister, Neville Chamberlain, met Hitler at Berchtesgarten on the 15th and offered Sudeten self-determination. The French convinced Prague to concede. But a week later Hitler insisted to Chamberlain at Godesberg that Germany must occupy the Sudetenland. By the 27th Hitler was threatening general mobilization. War seemed imminent. The Soviet Union informed the French that it would fulfil its 1935 treaty obligations to Czechoslovakia if France did. On 27 September France called up its reservists, while Daladier insisted on the radio that peace was not over. The next day Chamberlain suggested to Mussolini and Hitler a five-nation conference with France and Czechoslovakia. The Munich conference met from 29 to 30 September, but without the Czechs. Hitler's demands, including annexation of the Sudetenland, were largely met. An ecstatic 500,000-strong French crowd welcomed Daladier. On 4 October the Chamber of Deputies voted a motion of confidence in him by 535 votes to 75, the latter all communists bar two.

General relief in France, as in Britain, did not mean that all French were defeatist. For some Munich was a breathing space, but for others it was a policy. Following Chamberlain's signing of a non-aggression pact with Germany at Munich, France, following in Britain's wake, signed its own version in Paris on 6 December. In it the Franco-German frontier was declared definitive and the two powers agreed to solve future problems by consultation. The Soviet Union suspected Paris and London of having made a secret deal with Berlin allowing it free rein in the east in exchange for security in the west. Partly out of self-preservation Stalin would sign the

Nazi–Soviet pact in August 1939, denying France traditional Russian support against Germany.

Hitler flagrantly breached the Munich agreements. By 15 March 1939 the *Wehrmacht* had marched into Prague and occupied the rump of Czechoslovakia. France and Britain, guarantors of Czechoslovakia's new borders, did nothing, feeling that they did not have the military means to react. France's demographic deficit of the First World War was having a serious impact on the numbers of men of military age. Moreover, delays in rearming, especially aviation, resulting from strikes and reductions in the working week during the Popular Front, put France at a disadvantage to Germany, whose rearmament had been underway for years. However, the climate of opinion was beginning to change. In Britain the public now favoured a more vigorous stance against Hitler than the government. France's attitude also stiffened. It was clear that Hitler's ambitions went well beyond ethnic expansion. Poland was next in the firing line over the Versailles-created Danzig corridor with its German-speaking minorities. Paris and London decided to put an end to concessions and to launch a diplomatic offensive, beginning with the Franco-British guarantee to Poland on 31 March 1939. On 13 April Anglo-French guarantees were given to Greece and oil-rich Romania. On the 27th Germany claimed Danzig. On 28 April the House of Commons voted for the reintroduction of conscription. This was too late to stop Hitler, who realized that he had to make war quickly before Britain and France had galvanized their military positions. On 22 May in Berlin Germany and Italy signed the offensive military Pact of Steel.

In France opponents of war and supporters of greater concessions to Hitler were typified by Marcel Déat's article in *L'Œuvre* of 4 May 1939 entitled 'Die for Danzig? No'. But most opinion tended towards resistance to Hitler. In the event of war the Soviet Union's position became crucial. But relations with London and Paris were complicated by mutual suspicion resulting from the Munich agreements. On 14 April Daladier tried to convince the Soviets to come to the assistance of France and Britain should they have to help Poland. Negotiations took place in Moscow with British and French officials, but Stalin had another iron in the fire: a rapprochement with Germany underway since March and prefigured by negotiations for a commercial agreement in June and July. Daladier pushed for a military agreement, which a Franco-British military delegation began to negotiate in Moscow from 12 August. But the sticking point was Soviet demands for the Red Army to be allowed to occupy strategic bases in the independent Baltic States and to be able to cross Poland and Romania, which the latter continued to refuse. Meanwhile, the Germans, aware of these negotiations, accelerated overtures to the Soviets. Von Ribbentrop, the German Foreign Minister, aware of Hitler's deadline for an invasion of Poland set for 1 September, pressed his newly appointed Soviet counterpart, the anti-Western

Vyacheslav Molotov, for a non-aggression pact. He agreed in principle, as well as to the secret protocol setting out respective zones of influence in Eastern Europe on 18 August. The following day Stalin chose to go with the German deal, while continuing negotiations with the British and French delegation for a couple of days. On 23 August Ribbentrop was in Moscow to sign the Nazi–Soviet pact.

The Nazi-Soviet pact enabled Hitler to avoid a war on two fronts and Stalin to secure short-term peace and territorial gains. It remained for Hitler to begin his end game. On 20 August German reservists were called up; three days later Gauleiter Nazi Forster took over in Danzig. On the 25th Hitler threatened the French ambassador over French assistance to Poland. By the 30th London and Paris were trying to encourage negotiation between Berlin and Warsaw. On 1 September German troops invaded Poland. France mobilized and the French Chamber unanimously voted 70 billion francs in military credits. There was little sign of enthusiasm, few having forgotten the carnage of the First World War. On 3 September London and Paris issued ultimatums to Germany to evacuate Polish territory. With no German reply, the British government declared war on Germany at 11 a.m. and France the following day at 5 p.m. Since the last war France had vainly tried every tack from containment to conciliation. Hitler had known what he wanted. The French government had known only what it did not want, to spill French blood. For the third time in three generations France was at war with Germany.

Collaboration

Haunted by the memory of the First World War, France did not begin an outright offensive against Germany while it was tied up fighting in the east; it settled down behind the Maginot Line and waited for the German attack. Paris and London calculated that this would give them time to continue rearming. while the blockading of German ports by the Royal Navy suffocated the German economic war effort. The 'phoney war' in the west was finally broken on 10 May 1940 by the German *Blitzkrieg* through neutral Belgium. The German armies were victorious in six weeks, having skirted round the Maginot Line. For the third time in three wars France was forced to move its seat of government to the provinces, this time to Bordeaux on 10 June. But not only had the French armies been routed; the French state was breaking up. Cracks appeared in the French government between those in favour of seeking an armistice with Germany, led by the Vice-Premier, Philippe Pétain, and those in favour of continuing the struggle from North Africa with the French navy and Empire, led by Premier Paul Reynaud. The former won and Reynaud resigned. Pétain was charged by the President of the Republic, Albert Lebrun, with forming a government and in the night of 16–17 June called for a cessation of hostilities from Germany. On the 17th a little-known two-star general and junior minister of defence, Charles de Gaulle, found the cessation of hostilities intolerable and flew from Bordeaux to London. On 18 June he appealed via the BBC for the French to resist the German invasion. His appeal went largely unheard and unheeded.

On 21 June a French delegation led by General Huntziger was summoned to Marshal Foch's old railway carriage at Rethondes in which the Germans had signed the armistice of 11 November 1918. In the presence of Hitler, Marshal Keitel read to the French the German armistice conditions, which were signed the next day on behalf of the French government. France was to cease all hostilities. Three-fifths of French territory was to be occupied in the north and down the Atlantic coastline (Alsace and Lorraine were annexed). The southern zone was to remain 'free' under French control. France was to be disarmed and allowed an army for the maintenance of order of only 100,000 men, exactly what Germany had been allowed in the 1918 armistice. The two million captured French soldiers were to remain in German hands until a full peace was signed. The French navy was to be disarmed and remain under French control, as was the colonial empire. These two concessions were granted to no other German occupied territory and gave Vichy the illusion of independence and world power. But Germany took control of French foreign policy via Article 10, which stipulated that France 'agrees not to develop in the future any hostile action against the German Reich with its remaining armed forces or in any way'. France was to indemnify Germany in cash daily for the occupation. Although fundamentally undermining France's existence as an independent state and its rank in the world, the armistice terms were relatively lenient, given the scale and rapidity of France's defeat. It was the only defeated country to have signed an armistice; it was not administered directly by a German governor or commissar (unlike Poland and the Netherlands), was not fully occupied and did not have leaders imposed on it (unlike Norway with Quisling). It was even allowed a prestigious war hero and marshal as its leader. This apparent leniency and the presentation of the armistice as a prelude to a final peace treaty (like 1918) left many in France with the impression that concessions in the short term could enhance chances of a more favourable final peace settlement and even a privileged place in the 'New Europe'.[35] The armistice document remained the basis for Franco-German relations until the whole of France was occupied on 11 November 1942. On 10 July 666 *députés* and senators gathered at Vichy, the headquarters of the southern zone, to vote on a bill giving full powers to Marshal Pétain and the right to draw up a new constitution for 'L'Etat français'. With only 80 votes cast against the bill, the Vichy regime came into existence.

The Vichy period was for long presented as an aberration of French history, isolated from what went before and what came after. This view has been increasingly challenged. In terms of Franco-German relations, evidence of continuity with the past can be adduced. Ever since the nineteenth century some French had favoured close Franco-German relations. It is known that the same *députés* who voted for the Munich agreements voted for the Vichy regime in July 1940. But were those Quai d'Orsay diplomats who advocated conciliation, even an entente with Germany, in the inter-war years the same people who encouraged collaboration with Germany during the 'dark years' of 1940 to 1944?

Hitler may have perceived Franco-German relations as merely of victor to vanquished, in which France was to be a docile supplier of food, men and *matériel* to the German war effort, but this was not the picture from Paris. Unlike other occupied territories, Slovakia apart, the Vichy regime had a very clear political agenda called the National Revolution aimed at transforming a decadent and corrupt French society into 'a virile and moral France'. Defeat and occupation made this possible, as Vichy had the inclination and Germany provided the opportunity. No wonder that the 1940 defeat was referred to by some as the 'divine surprise', or that collaboration continued beyond 1942 when German defeat appeared likely. By binding Vichy to Germany and to its victory domestic politics, where Vichy had a certain freedom of manœuvre, conditioned French foreign policy.[36]

France experienced several forms of collaboration from administrative collaboration between the central French authorities and the Germans to protective collaboration, by which those such as Pétain hoped to attenuate the suffering of the French people and obtain better conditions generally for France. Government collaboration was indulged in to maintain France's great power status. This implied at least indirect participation in a German victory to allow France a privileged place in a future Hitlerian Europe.[37] Finally there was unadulterated ideological collaboration, mostly in Paris, by 'fascist' elements that enthusiastically embraced the Nazi 'New Order'.

Within the Vichy regime there was a group that believed that, even if Britain did quickly fall, as was widely predicted, the armistice provided a breathing space during which France should refuse any further collaboration with Germany and quietly prepare its revenge. They were led by General Weygand, Foch's trusty Chief of Staff in 1918, appointed Supreme Commander during the Battle of France in 1940 and Minister of Defence in the first Vichy government. Subsequently appointed to North Africa, Weygand secretly began to prepare France for a war of *revanche* until the Germans obtained his recall in 1941.

Ideological collaborators tended to be drawn from inter-war groups like the fascistic extra-parliamentary 'ligues'. They shared the anti-Bolshevism of the Nazis and their enthusiasm for a 'new Europe' and were mostly active in Paris, believing Vichy collaboration to be too pallid, paternalistic and reactionary. They sought tighter Franco-German collaboration through the influential German ambassador in Paris, Otto Abetz, an old exponent of Franco-German rapprochement. Other leading Paris collaborators had more of a history of supporting German, as opposed to Nazi, collaboration for its perceived intrinsic merit: Ferdinand de Brinon and Jean Luchaire claimed to be working for a Briandist conception of Franco-German reconciliation. The former, as Pétain's representative in Paris, was a long-standing Germanophile who, through his Comité France-Allemagne from 1933 to 1939, had fostered cooperation between French and German businessmen, politicians and intellectuals. He helped introduce Laval to Hitler. De Brinon would head the Vichy government transferred to Sigmaringen in 1944 as the Liberation began. The journalist Luchaire headed the collaborationist press in Paris and with Abetz had co-organized the Franco-German youth congress of 1930–32.[38]

Another Vichy tendency was that of the 'opportunistic' collaborators such as the former socialist turned Radical and Briandist minister of the Third Republic, Pierre Laval, a supporter of conciliating Germany. He had secured the vote of full powers to Pétain and engineered the birth of the Vichy regime. As Vice-Premier in Pétain's first government and Premier from April 1942, he was convinced of a German victory and of the need for France to side with it in the crusade against bolshevism to gain a privileged place in the 'New Europe', perhaps even as Germany's 'brilliant second'. Inventor of the term 'collaboration', Laval was in contact with Otto Abetz from July 1940. He worked to keep Vichy's policy firmly on the rails of collaboration and what was left of French assets geared to helping the German war effort. He infamously broadcast to the French people in January 1943: 'I hope for a German victory for without it bolshevism will establish itself everywhere.' His was also a European vision: 'A new Europe will inevitably arise from this war . . . As for me, a Frenchman, I wish that tomorrow we should be able to love a Europe in which France will have a worthy place.'[39]

Pétain's position was to sway from one tendency to the other. At Montoire on 24 October 1940 he shook hands with Hitler declaring: 'today I am going down the road of collaboration . . . this is my policy . . . It is I alone whom History will judge.' Yet he supported closer contacts with London, especially after the Battle of Britain in 1940. This was not to promote London's victory but to obtain concessions from it, such as relaxing the British blockade, neutralizing de Gaulle and generally taking the sting out of the British threat to France's remaining interests, notably in the Empire. Although on 13 December 1940 Pétain sacked Laval, putting him under house arrest, the British line did not triumph. Collaboration with Germany became subtler, with the Germans being kept informed of negotiations with Britain. Under Vice-Premier Admiral Darlan, the real power until April 1942, the backing of both the German and British horses continued. Collaboration with Germany tightened, with French production of aircraft for the Reich, meetings with Hitler in May 1941 and facilities afforded to Germany to defend Syria against the British and Free French. It was not the first or last time that France would hesitate about choosing between Germany or Britain. Darlan believed that France was 'caught between Germany and England'. For the moment Germany represented the greater threat and consequently deserved greater 'rapprochement'. But, following German setbacks during the Battle of Britain, in Greece and in Libya, Darlan was less convinced of a German victory. Believing that an Anglo-German war of attrition could in the long term benefit France, he noted: 'It is therefore possible and even probable that France's hour will come at the time of the final settlement. It will be able to play a real role of arbiter in the final settlement and to impose a French solution on the conflict, which will be neither the "new German order" nor will it be synonymous with Anglo-Saxon hegemony.'[40] With new German successes in spring 1941, he returned to believing in a German victory and hence collaboration, but remained reluctant to risk war with Britain. He told the French Cabinet on 14 May 1941 that such a policy would attain three objectives: 'Save the French nation, reduce to a minimum our metropolitan and territorial losses, play an honourable role – even important – in the future Europe.'[41] By December 1941 his attitude changed again after the German failure to take Moscow and the USA's entry into the war. He attempted to discover Churchill's attitude to France's potential participation in an Allied peace settlement. With Laval's return on 18 April 1942, the pendulum policy came to an end and a pro-German line triumphed. After the Allied landing in North Africa, the loss of Empire, the occupation of the southern zone in November 1942, Vichy lost all of its trump cards. Of the three original motives for state collaboration with Germany – maintaining France's rank in the world, protecting the French and maintaining the regime – by 1943–44 only the latter remained.[42]

According to Robert Frank, what the men of Vichy failed to comprehend, unlike General de Gaulle, was that the war was a world war. For Vichyites, ending the Franco-German war could save France. Then, by mediating in the Anglo-German war, France would place itself on the winning side whatever the outcome. Occasionally, old geopolitical reflexes surfaced when the men of Vichy believed that first the Soviet Union and then the USA could loosen the vice in which France was held between Britain and Germany.[43]

In the end, Vichy could not avoid collaboration with Germany, but in so doing made a colossal contribution to the German war effort. In total France financed the equivalent of one-fifth of the German war budget, worth annually 48 per cent of France's national income in 1939. In the spring of 1942, before coercive recruitment was introduced, 170,000 French were working in France for the *Wehrmacht*, 275,000 in construction programmes such as aerodromes and 400,000 in factories producing *matériel* for the German army, and another 185,000 laboured in factories in Germany. The latter increased substantially from 1942, particularly with the introduction at the beginning of 1943 of a compulsory work scheme, the Service du travail obligatoire. The Germans also benefited considerably from the French State, police and judicial authorities' help in the repression of Jews (75,000 of whom were handed over to the Germans), communists and resistance members. While not deriving great benefit from the small numbers of French volunteers who offered to serve on the Eastern Front in the Légion des volontaires français (3000) organized in Paris in the summer of 1941, or the *Waffen SS* (2000), the Germans saved themselves much effort and hatred by letting the French organize the political and para-military *Milice* to hound out Jews, communists and the Resistance.

The Resistance – representing the historical trend of refusing to have any truck with Germany – had no impact in impeding the German war effort before the summer of 1941.[44] Their numbers increased subsequently. Resistance members were not always motivated by rejection of Germany. The French Communist Party had a change of heart over Germany only following Hitler's invasion of the USSR in June 1941; others preferred Resistance to compulsory labour in Germany (*STO*). The socialists rallied to de Gaulle in 1942 and the disparate elements of the Resistance were united in 1943. With the fall of North Africa to the Allies in the winter of 1942–43, the Free French were able to increase their contribution to the Allied war effort against Germany. On 3 June 1944, three days before the Allied landings in Normandy, de Gaulle created the Provisional Government of the French Republic in an effort to demonstrate to everyone, the Allies, the Germans and the French, that the legitimate French state was again a player on the international scene. The symbolic liberation of Paris by French troops and their subsequent participation alongside the Allies in the final defeat of the German armies along the Rhine and Danube were more political than military acts. They were intended to convey the illusion that France was once again a great power able legitimately to take part in the final peace settlement on the winning side. Fear of humiliation at the hands of Germany would again condition France's attitude to its eastern neighbour in the peace settlement. But again circumstances would force France to move through cycles of wishing to crush, then contain and finally to conciliate Germany in the post-war world.

From hostility to containment

France was present at the signing of German capitulation in Rheims on 7 May and Berlin on 8 May 1945 alongside the major Allied powers. This was an act of the highest symbolism. By an extraordinary turn of political rather than military circumstance, in the space of nine months France had gone from being a collaborator to an Allied victor over Germany. With France liberated, the war over and Germany disarmed and occupied, as in 1918

France set about gaining maximum advantage from victory. Other than restoring its rank in the world – not a uniquely Gaullist ambition – France wished to neutralize the German threat. But after the Second World War its position in relation to the Allies was a good deal weaker than after the First from a diplomatic, military and financial point of view. It was clearly the least of the great powers and seriously dependent on their goodwill.

The first means of dealing with Germany was potentially through the major international conferences convened to organize peace and security. But this option was largely denied to France, which was not invited to Yalta in February 1945, Potsdam from July to August, or London in September 1945. Yet it was here that the Big Three, the USA, USSR and Britain, decided on Germany's fate. France had to be satisfied with becoming one of the five permanent members of the newly created United Nations' Security Council, even though this conferred no direct control of Germany. France set little store by it as a source of its own defence, as the failure of the League in the inter-war years had undermined its faith in collective security. A second means was for France to attempt to have its ideas on a future Germany adopted by the Allies. De Gaulle's aim (as in 1919) was to reduce German power by refusing a centralized Reich, and by creating client states in the Rhineland and a federal structure for what remained of the state after the amputation of territory to the east of the Oder–Neisse line. De Gaulle believed that the geo-strategic left bank of the Rhine should be under French, British, Dutch and Belgian control, while the Ruhr, with its coal deposits vital to the French, Dutch and Italian economies, should be detached from Germany and placed under international mandate, to avoid it ever again becoming the Reich's arsenal. The Sarre was to be given political autonomy. France obtained satisfaction only on the latter. Even that was temporary. In 1955 the inhabitants of the Sarre voted to return to the German fold, to which Paris agreed in the Franco-German treaty of 27 October 1956.

France was not satisfied with its share of reparations ($37 million by 1948). However, it did obtain, with British support at Yalta, an occupation zone in Germany along with the Big Three of some 42,800 square kilometres adjacent to its eastern frontier from south of Bonn to the Swiss border. This it administered more independently and in harsher fashion than those of Britain and the USA.[45] De Gaulle deemed it vital that, in order to take 'a share in the defeat, occupation, and administration of the Reich', French troops should participate in the invasion of Germany across the Rhine, which upset the Americans. More symbolically, it was a means of settling the moral scores so that the Occupier became the Occupied.

By the time he had resigned on 20 January 1946, de Gaulle had clearly set out the French position on the future of Germany. That position was broadly maintained by all French governments for the next three years and supported by all political parties, from extreme left to extreme right, albeit with the socialists taking a more nuanced position. There seemed little room for forgiveness or reconciliation after German occupation, with many French convinced, as Roger Gaborit told the French National Assembly on 12 June 1948, that the Germans needed not denazification but degermanization.[46] As after the First World War, France found no Allied support for crushing Germany and was in no position to demand it given its own weak diplomatic, military and financial state. Nor did France emerge from the war into a haven of peace, but into other forms of war. The newly established fragile Fourth Republic was unable to deal effectively with the problems of the cold war or, more importantly, decolonization. This weakened France's position still further vis-à-vis the Allies and Germany.

The third means France sought to guard against a re-emergence of a powerful German state and to contain it was by bilateral alliances. Until 1948 under successive governments and despite the departure of de Gaulle in January 1946, French diplomacy demonstrated that its old geo-strategic reflexes were still functioning. On 10 December 1944 it signed a mutual assistance pact with the Soviet Union. Half of its clauses concerned Germany; notably mutual assistance in the event of renewed German aggression after the war. Unlike in 1919, France's immediate post-war weakness reduced the likelihood of French hegemony over the continent. This helped in its search for security. Unlike its long quest of the 1920s, Paris did obtain an alliance with Britain. The Dunkirk treaty of 4 March 1947 had as its prime aim to guard against any future German aggression or policy likely to lead to a threat to peace (even non-compliance with economic treaty stipulations) that would provoke immediate mutual assistance. But with the onset of the cold war from 1947 Paris found it increasingly difficult to keep others focused on the German threat. Although the 17 March 1948 Brussels Treaty between France, Britain and the Benelux countries called for mutual assistance in the event of aggression from any source, the Soviet Union was the new threat. However, the Western European Union, which would emerge from the Brussels Treaty, did increasingly become a European forum to control German rearmament. Similarly, the NATO treaty of 4 April 1949, enthusiastically solicited by Paris throughout 1948 and ostensibly directed against the Soviet Union, had for France the added convenience of committing additional British and American troops to the European continent, where they automatically neutralized potential German aggression. Few people in France would have disagreed with the alleged quip by Lord Ismay, NATO's first Secretary-General, that the alliance was 'a device for keeping the Americans in, the Soviets out and the Germans down'.

As nervous about Germany in 1945–46 as it was about the emerging Soviet threat, France was determined at all costs not to repeat the policy errors of the early 1920s and successfully avoided diplomatic isolation as the cold war began. The French had hoped not to have to take sides in the developing quarrel between Soviets and Anglo-Saxons and held to the idea of maintaining the friendship of all the victors, geo-strategy having primacy over ideology. But the communist coup in Czechoslovakia on 25 February 1948 and the blockade of Berlin by the Soviets from 24 June until March 1949 forced it to take sides. The implications of this were acutely felt in France because of the strength of the French Communist Party with its quarter of the vote. Its four ministers had been ejected from the government following communist-supported strikes in the winter of 1947, giving rise to talk of a potential communist coup. Gradually Soviet expansion super-imposed itself on the German threat, but the latter by no means disappeared from French minds.

In exchange for control of the Sarre and international control of Ruhr coal, the French agreed in August 1948 to fuse their occupation zone with the already united American and British zones effectively creating a West German state. The federal structure desired by the French was formalized by the law of 8 May 1949. (Whether the French chose the anniversary of the defeat of Germany for that occasion is unclear.) The French also accepted the Petersberg Protocol of 24 November 1949. This allowed West Germany access to a series of international bodies from the Council of Europe to receipt of Marshall Aid, but it also ended reparations. There was no stopping German revival, even if for France not all the safeguards were in place. But already an alternative means of keeping Germany in check was coming to the fore – European integration. The influential Edouard Bonnefous of the UDSR party spoke for many when he warned parliament on 24 November 1949 that 'if the German revival is not integrated in the economic organization of Europe, it will be carried out against the other European countries'.[47]

External influences pushed the French further down the road of European integration. The cold war was, of course, not confined to Europe, though it impacted seriously on France's relations with West Germany. The onset of the three-year-long Korean War, in June 1950, pitted communist North Korea against pro-western South Korea. A divided Korea in which one half, communist-led, invaded the other was interpreted as a dummy run for a similar scenario in which Soviet-backed Eastern Germany tested the defences of West Germany. Supporting South Korea had diverted many of Britain's and the USA's best military forces and commanders to the Far East by 1952–53. The West German Federal Republic, formed in 1949, had no armed forces of its own. By 1951–53 arguments for West German rearmament appeared overwhelming to France's Anglo-American allies. This worried the French, for whom the spectre of a rearmed Germany was anathema. It came hard on the heels of French military and financial commitments to war in Indochina from 1946, ruinous to French economic recovery plans at home and an impediment to defending West Germany or France's eastern borders. French strategists and politicians were forced to acknowledge that theirs was a short-weight contribution to Western Europe's security so long as France remained snared in colonial entanglements.

As in the past – and future – an alternative means of neutralizing the German threat emerged: the Briandist solution of wrapping Germany up in a European supranational body to deny its sovereignty over its army. The French response was the Pleven Plan (named after the Premier René Pleven) of 24 October 1950 for a European Defence Community (EDC) between the Benelux countries, Italy, West Germany and France. The EDC would share command of a European army made up of all land and air forces other than those necessary for the defence of overseas territories, which in France's case was by far the largest. Though Winston Churchill had suggested the idea of a European army earlier in March 1950, France now appeared to support it and the Treaty of Paris was signed on 27 May 1952. For two years the French parliament would debate the Treaty's ratification, generating 'more political controversy since the Dreyfus Affair or the separation of Church and State'.[48] It gave vent to the most strident views demonstrating the extent to which the German threat was still alive. In October 1951 de Gaulle had criticized the project because the German army would be reborn without sufficient guarantees for French safety, while in February 1952 former Premier Edouard Daladier had described the project as dangerous for France and for peace. An oft-repeated phrase of the time was that the EDC 'rearms Germany and disarms France'. The fear was that a reborn German army would quickly regain pre-eminence in Europe, as the French army was deployed largely abroad in the Empire. When the Bonn agreements, restoring full German control over most of the Bundesrepublik's territory, were signed on 26 May 1952, and followed the next day by the Paris Treaty on a European army, there were strident protests in France. De Gaulle and his supporters claimed that France was being abandoned while Daladier described the Treaty of Paris as 'hiding the resurrection of Germany under the European flag'.[49] By 1953 the General Staff were opposed. Momentum gathered for de Gaulle's notion that the EDC would be 'Germany's thing'.[50] According to Raymond Aron: 'The European Defence Community was supposed to have established a "definitive" link between Germany and the West which would dispel the nightmare of reunification . . .'.[51]

However, the memories of 1940–44 were too fresh to contemplate any German rearmament, whatever the new Soviet threat. Prusso-German militarism was a genie that dared not be released from the bottle a third time. In the end the bill steered by the Radical Premier Pierre Mendès France and supported by most of the left (the communists apart) and opposed by the Gaullists was rejected by the French National Assembly on 30 August 1954.[52] As a compromise it was accepted that a rearmed Federal Republic of

Germany should have its armed forces dissolved in the Atlantic Pact by making it a member of NATO. Ironically, four years previously the French government had proposed the creation of a European army to stop Germany becoming part of that Pact.[53] But France was reassured by Britain's decision to resurrect the Brussels Pact and maintain its forces on the continent. In October 1954 the Paris agreements acknowledged German sovereignty. Germany and Italy were admitted into an extended Brussels Pact renamed the Western European Union. More important still West Germany pledged never to manufacture atomic, bacteriological or chemical (ABC) weapons on its territory and never to use force in order to secure reunification or a change in its borders.

France's policy of maintaining Germany in a state of total subordination had failed, just as it had after the First World War. It would have to be content with seeing its neighbour occupied by the four powers and divided for the foreseeable future, given the antagonistic political, social and economic systems in place in the two Germanys. One issue led the French government to accept the rearming of Germany with a degree of equanimity: the question of a French nuclear weapon, which Mendès France brought before the Cabinet on 26 December 1954. The French Premier's aim was to make France an independent nuclear power, with the added bonus of ensuring that Germany did not gain influence in the Western Alliance to France's detriment. Mendès France made clear that he was conscious of the gap between the atomic powers and the rest, 'as well as the advantage which France had in this area over Germany as a result of the latter's renunciation to build the weapon'.[54] The decision was taken to launch a secret programme of study and to build a proto-type. Germany would be allowed to rearm, but France would possess the ultimate deterrent.

Franco-German relations deteriorated during this period as a result of serious differences over the Sarre, whose economic attachment to France and political autonomy were hotly contested in Germany, notably on the left, and increasingly in the Sarre itself. French heavy-handedness in dealing with German protests provoked international criticism of a similar nature to that which greeted France's 1923 occupation of the Ruhr, with France described as behaving like a conqueror. The Sarre issue and the rearming of Germany encouraged Paris to shift towards a policy of reconciliation with Bonn. Fear that Germany might be seduced by a Soviet peace offensive and come to an arrangement with it edged France closer to its eastern neighbour.

From containment to conciliation

Reconciliation with Germany through European supranational agreements had started in April 1950, when Foreign Minister Robert Schuman took the initiative in proposing to 'eliminate the age-old opposition between France and Germany' through the creation of a coal and steel community. The Schuman Plan was not purely an altruistic gesture of friendship or simply 'the mystique of integration', as General de Gaulle pejoratively referred to it. The strategic interest of denying Germany control of what was effectively its arsenal was part of the calculation, with Schuman declaring that such an undertaking would 'make war henceforth impossible between the two countries'. The project called for federal integration in which France would exercise the leadership. Only two years earlier Schuman had suggested that there were several Germanys, which would be better organized as separate states. The birth of the Bundesrepublik, largely at the behest of the Anglo-Saxons, had by no means reassured French opinion, despite the new state's federal nature. On 14 November 1949 Schuman had attempted to soothe opinion by explaining that Germany would neither have an army, nor be a member of the Atlantic Pact, nor have the right to increase its steel production. The creation of the European Coal and Steel Community on 18 April 1951 by which French, German, Italian and Benelux production was pooled was less of a Damascene conversion to reconciliation than an example of French *realpolitik*, which had not been absent from Briand's European plan 20 years earlier.

Reconciliation was also inspired by a desire, in de Gaulle's words in July 1946, to see the balance restored by 'the old world between the two new ones', the USA and the Soviet Union. At the time de Gaulle was thinking of a Franco-British alliance as the foundation stone. But on 16 March 1950 he noted in a press conference that 'one would almost be blinded by the perspective of what would result from the combination of French and German qualities'. With the Soviet ally now the potential adversary of the Western world, of which the Federal Republic was now a member, Germany could replace Britain as the counterbalance to American might, given London's refusal to join the supranational ECSC.[55] But there was still opposition to the plan from employers' organizations, small and medium-sized firms and the communist CGT trade union. Parliamentary commissions were split over ratification, with Foreign Affairs and Finance in favour and Economics and Defence opposed.[56]

German membership of NATO on 22 October 1954 and the creation of the *Bundeswehr* on 15 July 1955, albeit deprived of ABC weapons and strategic bombers, encouraged the idea of smothering Germany still further in friendship. After the settlement of the Sarre problem in 1956, the way was clear for drawing Germany closer to France via further European integration. Differences were not absent from the conferences of Messina, Brussels and Venice on the road to the Common Market. Serious reservations were expressed in France about the threat of German competition in such a market, but professional organizations were overall fairly evenly divided on the question of signing the treaties of Rome creating the European

Economic Community and Euratom on 25 March 1957. The French
parliament readily accepted ratification in July. At a less public level steps
were taken towards Franco-German cooperation on military nuclear issues.
From January 1957 until May 1958 the German Defence Minister, Franz-
Josef Strauss, met his opposite numbers Maurice Bourgès-Maunory and
Jacques Chaban-Delmas to explore the possibility of Franco-German cooperation (with Italy) on developing military nuclear technology and delivery
systems. Nothing concrete emerged, but France had stood to gain most from
the agreement. Desperate for its own nuclear weapon and a credible delivery
system, France was banking on gaining access to German funding and
expertise, especially in rocket technology, for a project the outcome of
which was denied to Germany by the 1954 Paris agreements. As would often
be the case, French (but also German) national interests strongly motivated
cooperation.[57]

The return to power in May 1958 of General de Gaulle, an opponent of
a supranational Europe, worried Bonn. However, these fears proved ill-
founded. Not only would the EEC be created as planned on 1 January 1959,
but de Gaulle would make Franco-German entente a key feature of his foreign policy. He hoped to use reconciliation to make Germany a grateful and
faithful partner in his bid to dominate the European Community. He was
helped by his excellent relations with German Chancellor Konrad Adenauer,
who was welcomed like an old friend to de Gaulle's country home at
Colombey-les-Deux-Eglises on 14 and 15 September 1958. Despite very
different outlooks, the two men shared an understanding of the symbiotic
relationship between France and Germany: Bonn could help Paris in its
European and world power ambitions, while Paris could support Germany
over the status of Berlin and reunification with the Soviets.[58] For de Gaulle
a Europe dominated by France would give it a voice likely to be listened to
by the two superpowers. This vision of France restored to its rank among the
great powers necessarily demanded even closer relations with its hereditary
enemy. An alliance was the next logical step.

A series of state visits by Adenauer and de Gaulle in 1962 presaged the
signing of a Franco-German alliance. De Gaulle's state visit to Germany in
September was particularly revealing for the way he set out to enthuse the
crowds with speeches in German, having learnt the language of the enemy
as an officer cadet at the Saint Cyr military academy. As de Gaulle told the
crowds: 'For Charles de Gaulle to be here and for you to extend this cordial
and moving welcome to him, confidence must really exist between our two
peoples.' De Gaulle's visit symbolized the rallying of the French nationalist
tradition to Franco-German friendship. He praised the idea of a Franco-
German union, rehabilitated Germany and described it as a great country
that must again have an international role. He even acknowledged German
military virtues, but underlined that henceforth it was the duty of France and

Germany to be brothers. The visit was a spectacular success, with the anti-French *Der Spiegel* remarking: 'De Gaulle came to Germany as President of the French and leaves Emperor of Europe.'[59]

But there were weaknesses in this idyll. France and Germany could be unfriendly allies. The Germans remained suspicious of de Gaulle's 1958 call for a three-power directorate for NATO composed of France, the USA and Britain in which Germany obviously had no place. They had reservations about the General's support of a 'Europe of nations' rather than their more integrated concept. They were annoyed about his refusal to allow Britain into the Common Market fearing that this was a ploy to maintain French domination of the Community. A more fundamental problem was that Germany, divided, non-nuclear and on the border of a huge Soviet empire occupied by the Red Army, was unembarrassed about military dependency and remained committed to the Atlantic Alliance and good relations with Washington. Overall it was wary of the not unfounded belief that France's friendship was monopolistic and intended to keep Germany under its thumb.

But Berlin's feelings were not sufficiently strong to deter it from signing the Franco-German Treaty of 22 January 1963. This was considered by many to be a veritable alliance, whereby the 'two governments will consult before any decision on all foreign policy questions . . . with the aim of coming, as much as possible, to a similar decision'. Cooperation was to be fostered by a series of regular meetings ranging from heads of state to representatives from defence, education and youth. 'Following up the work begun before 1939 by Otto Abetz, the treaty really encouraged contact between the youth of the two countries, but the two countries never had a common policy.'[60] But the Bundestag quickly emptied the agreement of much of its value. It agreed to ratify the Treaty only if a preamble was added to set out Bonn's unwavering commitment to concepts about which France remained sceptical: close cooperation between Europe and the USA; integrated defence in NATO; European Union to include Britain. De Gaulle was bitterly disappointed by this preamble, which his biographer, Jean Lacouture, likened to having Karl Marx's *Das Kapital* prefaced by Ronald Reagan.[61] It was said that de Gaulle had hoped for more from his 'loyal' West German partner. However, according to the KGB agent of influence, François Saar-Demichel, de Gaulle had said privately, 'We extended our hand to the Germans so that we could at least be sure they were not holding a knife in theirs.'[62] But henceforth Germany reinforced co-operation with the USA. De Gaulle abandoned the idea of using Germany in his cold war strategy. He returned to a rapprochement with the Soviet Union, a Europe from the Atlantic to the Urals, coolness towards the USA, development of France's nuclear deterrent and French progressive withdrawal from NATO's integrated command. The spirit of the Treaty was dead. Without disintegrating, Franco–German relations soured, worsened by the replacement of the 87- year-old Adenauer by the Atlanticist Ludwig Erhard as Chancellor in October 1963.[63]

In 1964 France failed to consult Bonn over the spectacular recognition of the People's Republic of China. When Germany expressed a desire to see negotiations on a NATO multilateral force completed, France denounced it as a threat to European security and referred to the re-emergence of the German threat. At the same time de Gaulle warned against a renaissance of German expansionism and blamed Berlin for the failure of the Franco-German Treaty. The introduction of the Common Agricultural Policy (CAP) was a further source of disagreement. With half of the European Community's farmland and an exporter of agricultural produce, France was enthusiastic, whilst Germany, a net importer of meat and sugar, preferred to buy from the world market at cheaper prices. From the end of 1964 until the summer of 1965 discussions on the CAP were heated. Finally, on 30 June 1965 de Gaulle withdrew France from the meetings of the ECSC and the EEC and applied the policy of the 'empty chair', effectively blocking the Community's business. This Franco-German conflict would only be resolved by an agreement amongst all six members in May 1966. The Franco-German treaty was functioning only at a cultural level, even though economic and technological cooperation continued to develop.[64]

Franco-German differences were greatest on issues of defence, notably over French withdrawal from NATO's military command in 1966 and Germany's clear commitment to the Atlantic Alliance. West Germany was worried in particular by the development of France's independent nuclear weapon, mocked as the 'bombinette', but which worryingly had more credible short-range capability than a long-range one. By the fifth anniversary of the Franco-German Treaty German economic and monetary superiority was a serious source of anxiety in France, exacerbated by the destabilizing crisis of May 68 and German support for the franc. Despite the two countries going through the motions of periodic meetings, an embittered General de Gaulle refused to keep Germany informed of French diplomatic initiatives, such as contacts with Moscow or overtures to Britain in 1969.

With the de Gaulle's departure at the end of 1969 it was hoped that Franco-German relations could be put on a more equal footing. President Pompidou did not have de Gaulle's stature, or temperament; conversely the new Chancellor Willy Brandt seemed just the man to give Germany the authority to speak as an equal partner to France. The new problem for France was that the hitherto German economic giant and political dwarf had grown in political confidence. It now wished to negotiate directly with the German Democratic Republic and the Soviets to obtain reunification, thereby eliminating France as the self-appointed intermediary and interlocutor of the communist world. In 1970 Brandt's *Ostpolitik* re-established relations with the USSR and Poland; two years later negotiations were underway with East Germany and in 1973 an agreement was signed with Czechoslovakia. Germany recognized the borders imposed by the Allies in 1945 and began to re-establish itself on the international stage, joining the United Nations. France's fear, expressed by Pompidou in a press conference on 27 September 1973, was that *Ostpolitik* could lead to Germany turning eastwards away from Europe and securing reunification at the price of neutrality – or worse still a new Rapallo. Another worrying scenario for Paris was the prospect of German reunification and the subsequent departure of the Americans. As one unnamed source told *L'Express* in August 1973: 'At the Elysée, every conversation about foreign policy, no matter how it starts, always ends up conjuring up the German problem.'[65] In Pompidou's own words: 'The Germans must act tactfully, for one does not have to scratch too far for the French once more to uncover an old aversion.'[66] French anxiety was heightened by Germany's obvious military power. In 1971 the German army with 456,000 soldiers was the largest in European NATO and was continuing to grow in size and quality. The following year German defence estimates were 28.6 billion marks, while France's trailed at 22.9 billion marks.[67] Pompidou was said to have privately told an opponent of France's nuclear weapon: 'Don't criticize it too quickly. Perhaps one day, or perhaps in 20 years, it will give us a determining trump card to play against Germany who has none.'[68]

During similar moments in its history, France pressed for a rapprochement with Britain, allowing it into the Common Market in 1973. This process had begun in 1971. Meetings between Prime Minister Edward Heath and Pompidou evoked memories of a new entente cordiale, which worried Bonn. As early as June 1969 Pompidou privately told the influential editor of *Le Monde*, André Fontaine, that in order to counterbalance Germany 'there was no other solution than to lean on the United States, the USSR and Great Britain, whilst of course maintaining the best of relations with Bonn. You must understand that I cannot say that publicly.'[69] Franco-British relations continued to improve through the world oil crisis that resulted from the quadrupling of the oil price after the 1973 Arab–Israeli War. Franco-German relations, by contrast, were tense. The ostensible source of difference was the CAP, whose operation was perturbed by revaluation of the Deutschmark on 29 June 1973. But the subtext of the disagreement was *Ostpolitik*. Premier Jacques Chirac's Agricultural Minister told the weekly *Le Point* in August that he was 'preoccupied by Germany on account of the distance it is taking from Europe'.[70] Nevertheless, French and German leaders continued diplomatically to underline the importance of Franco-German entente. But at the beginning of 1974 the French preferred to devalue the franc by withdrawing from the European monetary 'snake' rather than accept several billion marks credit from West Germany to maintain its parity. Paris feared dependence on the German economic giant. But the differences over NATO remained a serious main stumbling block. In 1973 Gaullist Foreign Minister Michel Jobert attempted to seduce Germany into relaunching the Western European Union as the military arm of Europe rather than NATO, but the Germans roundly rejected it.

Germany displayed much discomfiture when France announced that it was to deploy *Pluto* tank-mounted nuclear missiles with a range of 120 to 150 kilometres along France's eastern border at the end of 1972. It was obvious to all, not least the Germans, that these missiles could only strike West German territory. Bonn asked for a say in their positioning and use, and was turned down. France merely promised its European partners protection with its nuclear arsenal. It might be claimed for Pompidou, as for de Gaulle and his predecessors, that the defence of France began on the Elbe, not the Rhine, but France still controlled the ultimate deterrent. France was not willing to follow Germany down the route of multilateral force reductions in Central Europe. It wished to maintain complete independence in defence matters. At the death of Pompidou in April 1974 Franco-German relations were in a parlous state.[71]

Friends again

With the Gaullist Pompidou's replacement in 1974 at the Elysée by the centrist and pragmatic Valéry Giscard d'Estaing and a new German Chancellor, Helmut Schmidt, Franco-German relations improved, resulting in the establishment of the European Monetary System. On defence, the Atlanticist and pro-European Giscard was more willing to abandon some of the Gaullist dogma of his predecessors and draw more closely to NATO and thus to Germany in order to reinforce European defence. Schmidt was far more of an Atlanticist than an *Ostpolitiker*, but no less in favour of an integrated Europe. Aware of the anxiety that a too prosperous and powerful Germany evoked in France and Europe, he believed that it was time for Europe to assert itself diplomatically, particularly after the poor American performance during the President Carter years. As usual European co-operation was predicated on a Paris–Bonn axis. But after the first oil crisis differences surfaced over Bonn's desire for hardline European measures to curb inflation and France's desire to relaunch monetary union by an inflationary large loan from the oil-producing countries in September 1974. That month Schmidt vetoed further increases in Community agricultural prices. This provoked violent reactions in the French press, which alluded to the German danger and to Helmut Schmidt as the new Bismarck. National interests were clearly visible: France had been a net beneficiary of the Common Agricultural Policy's price support mechanism from 1963 to 1973 to the tune of 5 billion deutschmarks, which was the size of West Germany's net contribution to it.[72]

Differences continued over defence and security. In 1975 Giscard d'Estaing brought in army reforms designed to increase the flexibility of French armed forces and give them a potential for action beyond national territory, ostensibly in the interests of European defence. In November that year Giscard also expressed anxiety at seeing France overtaken by Germany in conventional armaments. In June 1976 the Chief of the French Defence Staff, General Guy Méry, set out for the French five-year military programme law the military doctrine of the 'enlarged sanctuary' (*sanctuarisation élargie*), which seemed to imply that French nuclear cover would be extended to West Germany. Méry never in fact said that Germany was covered by the *force de frappe*; rather he reiterated the old Gaullist doctrine that French defence began on the Elbe not on the Rhine. This implied using French conventional and even tactical nuclear weapons on German territory to stop an approaching enemy – something of a double-edged sword for Germany. Franco-German defence cooperation had its problems. These worsened as Giscard's presidency came under increasing attack by the powerful Gaullists and anti-American socialists in the French parliament for being too Atlanticist. Consequently, Giscard refused to support Schmidt on the critical issue of the deployment of NATO's intermediate-range nuclear forces (INF) in December 1979, which were intended as a riposte to the deployment of the Soviet SS20s. The French also feared that the Soviets would use this as a pretext for including French warheads in arms control negotiations. As cold war tension increased from the end of the 1970s with the Soviet invasion of Afghanistan and the military crackdown in Poland in 1981, the USA, not France, looked like West Germany's most credible ally. France was reluctant to criticize the USSR for fear of upsetting détente with it, leading some to claim that this was the 'Finlandization' of France. By 1981 Giscard had been replaced at the Elysée by the socialist François Mitterrand and Schmidt in 1982 by the conservative Helmut Kohl.[73]

The accession of the first socialist President of the Fifth Republic on 10 May 1981 followed in June by a socialist majority in the National Assembly and a socialist government with four communist ministers might have been expected to mark a clear shift away from Atlanticist policies and by extension defence links with West Germany. However, the French Socialist Party's position on defence had changed since its 1972 position of opposition to French nuclear weapons and arms exports. It may have been in order to dispel fears among France's allies about the reliability of a socialist government with communist ministers, that once in power Mitterrand showed himself to be a strong supporter of the Atlantic Alliance, the *force de frappe* and a tough critic of the Soviet Union. These positions dovetailed perfectly with Kohl's views.

In 1983 the Franco-German 1963 Treaty on cooperation was spectacularly relaunched with a new Franco-German commission on security and defence. This was intended to bring together the two countries officials regularly on issues of arms, military collaboration and policy. On 20 January 1983 Mitterrand made a speech to the German Bundestag celebrating the twentieth anniversary of the Elysée Treaty in which he called on the Germans to support deployment of the Pershing 'Euromissiles' and denounced those who wished to 'decouple' Europe from the USA. With the French more committed to the notion of European cooperation and less intent on undermining NATO, the Germans agreed to measures to re-invigorate the Western European Union in 1984. At the same time the French established the Force d'action rapide (FAR), a rapid reaction force of some 47,000 designed to intervene directly in Central Europe. However, although the French claimed that the FAR was a commitment to the defence of Germany, simultaneous statements on the absolute autonomy of French defence rendered its role ambiguous.[74]

Paris and Bonn were, however, drawn closer together in the mid-1980s around fears about American President Ronald Reagan's Strategic Defence Initiative, or 'Star Wars', and anxiety about the potential of the USA's large budget deficits to weaken the US commitment to European defence. It was calculated that Europe ought to begin planning its own defence. This resulted in a flurry of meetings and agreements to encourage European, and especially, Franco-German defence. Paris even agreed to consult with Bonn on the eventual use of tactical nuclear weapons in Germany. In February 1987 large joint military manœuvres took place with French troops operating for the first time under German command and Germany reluctantly agreeing to the exercises taking place outside NATO structures. By 1986 Franco-German security relations were probably better than they had ever been. However, problems remained. The French feared pacifism in the German SPD and Green Party, they held different views from Berlin on the autonomy of French defence and believed that Germany was still too interested in *Ostpolitik* and the USA, rather than France. The Germans, for their part, believed that France was still too wedded to national independence and grandeur.[75]

Where the Franco-German tandem did find momentum was on European integration. Paris and Bonn were committed to the largest increase in Community supranationality since the 1950s. In France, the motivation came partly from the desire to tie down a Germany that in the early 1980s was continuing to outstrip France economically and financially. While the deutschmark had been revalued, the franc had been forced into almost annual devaluations from 1981 to 1983 as a consequence of inflationary socialist reforms. Mitterrand's socialist reforms had also run into the sands and he was casting around for a new initiative. Meanwhile, Chancellor Kohl, like his predecessors, was committed, in Thomas Mann's words, to 'a European Germany rather than a German Europe', which would dispel the ghosts of militarism and nationalism and ensure that Germany remain on the road to liberalism, wealth and peace. Furthermore, both leaders increasingly believed that further European integration could deliver peace and security while enabling the 'old continent' to compete economically and technologically with Japan and the USA.

In order to keep the British Conservative Prime Minister Margaret Thatcher, a champion of a 'single market', on board, it was decided at an EC summit in Brussels in March 1985 that a single market should be brought into operation by I January 1993. But this was to be in exchange for institutional reform to increase supranationality through the December 1985 Single European Act. French socialists and German Christian Democrats, together with the new French socialist President of the European Commission, Jacques Delors, were determined to protect individuals from the excesses of the single market. They pressed for a Social Charter to guarantee and harmonize citizens' rights across what was soon to become the European Union. Paris and Berlin also believed that the next logical step in European integration was European Monetary Union, given the rigours of the Exchange Rate Mechanism (ERM) in bringing down inflation in most member states since its creation in 1979. The Delors Report of April 1989 suggested a move towards currency union, which entailed the creation of a European central bank. But it was the dramatic events of the 'velvet revolutions' in Eastern Europe at the end of the 1980s, followed by demands in East Germany for reunification, that forced the French to push for further European integration. This was seen as the only means of limiting the independence of what would otherwise be a mighty Germany of similar proportions to its predecessors of 1914 and 1939.

Despite the ups and downs of the Franco-German relationship since the 1960s, the French are clearly aware of its politico-strategic value, despite differences on aspects of defence and diplomacy. From once having been anathema, Franco-German collaboration now seemed natural. While France sought to trumpet and display its power and prestige proudly and prominently, Germany wished to play its down or cover them up. Whereas France sought an international role, Germany was happy with a domestic and parochial one. What France sought in the area of security, such as independence, Germany eschewed. Whereas post-war France 'associated military force with victory, independence, power and glory, West Germany associated it with defeat, dependence, ignominy, and disaster'.[76] Perhaps it was precisely because of their divergent interests and the fact that they were rarely in competition in the defence and diplomatic fields that the Franco-German entente could be maintained. What has characterized Franco-German relations since 1955, or perhaps 1963, is wish-fulfilment. Both nations understand how important it is that the relationship should work. That overweening mutual desire for success explains the extra-ordinary lengths to which the authorities will go to make it work right down to the cultural dirigisme to draw the countries together at the level of ordinary citizens, and in particular youth. On the French side there is still a subcutaneous apprehension about 'the German problem', accompanied by embarrassment about discussing it. Opinion polls continue to suggest that the French feel a degree of solidarity and admiration for their eastern neighbour, suggesting a will to see the partnership work. Work it does at the level of trade where since 1960 France has been Germany's biggest export market, even if Germany became France's biggest export market only in 1968. The partnership is also reasonably successful at the level of investment, notably via subsidiaries. However, even here the French became worried in the early 1970s by the concentration of German investment in the east of France, which, though it had created over 26,000 jobs in Alsace-Lorraine by January 1973, caused Paris to let it be understood that greater dispersion would be more welcome.[77] Cooperation at company level is fairly well established, particularly by banks, in similar fashion to the late nineteenth century, but also in chemicals and pharmaceuticals. Joint manufacturing ventures are another area of increased cooperation since the 1960s. This is particularly true of military aircraft, with joint projects for the construction of planes such as *Transall* and *Alpha Jet*, or joint ventures in the nuclear and space industries. Here the French have benefited greatly from German expertise and funding to produce, for instance, spy satellites of great sophistication, such as *Hélios*, to break a flagrant dependence on the USA at the time of the 1991 Gulf War. The undoubted success of Franco-German economic relations should not hide the fact, however, that they still remain fairly limited for all that is trumpeted about the Franco-German alliance; Franco-British economic relations are not far behind, though much less talked about.

When all is said and done, what lies at the heart of France's relation-ship with Germany is war and insecurity. In attempting to discover how best to deal with that problem over the twentieth century France's relations with Germany went through a series of cycles from hostility to rapprochement. The fundamental ambiguity at the heart of France's rela-tions with its eastern neighbour would be demonstrated clearly again with German reunification.

Notes

1 Harold Nicolson, *Diplomacy* (London, Thornton Butterworth, 1939), p. 150.
2 Quoted in Dorothy Pickles, *The Government and Politics of France*, vol. II, *Politics* (London, Methuen, 1973), p. 228.

3 F. Roy Willis, *France, Germany and the New Europe 1945–1963* (Stanford, Calif.: Stanford University Press, 1965), p. vii.

4 Taylor, *Struggle for Mastery*, pp. xxiv–xxxiii.

5 Taylor, *Struggle for Mastery*, pp. xxiv–xxxiii.

6 Quoted in E. M. Carroll, *French Public Opinion and Foreign Affairs, 1870–1914* (London, Frank Cass, 1931), p. 87.

7 Quoted in G. P. Gooch, *Franco-German Relations, 1871–1914: The Creighton Lecture, 1923* (New York, Longman, 1923), p. 22.

8 Quoted in Gooch, *Franco-German Relations*, p. 21.

9 Poidevin and Bariéty, *Relations franco-allemandes*, pp. 151–2.

10 Quoted in Pierre Renouvin, *Histoire des relations internationales*, vol. VI, *1871–1914* (Paris, Amand Colin, 1955), p. 221.

11 Poidevin and Boriéty, *Relations franco-allemoneles*, pp. 167–8.

12 Christopher Andrew, *Théophile Delcassé and the Making of the Entente Cordiale* (London, Macmillan, 1968), pp. 119–35.

13 Poidevin and Bariéty, *Relations franco-allemandes*, pp. 177–80.

14 Quoted in Keiger, *France and the Origins*, p. 131.

15 Quoted in Keiger, *France and the Origins*, p. 135.

16 Keiger, 'Jules Cambon', pp.641–59; Keiger, *France and the Origins*, pp. 68–81, 129–35; Poidevin and Bariéty, *Relations franco-allemandes*, pp. 191–211.

17 Keiger, *Poincaré*, pp. 193–8.

18 Poidevin and Bariéty, *Relations franco-allemandes*, pp. 230–1.

19 Keiger, *Poincaré*, pp. 265–311.

20 Quoted in Marc Trachtenberg, *Reparation in World Politics: France and European Economic Diplomacy, 1916–1923* (New York, Columbia University Press, 1980), p. 335.

21 Poidevin and Bariéty, *Relations franco-allemandes*, pp. 266–9.

22 Quoted in W. R. Keylor, *The Twentieth Century World: An International History* (New York, Oxford University Press, 1984), p. 124.

23 Poidevin and Bariéty, *Relations franco-allemandes*, pp. 271–5.

24 Quoted in J Néré, *The Foreign Policy of France 1914 to 1945* (London, Routledge, 1975), pp. 284–6.

25 Quoted in Poidevin and Bariéty, *Relations franco-allemandes*, p. 275.

26 Poidevin and Bariéty, *Relations franco-allemandes*, pp. 281–5.

27 Poidevin and Bariéty, *Relations franco-allemandes*, pp. 285–6.

28 Poidevin and Bariéty, *Relations franco-allemandes*, pp. 287–93.

29 Quoted in Poidevin and Bariéty, *Relations franco-allemandes*, p. 295.

30 Quoted in Poidevin and Bariéty, *Relations franco-allemandes*, p. 297.

31 Poidevin and Bariéty, *Relations franco-allemandes*, pp. 301–3.

32 Quoted in Tacel, *France et le monde*, p. 153.

33 Tacel, *France et le monde*, p. 153.

34 Tacel, *France et le monde*, pp. 152–5.

35 Robert Frank, 'Vichy et le monde; le monde et Vichy: Perceptions géopolitiques et idéologiques', in Jean-Pierre Azéma and François Bédarida (eds), *Le Régime de Vichy et les français* (Paris, Fayard, 1992), pp. 100–1.

36 Frank, 'Vichy et le monde', p. 104.

37 Frank, 'Vichy et le monde', pp. 105–6.
38 Willis, *France, Germany*, pp. 2–3.
39 Quoted in Willis, *France, Germany*, p. 4.
40 Darlan to ministerial heads, n.d. (probably beginning 1941), quoted in Frank, 'Vichy et le monde', pp. 106–11.
41 Quoted in Frank, 'Vichy et le monde', p. 110.
42 Frank, 'Vichy et le monde', pp. 106–11.
43 Frank, 'Vichy et le monde', pp. 111–13.
44 Poidevin and Bariéty, *Relations franco-allemandes*, pp. 316–18.
45 Poidevin and Bariéty, *Relations franco-allemandes*, pp. 325–8.
46 Willis, *France, Germany*, pp. 17, 32.
47 Quoted in Willis, *France, Germany*, p. 68.
48 Pickles, *Government and Politics*, II, p. 231.
49 Quoted in Poidevin and Bariéty, *Relations franco-allemandes*, p. 329.
50 Doise and Vaïsse, *Diplomatie et outil militaire*, p. 531.
51 Quoted in Carmoy, *Les Politiques étrangères*, p. 48.
52 Poidevin and Bariéty, *Relations franco-allemandes*, pp. 328–30. The French Ambassador to the United States declared: `As far as we are concerned, we had no intention to promote, propose or accept the rearmament of Germany' (*Le Monde*, 8 Aug. 1950, quoted in Mendl, *Deterrence and Persuasion*, p. 23).
53 Alfred Grosser, *La IVe République et sa politique extérieure*, Armand Colin, Paris, 1961, p. 326.
54 Quoted in Mendl, *Deterrence and Persuasion,* p. 28.
55 Grosser, *IVe République*, pp. 231–8.
56 Poidevin and Bariéty, *Relations franco-allemandes*, pp. 331–2.
57 Philip Gordon, *France, Germany and the Western Alliance* (Boulder , Colo., 1995), p. 13.
58 Alfred Grosser, *La Politique extérieure de la Ve République* (Paris, Seuil, 1965), pp. 84–6.
59 All quoted in Grosser, *La Ve*, pp. 88–9.
60 Tacel, *France et le monde*, p. 238.
61 Jean Lacouture, *De Gaulle*, vol. III, *Le Souverain* (Paris, Seuil, 1986), pp. 308–9, quoted in Gordon, *France, Germany*, p. 14 n 17.
62 Quoted in Andrew and Mitrokhin, *Mitrokhin Archive*, p. 605.
63 Poidevin and Bariéty, *Relations franco-allemandes*, pp. 334–5.
64 Poidevin and Bariéty, *Relations franco-allemandes*, pp. 336–7.
65 Quoted in Haig Simonian, *The Privileged Partnership: Franco-German Relations in the Euopean Community, 1969–1984* (Oxford, Oxford University Press, 1985), pp. 180–1.
66 Quoted in Simonian, *Privileged Partnership*, p. 181.
67 Poidevin and Bariéty, *Relations franco-allemandes*, p. 338.
68 Quoted in Georges Valance, *France-Allemagne: Le Retour de Bismarck* (Paris, Flammarion, 1990), p. 187.
69 Quoted in André Fontaine, *Un seul lit pour deux rêves: Histoire de la `détente' 1962–1981* (Paris, Fayard, 1981), p. 158.
70 Quoted in Simonian, *Privileged Partnership*, p. 179.

71 Poidevin and Bariéty, *Relations franco-allemandes*, p. 339.
72 Poidevin and Bariéty, *Relations franco-allemandes*, p. 340.
73 Gordon, *France, Germany*, pp. 16–17.
74 Gordon, *France, Germany*, pp. 17-20.
75 Gordon, *France, Germany*, pp. 20–2.
76 Gordon, *France, Germany*, p. 11 and *passim*.
77 Poidevin and Bariéty, *Relations franco-allemandes*, p. 346.

6

The Anglo-Saxons

If ever there was a mythical beast that stalked the minds of the French in the twentieth century it was the 'Anglo-Saxons'. They continue to be the most 'imagined' of 'communities'. Even the French are unclear about which nations are included in that elusive term. Britain and the USA are always designated, sometimes the whole English-speaking world, occasionally Scandinavia and the Netherlands, perhaps even Germany. But the flexibility of the term is largely immaterial. Like individuals, nations define themselves as much by what they are not as by what they think they are. The historian of Franco-British relations P. M. H. Bell quotes the great patriotic French historian, Jules Michelet, who in the mid-nineteenth century was all too conscious of how animosity towards Britain was important in French nation-building.

> The struggle against England has done France a very great service by confirming and clarifying her sense of nationhood. Through coming together against the enemy the provinces discovered that they were a single person. It is by seeing the English close to, that they felt that they were France. It is the same with nations as with the individual; he gets to know and defines his personality through resistance to what is different from himself. He becomes conscious of what he is through what he is not.[1]

The patriotic French leader Raymond Poincaré, in a small book intended to cultivate patriotism and civic duty in school children, quoted the German (though it could just as well have been an 'Anglo-Saxon') philosopher Schopenhauer: 'Other parts of the world have monkeys, Europe has the French'; in order to be able to retort in existentialist mode 'We are insulted therefore we exist!'[2]

If from 1870 France's attitude to Germany was characterized by ambiguity that largely reflected military vulnerability, its attitude to Britain and then the USA was still more ambiguous and more complex. The term 'Anglo-Saxon' came to be used increasingly to denote the Anglo-Americans from the

1890s, notably after the American victory over the Spanish in 1898. By the end of the First World War the French had begun to believe in an 'Anglo-Saxon' conspiracy against them in everything from politics, diplomacy, economics and finance to culture, not least of which was the growing power of the English language. And yet the French, according to particular circumstances, would continue to refer to the Americans as their cousins or the British as their cordial friends. The explanation lay of course in international opportunism or French vulnerability, but also in what national features French leaders wished to promote or underline in themselves at a given moment. Thus the Americans were a republican sister-nation born of a revolution that had enlisted the support of Lafayette and that championed democracy and liberty, as witnessed by France's gift of the Statue of Liberty to New York in 1876. Britain was at times a long-established democracy, a bastion of European industry, civilization and culture, a warrior nation and close ally ready to fight for the greater good of humanity. What could be better than if all three worked together as beacons for other nations, as Condorcet mused in the late eighteenth century: 'Should not all nations one day aspire to that level of civilization which has been reached by the most enlightened, free, liberated and unprejudiced peoples, the French and the Anglo-Americans?'[3] However, both the USA and Britain could also be alien Protestant, Anglo-Saxon cultures in which mercantile self-interest and greed invalidated higher aspirations, and of which the English language was the insidious vehicle. The French revealed much about themselves and their self-perception in the way they related to the Anglo-Saxons. In the twentieth century the Anglo-Saxons enabled the French nation to continue to define itself and added further cement to its nation building.

The British

Ambivalence towards the Anglo-Saxons had as its starting point rivalry with Britain. That rivalry can be traced back as far as the Hundred Years War. By the late seventeenth century French pre-eminence in Europe was supreme in wealth, armed strength, culture and reputation. But from that time Britain's star was in the ascendant. In the eighteenth century its power increased dramatically as its population and wealth grew, until by the nineteenth it had overtaken France and become the first industrial nation with the largest empire. The historian François Bédarida tells us that it is noticeable that

> the climax of rivalry between the two peoples took place at the time when both were making their maximum contributions to European and world civilization, and some of these in common. The triple revolutions of the eighteenth century – intellectual, industrial and French – are the work of both countries.[4]

The important moment in the reversal of the two nations' positions was when dramatically rising British self-confidence passed shrinking French self-confidence on the way down. The triumphalism and self-satisfaction that characterized Queen Victoria's long and stable reign contrasted starkly with France's stagnant population, political and social divisions and generally increasing self-doubt. French wealth per capita may not have been far behind Britain's in the course of the nineteenth century, but dynamism and vitality were absent from it. As P. M. H. Bell remarks, 'The most terrible verdict on France was battle' with its defeat at the hands of Prussia in 1870. Of course there were many flaws in Britain's performance at the end of the century, but none substantially offset France's self-conscious relative decline. More galling to France perhaps in the twentieth century was the sense that, even when things started to go badly for the British, their egotism or the white knight of the USA allowed them to save the day, seemingly at France's expense. Conspiracy theorists aside, a mixture of envy and disappointment appeared to characterize France's attitude to Britain: envy at Britain's 'privileged' relationship with America and disappointment that Britain should, except in war, forsake its French neighbour.

The Anglophile political observer of Britain André Siegfried pointed out in his 1931 best-seller *La Crise britannique au XXe siècle* that Britain's relative economic decline, its dependency on world markets and its continued feeling of superiority over the 'continent' ensured that it was 'condemned to having a world policy'. But it was beginning to understand the difficulty in maintaining that position. Siegfried asked: 'So is she to turn towards the oceans, to try to share in the youth of the new Anglo-Saxon societies, or is she to return in the end to the old world, from which her culture sprang?' Siegfried believed Britain was most attracted by the 'Anglo-Saxon' option, even if it meant a junior partnership for itself, because the Americans when all said and done were not really foreigners but family. Nevertheless, he still believed that Britain could not break away completely from Europe. It would continue to avoid making the choice and juggle the two. France, he counselled with some disappointment, needed a strong and reliable Britain, but would have to make do with a semi-detached commitment.[5] This astute and well-publicized interpretation influenced many twentieth-century French decision-makers, not least General de Gaulle.

France and Britain have always been divided by a great deal of common history, much of it conflictual. From Crecy to Waterloo the chronic and prolonged bouts of warfare between the French and English are unparalleled in the history of any other two countries. They have been prisoners of that history. The school textbooks of the Republic from the nineteenth century were punctuated with examples of Franco-British rivalry making Britain, not Germany, the hereditary enemy. From Joan of Arc to Fashoda via Napoleon, French schoolchildren were weaned on the doings of 'Perfidious

Albion', a term attributed to the great seventeenth-century bishop Bossuet lamenting on Britain's lapsing into Protestantism. A widely used French school textbook devoted to Joan of Arc published in 1895 put France's enemies on an equal footing in reminding children pointedly: 'If there haven't been any English in France for a long time, there are Germans in Alsace-Lorraine.'[6] Yet behind that outward hostility there was a fund of shared ideals and culture that placed the two nations in their own estimation at the forefront of Western civilization providing for bouts of mutual admiration.

Fashoda

The 1898 Fashoda incident, which took the mythology of Franco-British rivalry a step further, followed a period of French celebration of the two nations' shared defence of Western civilization. In July 1898, as General Kitchener's army routed the dervishes at Omdurman in the Sudan, French newspapers praised this victory for 'Western civilization'. There was little mention of latent rivalry, soon to become apparent as the small expeditionary force of Captain Marchand and his 150 men sized up to Kitchener's large and victorious army at Fashoda. The French aimed to force the British out of Egypt and eventually to open up a vast African empire stretching from Algeria in the north to the Congo in the south, and from Senegal in the west to the Nile in the east. However Marchand's four-year-long trek from west to east to make a military demonstration suffered, if nothing else, from poor timing. Marchand was encroaching on territory regarded by Britain as in its sphere of influence ever since it had taken control of Egypt in 1882. Britain demanded Marchand's withdrawal. Despite popular outcry, at least in nationalist circles, the French government eventually backed down, calculating that France was in no position to engage in a war with the greatest naval power in the world. This was a severe blow to French prestige. But the French were soon diverted from Albion's perfidy by the domestic trauma of the Dreyfus Affair. Nevertheless, the Fashoda incident un-remembered in British historical consciousness subsequently loomed large in France's. The French took their revenge by openly sympathizing with the Boers during the Boer War of 1899–1902. French volunteers left to fight alongside the Boers, while elegant ladies sported felt hats 'à la Boer' and the elite French military academy at Saint Cyr dubbed its 1900 cohort of graduates the 'Transval year'.[7] The Fashoda incident had injected new venom into Franco-British relations with the President of the Republic, Félix Faure, telling a Russian diplomat soon after the incident that Britain had replaced Germany as France's real enemy. Certainly some of the anti-British propaganda of the Boer War was so virulent that the Germans reprinted it when they occupied France in 1940, which partly explains why Fashoda endures to this day. Even so mutual interest overcame temporary tension with the 1904 Entente Cordiale.

France's long-running foreign policy dilemma of a continental versus an imperial strategy had a strong effect on relations with Britain. By the turn of the century Germany's rise was increasingly seen as a threat in London and Paris. The German 1900 Navy Law confirmed Berlin's intention to build a fleet capable of challenging Britain's naval supremacy and threatening France's colonies. For Britain isolation was becoming more dangerous than splendid. In France the prospect of simultaneous tension with Germany and Britain was to have one enemy too many. In France some supported Franco-German reconciliation, but Alsace-Lorraine made that difficult. Conversely, Britain and France had not been at war with each other since 1815. Financial interests in the City of London were sympathetic to better relations with France. There was also a strong body of the Parisian elite sympathetic to Britain culturally. From the fictional English gentleman Phineas Fogg in Jules Verne's *Around the World in Eighty Days* to the more serious writings of Anglophiles, often Oxford educated, such as Jacques Bardoux, André Siegfried or Elie Halévy, Britain's stock was in favour. Mutual interest was behind the package of agreements that made up the Entente Cordiale.

Entente Cordiale

The Franco-British agreements of 8 April 1904 were more about the past than the future. Far from being an alliance, they merely settled a number of outstanding colonial differences over Newfoundland, West and Central Africa, Egypt, Morocco, Madagascar and the New Hebrides, as well as establishing respective spheres of influence in Siam and West Africa. A key idea was the barter of Egypt for Morocco. However, the agreement contained no statement of general policy and was in no way comparable to the Franco-Russian Alliance. Yet in retrospect it was a starting point for an ever-closer union between the two countries that would eventually lead to alliance at the outbreak of the First World War. The Entente Cordiale also became a reference point for improved Franco-British relations over the rest of the twentieth century.

It was France's Foreign Minister in 1904, Théophile Delcassé, who had ordered Marchand's withdrawal from Fashoda, and who gradually promoted the rapprochement with Britain. His original aim had been to bolster the 1894 Franco-Russian Alliance, even to tempt Italy out of the Triple Alliance to improve French international security. A strategy of improved relations with Britain evolved slowly. Despite, or perhaps because, of Fashoda, a number of steps were taken that helped improve relations between the two countries. From February 1899 the colonial lobby group, the Comité de l'Afrique française, which had had a hand in securing Delcassé's nomination as Foreign Minister, made persistent efforts to convince their man of the need for a colonial agreement with Britain based on a barter of English influence in Egypt for French influence in Morocco. A sign that Franco-British differences were only skin deep came only four months after the Fashoda incident, when the two countries signed an agreement in London 'in a spirit of mutual good entente' specifying respective possessions and spheres of influence in the Nile valley and West Africa. Anglophobia did resurface and peak from 1899 to 1900 during the Boer War. Nevertheless, Fashoda appears more of an aberration in relations between the two countries at this time.[8]

A measure of how superficial and sectarian the Fashoda uproar seemed to French opinion was that barely five years later King Edward VII was invited to visit France. An officially inspired media in the intervening years had softened up public opinion. The visit on 1–4 May 1903 was a clear success, with the King intoning: 'Providence has made us neighbours, let us make sure that we are friends.' President Loubet's return visit to Britain two months later was equally cordial, despite the minor diplomatic embarrassment of the representative of the Republic declining to don knee breeches for his audience with the King. Negotiation followed diplomacy. When finally signed, the Conventions were welcomed on both sides of the Channel, despite murmurs about France surrendering to Britain in Egypt. More important was how each side perceived the agreements. Delcassé wrote to a senior French Foreign Office official that the agreement 'should lead us, and I desire that it shall lead us, to a political alliance with England . . . If we could lean both on Russia and on England, how strong we should be in relation to Germany.' In Britain expectations were a good deal more muted. Though happy to have reduced imperial tensions with a rival, Britain was still not prepared to countenance an alliance. Differing perceptions and expectations of the agreement explain in part French frustration and disappointment over the next decade in not being able to secure an alliance with Britain. Nevertheless, Paris was helped in its mission to tie Britain down by events, the most significant of which was Germany's seemingly aggressive behaviour at Tangiers in 1905 and at Agadir in 1911.[9]

The First and Second Moroccan crises underlined the potency of the German threat and increased Britain's commitment to France. On both occasions London made clear to Germany that France would be supported. Germany's clumsy diplomacy also weakened the hand of those in France who favoured a rapprochement with Berlin and strengthened the pro-Britain lobby. Instead of being weakened, as Germany had hoped, the Entente Cordiale was reinforced. Whereas Britain had resolutely resisted a political alliance, from 1905 it agreed to secret military staff conversations with France.

Although the talks were in no way to bind the two governments, Paris saw in them firm and concerted British military support for France that was a step closer to an alliance. The secret General Staff talks were underway from December 1905 and were intended to map out possible joint action in a conflict in which both countries might become involved. Intended only as a temporary measure to provide for a possible conflict during the Algeçiras conference, they became a key feature of the Entente. The conversations lapsed from 1906 to 1910, but then flourished when Brigadier-General Henry Wilson became Director of Military Operations in August 1910 and fostered closer relations with the new French High Command in 1911. Nevertheless, as late as August 1911 Wilson was obliged to admit to the Committee of Imperial Defence that he had no precise details of French war plans. Prompted by Agadir, the new Chief of the General Staff General Joffre gave a greater place to Britain's assistance than his predecessors. His new plan contained detailed provisions for the concentration of the British Expeditionary Force of 150,000 men in north-east France. Nevertheless, the British Foreign Secretary ceaselessly repeated to the French that the secret talks – so secret that until 1912 most of the British Cabinet were unaware of their existence and would probably never have approved them anyway – in no way bound either country to come to the other's assistance in the event of war. French diplomats and political leaders chose either to ignore those statements or to continue enticing Britain into more of a commitment against its will.

The consequence of seeing things as France wished to see them produced frustration, disappointment and bouts of irascibility towards Britain. The British ambassador to Paris, Sir Francis Bertie, explained this to the British Foreign Secretary, Sir Edward Grey as early as 1906.

> One must take the French as they are and not as one would wish them to be. They have an instinctive dread of Germany and an hereditary distrust of England, and with these characteristics they are easily led to believe that they may be deserted by England and fallen upon by Germany.[10]

The French were understandably upset at Lord Haldane's mission to Germany in 1912 to discuss an agreement to limit naval rivalry. They mounted a diplomatic counter-attack, which led to a Franco-British naval agreement in November 1912, whereby the French concentrated their main naval forces in the Mediterranean while Britain transferred part of its Mediterranean squadron to the North Sea to protect the French coastline. Though the British continued to insist that this in no way bound Britain to side with France in a conflict, agreeing only to consult in the event of a potential conflict, it certainly gave France a strong moral claim to British support should war break out. Enshrined in the so-called Grey–Cambon letters, this arrangement was a clear example of differing cultural values and attitudes that not for the last time would lead to misunderstandings between the two countries. Britain had insisted pragmatically that such an understanding could be merely verbal, as it did not commit either country to assist the other in the event of a conflict. The French accepted that, but insisted that it should be in writing. The rational French believed that what was written was more positive because it had the sanctity of text; as so often in French thinking, form was greater than substance. The British Prime Minister referred to the formula as 'a platitude', but there was no doubt that the French believed that they had secured a greater British commitment. The ultimate question as to what Britain's attitude would be in the event of war was, as Sir Edward Grey had repeatedly insisted to the French ambassador, dependent upon public opinion and parliament. In the British Cabinet's view, this was still the case when on 1 August 1914, barely two days before France was at war with Germany, Paul Cambon insisted that Britain had a moral obligation to defend France's northern coastline because France had transferred its fleet to the Mediterranean. Not even Cambon's recourse to emotional blackmail paid off when he asked 'whether the word "honour" should be struck out of the English vocabulary'. In the end it was not the entente with France that decided Britain's entry into war on 4 August 1914, but an almost forgotten treaty to uphold Belgian neutrality dating from 1839. Paul Cambon might well describe 2 August as 'the day through which I passed the darkest moments of my life'.[11] Only the day before he had spluttered to Sir Arthur Nicolson: 'They are going to ditch us. They are going to ditch us.'[12] Cambon and his political masters were guilty of overconfidence in a British commitment that stemmed more from wishful thinking than sound analysis of Britain's interests and way of doing things. Reliance on Britain had this time paid off, but only in the final hour. Rose-tinted memories of the two countries side by side in the ensuing war were, in the short term, to expunge the memory of how misplaced that reliance could have been. But frustration with Britain as a partner was not completely eradicated. In the inter-war years memories of those days of acute uncertainty would return. They convinced the French that Britain needed to be tied down by a formal alliance. Britain drew the opposite conclusion.

The French had gone to extraordinary lengths to ensure that in the event of war Britain would be at its side, demonstrating early signs of the dependency syndrome that François Bédarida would describe for the 1930s as the 'English governess'. In February 1912, when Premier and Foreign Minister Poincaré had summoned an informal group to the Quai d'Orsay for a review of France's defence posture, Joffre had advocated a French offensive across lower Belgium should Germany threaten France. The War and Navy ministers supported that strategy, but Poincaré rejected it. He feared that it would forfeit for France any hope of securing British support in a war against Germany. Similarly, on 31 July 1914, when Germany was rumoured to be preparing mobilization, the French Cabinet agreed that covering troops be ordered to take up positions along the Luxembourg–Vosges frontier. However, strict instructions were issued to the troops not to approach closer than 10 kilometres to the frontier. Joffre protested that such a withdrawal formed no part of Plan XVII and that every 24-hour delay in mobilizing the eastern army corps was equivalent to a 15- to 20-kilometre loss of French territory. The gesture was intended above all to influence British public opinion, as Paul Cambon emphasized to Grey on 1 August. It clearly demonstrated the extent to which French decision making was conditioned by Britain.

Wartime alliance

To a large extent Britain's intervention in the first stages of the war was valued more in psychological than material terms. When in 1909 Henry Wilson had asked General Foch, 'What would you say was the smallest British military force that would be of any practical assistance to you in the event of a contest such as we have been considering?', Foch replied immediately, 'One single private soldier and we would take good care that he was killed.'[13] But Britain's symbolic importance as an ally was soon overtaken by the need for its military support. Even before the 150,000 strong British Expeditionary Force took up its position on the French left in northern France, it was being criticized as inadequate, given France's swift conscription and mobilization of 3,800,000 men. The strains in Franco-British relations that were a feature of the whole war resulted from a lack of joint preparation, poor allied communications and the inability of each ally to understand the other's strategic priorities and operational plans. In France the delay and indecisiveness of Britain's decision to intervene imbued French military leaders with the view that the British contribution was too little and too slow. Whereas British commanders such as Sir John French – whose name did not reflect any gallic sympathies – saw their counterparts as unreliable, secretive, domineering and obtuse, the French returned the compliment by believing the British to be cautious, temperamental and unreliable in their military commitment to the alliance. The French were nominally in authority, given the size of their military contribution. Although Britain was committed politically to the alliance by the Pact of London of 5 September 1914 and militarily to the continent, it continued to assert its military independence on the Western Front and elsewhere, finding it difficult to reconcile national interests with alliance ones. The delicate relationship between the allied Commanders-in-Chief continued to be strained. It was in microcosm the consequence of two countries with very different strategic priorities, and very different traditions having to work as allies in what was essentially a long coalition war. Britain's strategic position on the northern French coast determined its Western Front strategy: to defeat Germany by a war of attrition through economic blockade and defend itself against invasion. France's strategic priority was to remove the enemy from French soil as quickly as possible. Not surprisingly, for the French, Britain did too little too late, while for the British the French expected too much too soon. But the two allies learned their lessons. At the outbreak of war in 1939 an allied Supreme War Council similar to that of 1917 was established to coordinate Anglo-French policy and military strategy, and the British Expeditionary Force was placed under the control of the French Commander-in-Chief.[14]

British military subservience to France on the Western Front would be reversed by 1917. With compulsory conscription replacing voluntary enlistment in 1916, British forces gradually assumed the senior role. After the disastrous Nivelle offensive of April 1917 and subsequent mutinies – of which Haig was informed – the French reluctantly surrendered control over operations on the Western Front to Britain. They were compensated in part by Foch's appointment as Supreme Allied Commander in 1918, which unified and improved command. French political and military leaders clung to the impression that they had made all of the sacrifices only to have control of the war wrested from them in the final hour. That the British would always fight to the last Frenchman was only partly moderated by final victory. Even so, with American entry into the war from 1917, French political and military leaders like Clemenceau feared France's bargaining position would decline with a strong American presence at the peace table. In November 1918 France had 102 divisions, but by 1919 the Americans planned to have 100 divisions in place. A speedy end to the war without a clear defeat of Germany was preferred to a peace dictated by the Anglo-Saxons. Pre-empting Charles de Gaulle's preoccupation with the French liberating Paris themselves in 1944, Foch's Chief of Staff, General Weygand, reflected the fears of many: 'French soil would not have been liberated by a pre-eminently French victory: this victory would have been above all Anglo-Saxon, especially American.'[15]

All military alliances are characterized by friction. But it could be said that France and Britain acquitted themselves extremely well of the military effort. Their performance on the economic front was even better. Inter-allied structures were put in place as a result of the disastrous loss of men, *matériel* and industrial potential, which had forced France into a growing reliance on British economic support. Inter-allied commissions oversaw wheat, sugar, coal, credit and shipping. This drew the two nations' economic systems closer than they had ever been. It was so effective as to be pointed to after the war as worthy of continuation by those such as Jean Monnet who had participated in its administration as French representative in London. Before the First World War Britain was the biggest market for French goods. With the German and Belgian markets cut off, and the Russian market restricted, Britain's share of France's total exports increased from 13 per cent in 1913 to 24 per cent in 1919. Even before the war Britain was France's chief source of raw materials for coal, rubber, wool, iron and steel. By the end of the war, the drive for inter-allied cooperation had been extended to almost every sphere of commercial and industrial activity.[16] But this put much of the French economy under indirect British control. Worse still, from 1917, with America's growing importance in the alliance and inter-allied commissions, French dependency on the Anglo-Saxons was economic, financial and military. It became obvious at the peace conference that the dependence was also political. Clemenceau predicted that 'France will have to make sacrifices, not to Germany but to her allies'.[17] In the event it made sacrifices to both.

An Anglo–Saxon peace

Brothers in arms France and Britain might have been during the war, but fraternal relations did not always characterize the peace. After 1919 French foreign policy was typified by a persistent but futile quest for an alliance with the USA and Britain to strengthen its position against Germany. Disintegration of the wartime economic entente between the USA and its European partners after the November 1918 armistice was, as William Keylor has emphasized, 'a major disappointment to France'.[18] Clemenceau relinquished security on the Rhine in exchange for an Anglo-American guarantee treaty, only to see this slip away as the US Senate refused to ratify the Versailles Treaty in 1920 and the USA returned to its traditional isolationism. As the British guarantee was contingent on US participation, the French found themselves exposed to what they still perceived as the 'German menace'.

This was a double blow to the French. Not only did they make sacrifices for a pledge that never materialized; they experienced further disappointment and frustration at Anglo-Saxon leniency towards Germany. The USA and Britain, benefiting from geographical detachment, felt less threatened by Germany. Clemenceau implored his Anglo-Saxon allies:

> After expending the greatest effort, and suffering the greatest sacrifices in blood in all history, we must not compromise the results of our victory . . . I beg you to understand my state of mind, just as I am trying to understand yours. America is far away and protected by the ocean. England could not be reached by Napoleon himself. You are sheltered, both of you; we are not.[19]

Furthermore, because Anglo-Saxon financial interests required the recovery of German prosperity and its return to the community of nations as a trading partner, their approach to enforcement of the Versailles reparations clauses differed sharply from the more punitive French demands. In French eyes the Anglo-Saxons were guilty of hypocrisy when presenting material interests with a veneer of idealism. Self-determination and the League of Nations, which Foch referred to as 'a queer Anglo-Saxon fancy',[20] were brandished at the 'aggressive' French. Charging the French with wishing to use a post-war alliance to keep Germany down and re-establish hegemony on the European continent was an Anglo-Saxon perception not without self-interest. The French felt doubly wounded by what they perceived as a betrayal of their security and friendship. Once again vulnerability, dependence and frustration manifested itself in criticism of the Anglo-Saxons. French politicians and public opinion were convinced that if France had not secured peace terms commensurate with its war effort then responsibility lay with the Anglo-Saxons. Ironically, impractical British liberal internationalism and its offshoot Wilsonian idealism had triumphed over French realism. It had done so largely because France was so encumbered with wartime debt owed principally to the Anglo-Saxons that its freedom to enforce German reparation repayments fell victim to Washington's and London's magnanimity towards Berlin. The only remaining instrument for controlling Germany slipped from France's grasp, as the unavailing Ruhr intervention in 1923 starkly revealed.

The problem was that Germany's defeat, Russia's eclipse and the USA's retreat from international affairs made London and Paris once again the main rivals in the international system. The French might bluster that Britain was resorting to its traditional policy of divide and rule on the continent, but there was a large body of international opinion, albeit stoked by German propaganda, that believed that France wished to reassert its dominance of the European continent. In 1922 British air staff considered war with France 'the greatest menace to this country' given its possession of the largest airforce in the world. Such fears had already put paid to the Channel Tunnel project in 1920. A Foreign Office memorandum for circulation to the Cabinet claimed: 'The Foreign Office conclusion is that our relations with France never have been, are not, probably never will be, sufficiently stable and friendly to justify the construction of a Channel Tunnel.'[21] Differences were not only imagined. Britain and France clashed over Germany, but also over Eastern Europe, the Middle East and even further afield. British self-righteousness was well matched with French intellectual arrogance. Much of French distrust of others stemmed from its sense of vulnerability, but also from its own belief in France's predestination to greatness. One of the Quai's principal officials astutely analysed that if France wished to lead Europe it had to dispel mistrust of itself, 'which derives from the mistrust that she herself feels towards others'.[22] But his was a lone voice. Not surprisingly, French relations with the Anglo-Americans did not thrive during the 1920s. The French felt further humiliation at the Washington conference on international disarmament (12 November 1921–6 February 1922), when they were forced to accept new international parities in capital ships: Britain 5; USA 5; Japan 3; France 1.75; Italy 1.75. France viewed this as essentially an Anglo-Saxon-imposed equality with Italy. The head of the British delegation to the conference, Arthur Balfour, commented perspicaciously during the negotiations:

> it means that [the] French are at last convinced that [the] Lafayette credit upon which they have counted so heavily, has been completely exhausted and have come to appreciate [the] realities of [the] position which they occupy in [the] American mind.[23]

To fill the vacuum left by the absence of an Anglo-Saxon (and a Russian) security guarantee, France spent the 1920s building a network of lesser European allies chiefly in Eastern Europe and the Balkans. Although this arc of eastern allies looked superficially impressive, states such as Poland, Czechoslovakia, Romania and Yugoslavia were divided among themselves. Worse still, French treaties with them frightened British governments anxious not to be drawn into the quarrels of 'small far-away countries' of which Britons knew little and cared less. France's problem was that it had a greater need of an alliance than Britain, but found concessions difficult. As Clemenceau had said, peace would mean making sacrifices not to Germany but to its allies. As before 1914, Paris was attempting in 1922 to force London into an alliance that was not based on an accurate assessment of Britain's interests or public opinion. More serious still, failure to assess its potential ally went hand in hand with an inability objectively to assess itself, its policy objectives and the sacrifices it needed to make to achieve an alliance. The fault lay on both sides; but both sides were not equally in need of an alliance. Ironically, France found it easier to know its enemy than its friend.

French leaders nonetheless maintained their quest to rebuild the elusive alliance with Britain. However, London would not countenance such a move without there first being a settlement of the two countries' outstanding differences around the globe. In 1922 the British Foreign Secretary, Lord Curzon, suggested an Entente Cordiale-style settlement, but his French counterpart, Raymond Poincaré insisted on a defence pact. This was at a time when Paris and London were at loggerheads over the Chanak Crisis, in which battles between Greece and Turkish nationalists saw Britain siding with the former and France with the latter. Mutual frustration came to a head in September 1922 when a face-to-face row broke out between Poincaré and Curzon, with the latter collapsing in tears before the British ambassador, Lord Hardinge, muttering, 'Charley, I can't bear that horrid little man, I can't bear him.'[24] This was not how to win friends and influence allies. It was in miniature a fine example of the two countries' inability to see eye to eye. Despite each country intercepting and deciphering significant amounts of the other's diplomatic traffic, mutual understanding did not emerge.[25] But knowing one's ally did not always mean understanding it.

The French made little effort to understand the USA, preferring to live off an imagined special relationship dating back to Lafayette. At a time when the Atlantic sea crossing took four to five days, when no regular air service existed with the USA until 1939 and no telephone link until the late 1920s, the French Foreign Ministry had only three staff on its American desk and only one French newspaper had a special correspondent in the USA.[26] As for the British, the French Foreign Ministry did countenance making attempts during the inter-war years to use the French community established in Britain to develop a better understanding of its cross-Channel neighbour by developing 'agents of influence' and by extending its intelligence services to Britain, but little came of it. Such ignorance and insularity merely reinforced stereotypes, conspiracy theories and a sense of vulnerability to their Anglo-Saxon rivals. Reparations were a case in point. A majority of the French elite and public opinion failed to acknowledge why the Anglo-Saxons would not allow Germany to be too cowed, always putting it down to an Anglo-Saxon plot. Similarly, when the franc was under attack in 1924 and 1926, they blamed Anglo-Saxon financiers intent on forcing France into a more lenient position on reparations, or claimed more fatuously that this was to enable the British and Americans to take advantage of cheap holidays in France. During these years French satirical cartoons targeted the Anglo-American invasion with children depicted as listing Paris as one of the British colonies or French restaurant customers having to endure overdone roast beef because 'the English prefer it like that!' A best-selling book by the Oxford-educated confidant of Raymond Poincaré Jacques Bardoux attributed the 1924 left-wing victory of the *Cartel des gauches* to the British intelligence services.

To be fair, not all French claims were fanciful. In 1923–24, British politicians, Foreign Office and Treasury officials had seriously contemplated starting a run on the franc to force Poincaré's hand on reparations. The British saw to it that Poincaré was aware of such an eventuality. However, in 1928, following Poincaré's restoration of confidence in the franc, foreign currency came flowing back into the Bank of France's coffers. France now possessed massive holdings of pounds and dollars, which were tightening credit in these currencies on the international markets. Indeed, the Bank of France had accumulated enough sterling to buy up the entire gold reserves of the Bank of England; something it was entitled to do since the pound's return to the Gold Standard in 1925. Poincaré was not shy in turning the financial weapon on the British, who were forced to accede to a greater international financial role for the Bank of France in Eastern Europe. France's massive financial reserves also spared Poincaré having to go cap in hand to France's Anglo-Saxon creditors for additional loans, thereby safeguarding French independence and international dignity.[27] Currency would continue as an instrument of diplomacy in relations between the Anglo-Americans and the French, as demonstrated by the 1956 Suez Crisis and General de Gaulle's anxiousness to maintain large French gold reserves during the 1960s.

The English governess

As American isolationism increased after the 1929 Wall Street Crash, so France increasingly aligned itself with British foreign policy, still craving the elusive alliance. Lacking firm support in March 1936 during Germany's remilitarization of the Rhineland, France stepped onto the path of appeasement already being trodden by Britain. Historians such as François Bédarida have described France as slavishly following Britain after 1936 and conceding all diplomatic independence to the tutelage of 'an English governess', so that French appeasement was 'made in London'.[28] Others such as Robert Young have argued that Paris was left with some room for manœuvre. What is certain is that the East and Central European alliances, which France had contracted in the 1920s, now seemed a liability. In 1938 France could muster only a diplomatic protest to German annexation of Austria and, at Munich in September, colluded with Britain to induce Czechoslovakia (France's ally by treaty) to accept dismemberment by Germany – a precursor to Hitler's destruction of the Czechoslovak state in March 1939. Nevertheless, during this period France did begin to rebuild its armed strength. To Hitler's astonishment, Edouard Daladier's government took France into war that September. Yet France was still operating in Britain's wake. Whereas in 1914 Britain had followed France into war; in 1939 it was the reverse. Only in those extreme circumstances of renewed hostilities against Germany did Britain agree to resume the alliance with France. Even then, as in 1914, Britain's pre-war aloofness from the continent and its imperial priorities ensured that its military aid to France in 1939–40 was modest and did not compensate for Germany's greater number of mobilized troops.

Anglo-French Union

The ambivalent Franco-British relationship never ceased to swing in opposite directions. On 16 June 1940 a remarkable British project was presented to the French Cabinet at Bordeaux for an 'indissoluble union' between France and Britain. It was the culmination of a series of initiatives, which since the start of the Second World War had drawn the two countries together in a manner not witnessed since the First World War. From the war's onset a Supreme War Council and machinery for joint economic planning were put in place. On 6 December 1939 an Anglo-

French Coordinating Committee was established, chaired by Jean Monnet. This was followed on 16 February 1940 by an Anglo-French trade agreement and on 8 March by an Anglo-French industrial council. Efforts were made to coordinate the resources of the two empires. On 28 March the Supreme War Council published a communiqué committing the two governments not to 'negotiate nor conclude an armistice or treaty of peace except by mutual agreement' and to agree on 'a community of action' for post-war settlement and reconstruction. *The Times* noted that: 'Anglo-French unity has already reached a more advanced point than at any period during the last war, and what is more it is realised in both countries that this point is but the first step towards a closer and more lasting association.' In *Le Figaro* newspaper of 30 March 1940 Vladimir d'Ormesson commented: 'England is now in Europe.' Suggestions were made for a union of the two countries along the lines of the old Austro-Hungarian dual monarchy. The final text for an Anglo-French Union, endorsed by the British War Cabinet, stated:

> The two governments declare that France and Great Britain shall no longer be two nations, but one Franco-British Union. The constitution of the Union will provide for joint organs of defence, foreign, financial and economic policies. Every citizen of France will enjoy immediately citizenship of Great Britain; every British subject will become a citizen of France.[29]

However, the day following the text's presentation to the French Cabinet the military debacle forced the French to request an armistice from Germany on 16 June. The 'stupendous' project, as de Gaulle enthusiastically referred to it, for a Franco-British Union was dead. It would never be resurrected. In France the project elicited divergent views, a reflection of the ambivalence with which Britain was viewed. Anglophobia was on the increase, old imperial rivalries surfaced, as did Dunkirk and the belief that the British would always fight to the last Frenchman. Others believed that Britain would soon be defeated and that its settlement with Germany would be at the expense of French interests. Thus French opponents of the project referred to it as an attempt to 'reduce France to the rank of a dominion'. Enthusiasts such as de Gaulle and French Premier Paul Reynaud, who resigned rather than accept the armistice, were in a minority. There is no doubt that the project would have had far-reaching implications for Franco-British relations, but also for the future of Europe, as the American Deputy Ambassador in France, A. J. Drexel Biddle, reported to Washington: 'It was far-reaching in scope: it meant in reality a fusion of two great Empires. It might have marked the beginning of a United States of Europe.'[30] How does one explain such a momentous proposal? During the phoney war European federation ideas provided fashionable solutions for the continent's ills. More realistically and immediately Churchill sought to galvanize the French with some tangible commitment for the forthcoming conflict and beyond. The French had always craved this, which probably explains why French personalities and politicians such as de Gaulle and Reynaud welcomed it. But for all the lyrical prose of *The Times* leader of 22 April and its talk of an 'ever closer union', all that would remain of the project would be that phrase later to become one of the tenets of European integration.[31]

Distrust and dependency

Aware of their need for an arsenal abroad, and notwithstanding American isolationism in the 1930s, some French leaders such as Foreign Minister Georges Bonnet and Jean Monnet (the latter a member of the Tardieu–Joffre mission to Washington in 1917–18) appealed to the US President, Franklin D. Roosevelt, during the phoney war. Once again the 'spirit of Lafayette and Rochambeau' – almost two centuries of Franco-American friendship – was invoked to recall how France had assisted America in its war for independence. Though sympathetic to France, Roosevelt was prevented by congressional hostility to American entanglement in Europe from providing practical assistance. Even in the June 1940 crisis, desperate telegrams containing personal pleas from Reynaud, the French Premier, failed to draw the USA into war alongside France. In the post-war world the lesson of how America did not come to France's aid in its hour of need would not be lost on Frenchmen such as General de Gaulle.

Disappointment with the Anglo-Saxons increased as the war advanced. The year 1940 saw a new rupture in Franco-British relations. Evacuation of the British armies back to Britain from Dunkirk symbolized, for many French, the perfidiousness of an Albion ready to cut and run from the continent, leaving France to fend for itself in a German-controlled Europe. An added source of bitterness was that, of the 165,000 troops taken off the beaches at Dunkirk by 31 May 1940, only 15,000 were French. Although between 29 May and 4 June, with Churchill's encouragement, almost equal numbers of French and British troops were evacuated (139,000 each), some 30,000–40,000 French troops were left behind to surrender, making 'Dunkirk' more a betrayal than the deliverance it was for the British.[32] Later that year the British sinking of the French fleet at anchor in Mers-el-Kébir, under Vichy control, killed some 1300 Frenchmen and was a propaganda gift to the Vichy regime. Even today Mers-el-Kébir figures alongside Fashoda as a byword for British perfidy.

The Americans, too, were objects of suspicion. Not only did they retain ambassadorial relations with Pétain's Vichy France until 1942, but de Gaulle's Free France got short shrift in Washington. 'How can one deal with a man who thinks himself Napoleon and Joan of Arc?', asked a bemused and irritated Roosevelt. Largely because francophile Churchill admired de Gaulle's stubborn courage and understood that he was all that Britain had to work with for the moment in the way of a sympathetic Frenchman, Britain gave more support to Free France. BBC broadcast facilities were put at de Gaulle's disposal to help him rally resistance inside occupied and Vichy France. Britain supplied weapons and training facilities for de Gaulle's Fighting French forces. The problem was that even by August 1941 de Gaulle's followers numbered only 30,000. That month a bungled Anglo-French expedition, undermined by disagreements between de Gaulle and Churchill, failed to capture the strategic West African port of Dakar from Vichy. Because the bulk of the French Empire continued to support Vichy, the British felt they could not alienate Pétain completely, much to de Gaulle's annoyance. De Gaulle grudgingly relied on the British for his survival from 1940 to 1942. He resented their not sharing military plans with him over the British invasion of the French colony of Madagascar in May 1942 and the Anglo-American invasion of North Africa in November 1942. Differences continued until the end of the war, with a serious clash over France's two mandated territories in the Middle East, Syria and Lebanon, which an Anglo-Free French force had seized from Vichy control. The British agreed with de Gaulle's representative, General Catroux, to grant independence to the Arabs in the two mandates, which de Gaulle viewed as interfering in French colonial matters. The Levant remained a running sore between de Gaulle and Britain until August 1944.

The Americans remained sceptical, even hostile, about de Gaulle. In 1942 they put up an alternative to him, the more senior, but politically undynamic, General Henri Giraud. They did not recognize de Gaulle's leadership of the French Committee of National Liberation until 1943. Nevertheless, American military aid was vital to de Gaulle's cause and kept him to heel. Over the course of the war French armed forces received over $2 billion in American 'lend-lease' supplies – 8 per cent of all the US War Department's lend-lease aid, a greater share than China.[33] Distrust and dependency were hard for de Gaulle to tolerate. The legacy soured de Gaulle's long-term view of the USA. He concluded that the Americans were driven by non-European interests and were potentially untrustworthy.

His view of Britain was only marginally better. His numerous differences and rows with Churchill about not being treated as an equal partner on a par with major allies such as the USA soured relations between the two men. British files declassified in January 2000 reveal the extent of the differences. In May 1943 in a series of 'most secret cyber [*sic*]' telegrams from Washington, Churchill asked the Cabinet whether 'we should allow this marplot and mischief-maker to continue the harm he is doing'. Urging the Cabinet to cut off all financial aid to the Free French and accusing de Gaulle of 'fascist tendencies', he boomed: 'I ask my colleagues to consider urgently whether we should not now eliminate de Gaulle as a political force and face Parliament and France upon the issues.' The Cabinet rejected Churchill's idea, claiming astutely: 'We would find ourselves accused . . . of interfering in French internal affairs, with a view to treating France as an Anglo-American protectorate.'[34]

Although unaware of this exchange, de Gaulle was party to the rows and deeply suspicious by 1943 that the Anglo-Saxons wished to block his plan to restore France to great power status at the end of the war. He was adamant that France should not emerge from the war as a rescued client state of the Anglo-Saxons. He was incensed to discover on 4 June 1944, two days before D-Day, well-advanced plans to impose an Allied Military Government of Occupied Territory (AMGOT) regime on liberated France; the currency ('counterfeit money' according to de Gaulle) already printed and prepared for distribution. Replacing German occupation by an Anglo-Saxon one was too much for the General. He eventually secured the administration of liberated France by commissioners of the Republic acting in the name of his provisional government. He also won the right for Free French tanks commanded by General Leclerc to lead the liberation of Paris in August 1944, symbolizing France's 'liberation by itself'. Two days after being notified by the British, American, Canadian and Soviet governments that they had, at last, officially recognized his government, he was asked at a press conference: 'Could you give us your impressions on the recognition of the French government by the allies?' Back had come the sardonic reply: 'I can tell you that the government is satisfied that it is to be called by its name.'[35]

Post-war

De Gaulle wished to consolidate liberated France's position by carrying on the fight against Germany and gaining recognition of France's status as one of the 'Big Four' powers able to shape the post-war European settlement. Disguising his irritation at his treatment by the Anglo-Saxons and with his eye firmly fixed on the post-war settlement, he told the Provisional Consultative Assembly in Algiers on 25 July 1944:

> There is, between England and us, a clear community of European and world interests, which no defunct rivalry on some point of the globe should be able to disrupt. There is between the United States and us an identity of ideals, both a rational and instinctive friendship, which should, in my opinion, be essential elements in the forthcoming reorganization of the world.[36]

Nevertheless, he remained sceptical about an Anglo-Saxon commitment to France. Preferring not to put all his eggs in one basket, and displaying French security's reflex since the 1890s, de Gaulle relished playing the 'Russian card', especially when it doubled as a snub to the Anglo-Saxons. In a letter to Stalin in 1944 de Gaulle remarked 'Between France and the Soviet Union there are no matters in direct dispute. Between France and Great Britain, there always have been and there always will be.'[37] That December he signed the Moscow Treaty thinking that Russia would again be important in France's European security policy and to provide leverage against Britain and the USA. The cold war put paid to that.

Although excluded from the 1945 Yalta and Potsdam conferences between the USA, Soviet Union and Britain, de Gaulle still achieved much of his ambitious agenda, gaining for France a leading role in German occupation and the United Nations. He laid blame for the post-war division of Europe squarely on the Yalta decisions and specifically at the feet of the Americans with their 'non-European' perspective. He made a virtue out of necessity from his exclusion by the 'Big Three', insisting that this independence allowed France to defend 'European' interests on the international stage, just as in the 1960s he would present France as the defender of all 'small' powers against the great.

Autonomy from the Anglo-Saxons

De Gaulle's jaundiced view of wartime Anglo-Saxon behaviour conditioned his thinking on foreign and defence policy during his 'wilderness years' from 1946 to 1958, and more seriously during his presidency from 1958 to 1969. Intent on reducing French dependence on the Anglo-Saxons, France embarked on an independent foreign and defence policy for which he found a broad welcome among the French political community and public. This was in part because during the Fourth Republic France had experienced further setbacks at the hands of the Anglo-Saxons, and particularly the Americans. In the post-Second World War world, as after the First, the Americans, and to a degree the British, quickly stopped regarding Germany as a threat and promoted its industrial revival. The Anglo-Saxons attempted to convince the French that the Soviet Union was the greatest threat to peace and West Germany a potential barrier to communism. The French did not see cold war developments in those Manichean terms. They recognized Stalin's brutality and resented Soviet domination of Eastern Europe; they also viewed the Anglo-Saxons as overbearing and even unnecessarily antagonistic to the Soviet Union. Dissatisfied with British military thinking in the 1948 Brussels Pact, Paris wanted a firm military guarantee to defend the Rhine and a prominent say in strategic planning. Even NATO's formation in April 1949 did not satisfy French security concerns about Germany or even what would happen in the event of a Soviet attack. The number of US divisions in Western Europe began to be significant only with the Korean War. Even then Paris was pressured into accepting German rearmament in exchange. Doubts remained as to the reliability of American support in the final hour.

During the final crisis of the Indochina War, with a French garrison at Dien Bien Phu on the verge of surrender to the Vietminh communists in April 1954, the ostensibly anti-communist Eisenhower administration refused pleas from a desperate French Foreign Minister, Georges Bidault, to provide American atomic weapons to break the encirclement. In November 1956, American hostility to the Franco-British–Israeli military intervention against Egypt's President Nasser at Suez forced a humiliating French and British withdrawal from the canal zone.

Suez demonstrated France's and Britain's inability to influence world affairs effectively. But the French and British governments drew radically divergent lessons from this debacle. London toed the American line there-after, drawing especially close in nuclear cooperation and procuring American Polaris missiles via the Anglo-American Nassau agreement of December 1962. Paris came to three very different conclusions. First, the Franco-British axis, pursued by those such as Guy Mollet, no longer appeared viable. Second, European weakness relative to the superpowers clearly demonstrated the need for greater European solidarity. 'Europe will be your revenge', German Chancellor Konrad Adenauer is supposed to have told French Premier Guy Mollet the very day the Suez operation was halted.[38] Finally, the failed Suez operation called into question the principle of integration, which was the basis of the Atlantic Alliance's military organ-ization. One senior French diplomat concluded that 'France's security depends entirely on the American alliance'.[39] France felt it had lost its independence and could only hope, at best, to influence the USA.

De Gaulle's resentment was greatest for what he viewed as the Anglo-Saxon monopoly of nuclear weapons. In September 1958 he suggested to President Eisenhower that a directorate of the USA, Britain and France should take decisions on the use of nuclear force. Rejection led him to accelerate development of France's nuclear weapon, which was finally tested in February 1960. American attempts to starve the French nuclear programme by denying it access to American know-how and technology further irritated the General. The 1962 Nassau agreement between London and Washington, whereby Britain became America's privileged partner in atomic weaponry, was for de Gaulle another classic example of the Anglo-Saxons sticking together and deeming the French not clubbable.

France resolutely pursued its independent nuclear deterrent, distancing itself from the 'Anglo-Saxon' Atlantic Alliance. De Gaulle took this policy to its logical end by withdrawing France from NATO's integrated military command in March 1966 and ordering the withdrawal of its 26,000 troops from French territory. As ever, de Gaulle's actions were a mixture of theatre and symbolism. He added insult to injury by provocatively embarking on a state visit to the Soviet Union three months later and publicly voicing his desire for improved bilateral relations with Moscow. His action resonated broadly with French public opinion, where intellectuals on the left like Jean-Paul Sartre, and on the right like André Malraux displayed a visceral dislike of the USA. When in 1961 London announced it would apply to join the European Community, General de Gaulle vetoed Britain's application in 1963 and 1967 on the grounds that Britain was insufficiently European and would be the USA's 'Trojan Horse' in Europe. De Gaulle had never forgotten Churchill's 1944 retort to him that 'every time we have to choose between Europe and the open sea we shall always choose the open sea'.[40]

The relationship with the Anglo-Saxons remained ambivalent. The USA did not give the French direct military help in Indochina, but they financed 90 per cent of the Indochina War. Despite claiming to develop an independent nuclear deterrent, France relied ultimately on the American nuclear umbrella. This did not stop de Gaulle delivering a series of calculated snubs to the USA. In 1964 he pointedly recognized America's bugbear, the People's Republic of China. In the same year he visited a string of Latin America countries, exalted their Latin cultural specificity and, without naming the USA, called on them to reject all hegemony and invited them to walk with France *el mano en el mano*. In 1966 he visited Moscow and championed Third World interests against 'American imperialism'. He openly criticized American involvement in Vietnam, convinced that US forces could not succeed where the French professional army had failed. He publicly denounced dominance of the dollar in international trade. He sided with the Arabs against American-backed Israel in the 1967 Six-Day War. That year in Montreal he publicly proclaimed 'Vive le Québec libre!' and expressed disapproval of Anglo-American oppression of the Canadian province. On the basis that irritation precedes existence, by de Gaulle's death in 1970, France felt it had pulled itself up again to great power status and could look the Anglo-Saxons in the eye.

Improved relations

It was when the Anglo-Saxons were getting weaker that France's relations with them improved. When US power seemed less threatening at the end of the 1960s, de Gaulle had seemed more prepared to draw closer to Washington. The year 1969 was the onset of American financial weakness and the beginning of chronic US balance of payments deficits leading to the August 1971 decision to allow the dollar to float. President Pompidou, speaking in the name of Europe, was able to broker a stabilization of the dollar with President Richard Nixon in December via a revaluation of the pound, deutschmark and franc. The sound working relationship with Washington under Pompidou deteriorated with the French President's health from 1973 as he gave greater latitude to his arch-Gaullist Foreign Minister Michel Jobert. Relations improved under the 'Atlanticist' Valéry Giscard d'Estaing.

There were no fewer than four meetings with Presidents Ford and Carter and a host of others at the annual summits of Western developed nations from 1975 to 1980. The dramatically expanding French economy was opened up to direct American investment – anathema to de Gaulle – while Paris and Washington had friendly discussions about controlling the effects of the world economic crisis followed the quadrupling of the oil price between 1973 and 1975. It was not quite the partnership de Gaulle had always coveted, but France felt it was dealing with the USA on more equal terms.

Similar magnanimity was displayed to Britain, whose economy had continued its relative decline during the late 1960s. In 1973, about the time that France overtook Britain in per capita GNP, Pompidou lifted de Gaulle's veto on Britain's membership of the European Community. Pompidou was looking to Britain as a means of counterbalancing growing West German economic and political power in the Community. Pompidou's successor Valéry Giscard d'Estaing was a conservative but not a Gaullist; he prioritized relations with Germany. Relations with Britain's Conservative Prime Minister since 1979, Margaret Thatcher, were poor, but her relations with Giscard's socialist successor from 1981, François Mitterrand, were good. Franco-British relations improved on many fronts, except Europe. That long-standing symbol of Franco-British proximity and divide, the Channel Tunnel, was finally opened to the public in summer 1994. Franco-British defence cooperation tightened in the 1980s and 1990s from the 1982 Falklands War to joint armaments construction projects.

Under Mitterrand relations with the USA were good. France relaxed its traditional protectionism and embraced the liberalized international economy. In the early 1980s Mitterrand supported the deployment of American intermediate-range nuclear missiles in West Germany to counter Soviet SS20s. Despite friction with Washington over France's criticism of the US invasion of Grenada in October 1983 (also criticized by Britain) and Mitterrand's championing of Sandinista guerrillas in Nicaragua, relations were increasingly cordial, with the French President visiting the USA in 1981 and 1984.

Cultural clashes

For the average Frenchman differences with the Anglo–Saxons crystallized around cultural and linguistic issues. Under de Gaulle the American threat had been perceived principally in terms of technological domination and economic hegemony. The journalist and politician Jean-Jacques Servan Schreiber encapsulated it in the 1967 best-selling polemic, translated the following year, *The American Challenge*. But again ambivalence was at the core of French relations with America. The early 1980s were characterized by

French 'Americanomania', reflected in everything from college sweatshirts to fast-food chains. All political parties other than the communists and National Front lobbied hard for the Disney Corporation to locate its Western European theme park, Euro-Disney, in France. However, there was widespread French support for the stand against the encroachments of Anglo-Saxon cultural norms and the debasement, and so-called Coca-Cola-ization, of French, European and world values. Mitterrand's high profile Minister for Culture and Francophonie, Jack Lang, inveighed against American cultural imperialism. To combat the decline of French as an international language at the hands of English, and to promote French universalist values, *la Francophonie* was revitalized and grew in nothing if not ambition from 1970. During the Uruguay round of the GATT negotiations (1986–93) the French championed the notion of 'cultural exceptions' for film and agriculture. France seemed to have found a new international role as the self-appointed promoter and sponsor of the notion of cultural specificity in the face of a bland Americanization.

Over the twentieth century France has entertained a complex and uneasy relationship with the Anglo-Saxons. Dorothy Pickles described the Franco-British relationship as the 'uneasy entente', a long history of misunderstandings.[41] The same could be said of France's relations with the Anglo-Saxons. The two communities rarely seemed in step. It is something of a cliché, but France has entertained a love–hate relationship with the Anglo-Saxons. The French admire Britain's and America's contribution to civilization, but, as Alfred Grosser remarked, feel 'a kind of permanent irritation against powers stronger than France'. This goes some way to explaining France's troubled relationship with Britain from the nineteenth to the mid-twentieth century when Britain was more powerful than France and why the Franco-American relationship was so poor after 1917 and especially after the Second World War when the USA was clearly a superpower. Grosser concludes: 'Many Frenchmen feel affection for the United States because of La Fayette, and resentment because of Marshall aid.'[42] But the relationship is symbiotic. In the twentieth century France has used the Anglo-Saxons to reaffirm its national identity and give it a platform for what it claims to represent on the international stage. France continues to define itself internationally by resistance to what it is not, or thinks it is not. This explains its proclaimed resistance at the beginning of the twenty-first century to all things Anglo-Saxon from the English language to 'la mal bouffe' and the 'MacDonaldization' of the world. If the 'Anglo-Saxons' had not existed, the French would have had to invent them.

Notes

1 Quoted in P. M. H. Bell, *France and Britain, 1900–1940: Entente and Estrangement* (London, Longman, 1996), p. 1.
2 Raymond Poincaré, *L'Idée de patrie* (Paris, 1910), pp. 6–22.
3 Quoted in François Bédarida, 'Postface', in Douglas Johnson, François Bédarida and François Crouzet (eds), *Britain and France: Ten Centuries* (Folkestone, Dawson, 1980), p. 364.
4 Bédarida, 'Postface', p. 364.
5 Bell, *France and Britain*, pp. 11–14, 116, 198–200.
6 T. Cahu, *Histoire de Jeanne d'Arc* (Paris, 1895), p. 76, quoted in Christian Amalvi, *Les Héros de l'histoire de France* (Paris, Editions Phot'œil, 1979), p. 284.
7 Pascal Venier, 'Delcassé et les relations franco-britanniques pendant les débuts de la guerre de Boers', in Rémy Paech, Claudine Pailhes and Louis Claeys, *Delcassé et l'Europe à la veille de la Grande Guerre* (Toulouse, forthcoming).
8 J. F. V. Keiger, 'Omdurman, Fashoda and Franco-British Relations', in Edward Spiers (ed.), *Sudan: The Reconquest Reappraised* (London, Frank Cass, 1998), p. 163.
9 Bell, *France and Britain*, pp. 23–33.
10 Quoted in K. I. Hamilton, 'Britain and France', in F. H. Hinsley (ed.), *British Foreign Policy under Sir Edward Grey* (Cambridge, Cambridge University Press, 1977), p. 118.
11 Quotes in Keiger, *France and the Origins*, pp. 162, 116.
12 Quoted in Bell, *France and Britain*, p. 57.
13 Quoted in Williamson, 'Joffre Reshapes French Strategy', p. 150.
14 William Philpott, *Anglo-French Relations and Strategy on the Western Front 1914–18* (London, Macmillan, 1996), pp. 13, 29, 50–1, 94, 164.
15 Quoted in Adamthwaite, *Grandeur and Misery*, p. 43.
16 John F. Godfrey, *Capitalism at War: Industrial Policy and Bureaucracy in France, 1914–1918* (Leamington Spa, Berg, 1987), pp. 44–81.
17 Quoted in Adamthwaite, *Grandeur and Misery*, p. 38.
18 W. R. Keylor, 'France's Futile Quest for American Military Protection, 1919–22', in M. Petricioli and M Guderzo (eds), *A Missed Opportunity? 1922: The Reconstruction of Europe* (Berne, Peter Lang, 1995), pp. 61–80.
19 Quoted in Adamthwaite, *Grandeur and Misery*, p. 40.
20 Quoted in Adamthwaite, *Grandeur and Misery*, p. 53.
21 Foreign Office memorandum on the Channel Tunnel, 1 May 1920, in Rohan Butler and J. P. T. Bury (eds), *Documents on British Foreign Policy 1919–1939* (hereafter *DBFP*), 1st series, vol. XII (London, HMSO, 1960), Document no. 14.
22 Quoted in Adamthwaite, *Grandeur and Misery*, pp. 73–5.
23 Balfour to Curzon, 20 Nov. 1921, *DBFP*, vol. XII, Document no. 437.
24 Andrew, *Secret Service*, pp. 423–4.
25 Andrew, *Secret Service*, p. 37.
26 Adamthwaite, *Grandeur and Misery*, p. 78.
27 Keiger, *Poincaré*, pp. 332–3.
28 François Bédarida, 'La "Gouvernante anglaise"', in René Rémond and Janine Bourdin (eds), *Edouard Daladier, chef de gouvernement (avril 1938–septembre 1939)* (Paris, FNSP, 1977), pp. 228–40.

29 Quoted in Max Beloff, 'The Anglo-French Union Project of June 1940', in *Mélanges Pierre Renouvin: Etudes d'histoire des relations internationales* (Paris, PUF, 1966), p. 215.
30 Quoted in Beloff, 'The Anglo-French Union Project', p. 219.
31 Bell, *Britain and France*, pp. 228–9.
32 Bell, *Britain and France*, pp. 238–40.
33 John Young, *France, the Cold War and the Western Alliance, 1944–1949: French Foreign Policy and Post War Europe* (Leicester, Leicester University Press, 1990), p. 4.
34 'They were Allies, but Churchill Loathed de Gaulle and Wanted him Eliminated', *Daily Mail*, 6 Jan. 2000.
35 Quoted in Grosser, *Affaires extérieures*, p. 7.
36 Charles de Gaulle, *Discours et messages*, vol. 1, *Pendant la guerre. Juin 1940–Janvier 1946* (Paris, Plon, Livre de Poche, paperback edn, 1970), pp. 460-1.
37 Quoted in Pickles, *Government and Politics*, p. 223.
38 Quoted in Maurice Vaisse, 'Post-Suez France', in W. R. Louis and R. Owen (eds), *Suez 1956: The Crisis and its Consequences* (Oxford: Oxford University Press, 1989), p. 336.
39 Quoted in Vaisse, 'Post-Suez France', p. 338.
40 Quoted in Pickles, *Government and Politics*, p. 225.
41 Dorothy Pickles, *The Uneasy Entente: French Foreign Policy and Franco-British Misunderstandings* (Oxford: Oxford University Press, 1966), pp. 1–2.
42 Grosser, *IVe République*, p. 176.

7
Russia

The ambivalence that has characterized France's relations with the 'Anglo-Saxons' has not been absent from relations with Russia. Russia was both friend and foe over the twentieth century. The key to an understanding of those relations has been Germany and a mutual geopolitical suspicion of Germany, situated in the centre of the European continent. As pillars at the extreme ends of the European continent, France and Russia have had few reasons to quarrel on geopolitical grounds. On 30 November 1828 Chateaubriand wrote:

> There is sympathy between Russia and France . . . Situated at the two extremities of Europe, France and Russia share no borders; they have no potential points of conflict; they are not commercial rivals and Russia's natural enemies of Russia (the English and the Austrians) are also France's. In peacetime, if the French government remains Saint Petersburg's ally, then nothing can move in Europe.[1]

Later on in the nineteenth century that complementarity had not dwindled.

> The alliance of France and Russia is something so natural that it would be madness not to expect it; of all of the powers, they alone, by reason of their geographic position and political aims, have the minimum of causes for dissension, since they have no interests which are necessarily in conflict.[2]

This statement by Bismarck to the Prince-Regent of Prussia on 26 April 1856 was the favourite quotation of one of France's longest-serving Foreign Ministers, Théophile Delcassé, who, while at the Quai d'Orsay from 1898 to 1905, zealously nurtured the Franco-Russian Alliance. As the twentieth century progressed, those geopolitical sympathies did not evaporate, even if they were often obfuscated by ideological differences. It all began at the turn of the nineteenth century when for a quarter of a century onwards the Franco-Russian Alliance became the cornerstone of France's security policy.

The Franco-Russian Alliance

It was France's isolation on the international scene, engineered by Bismarck, which made any alliance partner attractive. France's twenty-year search for security was eventually rewarded at the beginning of the 1890s following Bismarck's retirement from public life. The web of alliances put in place by the Iron Chancellor began to unravel. During the 1880s the Russian economy, though predominantly rural, had reached the 'take-off' phase. Russia needed capital for further investment. Germany had been Russia's traditional banker, but economic relations between the two countries worsened. The Russian autocracy's scruples about associating with republican governments began to waver with the lure of French gold. Loans to Russia also appealed to French bankers, who could count on better returns on their investment from a secure creditor. The first contract between French banks and the Russian government was signed in November 1888.

There was no hurry on either side to develop political relations. France feared reprisals from its enemies and Russia remained suspicious of the Republic, its internal stability and the nationalism whipped up by the Boulanger Affair. As economic and financial relations intensified in January 1889 and May 1891, as the furore surrounding the Boulanger Affair abated and as Russo-German relations worsened, so France's appeal as a potential ally increased. In 1889 Tsar Alexander III even allowed Russian industrialists and entrepreneurs to participate in the International Paris Exhibition organized to celebrate the centenary of the French Revolution. Within two years France had lent Russia two billion francs. French middle-class opinion was further seduced by closer relations with Russia by the growth of cultural interest in the Russian Empire. Jules Verne's *Michel Strogoff*, first published in 1877, was complemented by the popularity of Russian novels, particularly by Tolstoy and Dostoyevsky. The number of translations of Russian books increased from three or four per year in the period from 1880 to 1885, to twenty-five in 1888. As the French public was acquainted with the Russian Empire, so the right-wing press began to stress its qualities of order and military might, while the centre-left emphasized its ability to act as a counterweight to Germany.[3]

In August 1890, at Russian army manœuvres, Russian generals hinted to the Deputy Chief of the French General Staff of the possibility of a Franco-Russian military convention. The idea's attraction for the Russians was increased a year later when in March 1891 the new German administration abandoned the Iron Chancellor's policy of friendship with Saint Petersburg and refused to prolong the Reinsurance Treaty. That very month the Tsar conferred Russia's highest decoration on the French President of the Republic. With worsening Russo-German economic relations, closer links between London, Rome and Berlin and the pre-term renewal of the Triple

Alliance on 6 May 1891, Russia felt as isolated as France. Even though Saint Petersburg would have preferred only an entente with Paris, it was increasingly pressed for an alliance. More and more decorations followed. In July the French fleet was enthusiastically welcomed in Kronstadt and the Tsar stood bare-headed while the revolutionary 'Marseillaise' was played. On 27 August 1891 France pressed Russia into an exchange of letters in which it was agreed that the two states consult 'on all questions likely to upset the general peace'. Though not a formal alliance, it was a start. As the French Foreign Minister, Alexandre Ribot, remarked: 'The tree is planted.'[4] After much French pressure, the Tsar agreed in July 1892 to open discussions on a military convention.

General de Boisdeffre was dispatched to Russia to negotiate with the Chief of the Russian General Staff, General Obruchev. But difficulties remained. In the event of a war with the Triple Alliance, France wanted Russia to direct its forces principally against Germany, whereas Russia viewed Austria-Hungary as its principal adversary. A compromise was found and on 17 August 1892 the secret Franco-Russian military convention was signed. This defensive alliance was to have the same duration as the Triple Alliance. The main clauses stipulated that, if France were attacked by Germany, or by Italy supported by Germany, Russia would employ all its available forces to attack Germany. Likewise, if Russia was attacked by Germany, or by Austria supported by Germany, France would turn all its forces against Germany. A second clause stated that, should the forces of the Triple Alliance, or one of its members, mobilize, then France and Russia, at the first news of the event and without the necessity of prior concert, should mobilize their forces immediately and simultaneously and move them as close as possible to their frontiers. A third clause stated that the available forces to be employed against Germany on the part of France should be 1.3 million and on the part of Russia 700,000–800,000 men.

It took another eighteen months before the secret convention was ratified. France remained anxious about having to mobilize if Austria-Hungary mobilized against Russia without Germany, even though it was not obliged to go to war. But it was the Tsar who dragged his feet, having second thoughts about being allied to a state now going through the Panama scandal, in which leading politicians and even his ambassador were implicated. However, Germany provided the spur with its increased military spending and a renewed tariff against Russia. Alexander III approved the agreement on 27 December 1893 and the French reciprocated on 4 January 1894.

The Franco-Russian Alliance, the existence of which was not made public until 1897 and the clauses of which remained so secret that few French ministers knew of their details until the First World War, ended the Bismarckian system of alliances on which German hegemony of Europe depended. Above all, the Alliance put over 20 years of isolation behind France. It was to be the central pillar of French security up to the First World War.

The Alliance made Russia the counterweight to Germany and in the event of war with France would force Germany to fight on two fronts to its east and west. The Dual Alliance was reinforced and reshaped in two stages between August 1899 and 1901. It was extended to cover preserving peace and the balance of power in Europe and in July 1900 was even extended to cover the contingency of war with Britain. France's Foreign Minister, Delcassé, was motivated by the desire to check eventual German claims to the lion's share of the declining Austro-Hungarian Empire when, as everyone expected, it broke up. Delcassé's fear was that this would not only allow Germany to dominate the continent from the North Sea and the Baltic to the Alps and the Adriatic, but also provide it with an outlet to the Mediterranean, where he believed that France should be a leading power.

Throughout the period up to the First World War France attempted to improve Russia's military capability and speed up its mobilization times. The French calculated that Russia's enormous military potential could be realized only by massive investment to modernize its armed forces, and equipment and by extending its railways westwards to speed up mobilization. Enormous French investment and loans continued to pour into Russia as relations with Germany deteriorated after the First and Second Moroccan crises. Of course, Russia often disappointed France, militarily and diplomatically. In the Russo-Japanese War of 1904–5 Russia was defeated and its fleet humiliatingly sunk at Tsushima, undermining its credibility as a great power and as an ally to France. In the French stand-off with Germany at Agadir in 1911 Russia afforded its ally little diplomatic support, which Saint Petersburg saw as repaying Paris for its lack of support during the 1908–9 Austro-Russian Bosnian Crisis. Nevertheless, in July 1912 a Franco-Russian military convention between General Staffs defined the modalities for closer navy and army cooperation and set targets for a reduction in Russian mobilization times. A further loan was granted to extend Russia's railway network up to its Western Front. However, although under Raymond Poincaré as Premier and Foreign Minister in 1912, and then as President of the Republic from 1913, every effort was made to tighten up the Franco-Russian Alliance, he insisted that Russia should not be allowed to drag France into a conflict in which it had no interest. In the 1914 July Crisis France was careful to ensure that its Russian ally did not jump the gun and precipitate war. But nor was France willing to abandon its ally in the face of German threats. In the end, it did not do so and the Alliance became operational. Having declared war on Russia on 1 August, two days later Germany declared war on France for not withdrawing support for its ally. France was at war alongside Russia, accompanied by Britain from 4

August. The Dual Alliance had stood a diplomatic showdown; it would not stand the test of war.

Wartime alliance

Geopolitics brought France and Russia together in peacetime, geography would prise them apart in war. It was precisely because the two great powers were on opposing sides of Germany that they were of value to each other. But in a coalition war, being separated by more than half of Europe made it extremely difficult to coordinate military strategy, let alone share armaments and munitions. Furthermore, although they had an apparently large lead in army strengths at the outset of war, clever German use of reservists in the front-line fighting and reckless Franco-Russian offensives in autumn 1914 reduced this advantage. Nor were France and Russia well placed in terms of industrial strength needed for a lengthy war of attrition. It was only thanks to British, and later US, industrial and financial might that they had any chance of beating the Central Powers. By the end of 1915 the growing Russian army was, however, no match for the tactically and logistically superior Germans. Russia suffered a series of devastating blows and was driven out of Lithuania, Poland and Galicia. Only when the Germans reduced their pressure on the Eastern Front to concentrate on bleeding the French to death at Verdun in 1916 were the Russians able to mount what would be their last great offensive under General Brusilov against the dis-organized Habsburg army. In such cases the Alliance came into its own, forcing the Germans to keep up an unsustainable momentum on two fronts, rightly calculated to be their weakness since the Alliance's inception. Germany eventually realized with the replacement of Falkenhayn by Hindenburg and Ludendorf in August 1916 that they had to switch to a defensive stance on the Western Front and transfer troops to the east to pursue victory. The Russians and the French had taken the brunt of the fighting in the first two years and by 1917 the strain was beginning to show. The French army was severely weakened, as the Nivelle offensives showed, while trained Russian manpower was increasingly expended, with 3.6 million casualties and 1.2 million prisoners by the end of 1916, not to mention being hamstrung by increasingly poor logistics. Russia was further weakened by its geographical exposure along hundreds of miles of border to repeated German attacks and a general strategic isolation that often left it bereft of military and economic aid from its allies. Even when it set about producing more from its own war industries, its inadequate transport system, divided political leadership, and minuscule and inefficient bureaucracy blunted the effort. The tsarist regime hastened its demise by printing ever more paper to pay for the war, thereby fuelling inflation, which, added to the inadequate food supplies, triggered strike after strike. The defeat of the

Kerensky offensive in July 1917 together with unrest in the cities accelerated internal revolution and a merciless civil war. The Bolsheviks' internal victory in November 1917 eventually led them to acknowledge external defeat by the Treaty of Brest-Litovsk in March 1918. The Dual Alliance was broken, ending Franco-Russian cooperation for many years to come.

The inter-war years

Poincaré, France's President until 1920 and subsequently Premier and Foreign Minister for much of the 1920s, deeply regretted the demise of the Franco-Russian Alliance. It had given France security before the First World War and had averted a French defeat in 1914 by heroic efforts on the Eastern Front. The Bolshevik Revolution and the Soviet Union's pariah status in the international system was a severe blow to France, which had lost its counterweight to a still unbowed Germany. Outstanding Russian debts and tsarist bonds owed to France, which the Bolsheviks had repudiated in 1918, did not help things.

One of the most serious blows to France was the rapprochement between Russia and Germany. Given the German government's own sense of marginality on the international scene, it was less scrupulous in wishing to deal with Russia. In 1920 Soviet–German trade relations began to develop and in 1922 Germany concluded the Rapallo Treaty with Soviet Russia. The German government hated Versailles more than it feared communism. As with the 1939 Nazi–Soviet pact, the German government saw Russia as a necessary evil to counterbalance France and Britain. France was the most vociferous in denouncing the secret agreement, which gave its enemy an ally. By 1924 the Herriot government, along with the British, recognized the USSR diplomatically. In February 1925 a Franco-Soviet conference opened in Paris to examine the debts question. Even though Britain broke off diplomatic relations with Moscow in May 1927 over the Zinoviev letter, France entertained a limited improvement of political and economic relations with the USSR. Nevertheless, in domestic politics an anti-communist witchhunt was underway, which targeted the French Communist Party and raised the question of Soviet infiltration. 'Communism is the enemy,' proclaimed Interior Minister Albert Sarraut. Other French officials took a more long-term view, believing that a Franco-Soviet rapprochement would enhance future French security against Germany. In the end, Franco-Russian negotiations came to nothing, blighted by the question of the reimbursement of 1.2 million French bondholders, Soviet debt to France and the anti-communism of 1927.[5] The French turned down the offer of a Franco-Soviet non-aggression pact, repeated in 1930. This was despite the Soviet Union having signed the 15-nation Briand–Kellogg Pact of August 1928 outlawing war, which had improved Soviet relations with Western powers. For the moment the Soviet Union's attraction as a potential ally was outweighed by greater ideological fears about the nature of the regime. This was in the era of Locarno, when the German menace appeared to have abated. Things would change after Hitler came to power in 1933.

The thawing of Franco-Soviet relations was underway with the appointment of France's first ambassador to the Soviet state in 1932, quickly followed by a Franco-Soviet non-aggression pact in November 1932. In February 1934 Louis Barthou became Foreign Minister in the Doumergue government and proposed a series of League-sponsored regional and bilateral pacts to bolster French security. A Franco-Soviet alliance loomed. Barthou was reinforced in his aim by Hitler's call in March for an increase in Germany's military budget and an army of 300,000. Charles de Gaulle reckoned that 'we do not have the means to refuse Russian support, whatever distaste we may have for their regime'.[6] However, as attractive as the anti-fascist colossus of Eastern Europe might appear militarily with its enormous reservoir of men, French ideological suspicion of Moscow had not evaporated, especially within the military. More importantly, from a strategic point of view the Soviet Union and Germany had not shared a common land frontier since 1919, making it geographically difficult for the former to afford France military assistance in the event of conflict. Others doubted Soviet capabilities after Stalin's political purges were extended to the Red Army High Command in 1937 and calculated that if support were forthcoming it would arrive too late. Worse still, on 9 October 1934 the Franco-Russian Alliance's champion, Barthou, was assassinated in Marseilles, allegedly by a Croatian terrorist who had targeted the King of Yugoslavia at Marseilles during a state visit.

His successor Pierre Laval pursued the Franco-Russian axis diplomatically. This resulted in the more wide-ranging commitments of the mutual assistance pact of 2 May 1935, which was to come into operation should either party be the subject of threat or aggression. But this arrangement fell well short of the Franco-Russian Alliance of 1891–93. There were those such as the Air Minister in the June 1936 Popular Front government, Pierre Cot, who continued to insist that it should be converted into a full-scale military alliance. Cot attempted to convert the military chiefs to embark upon staff talks and joint planning with the Red Army. He believed that the Soviet Union's military might could be melded with that of France's East–Central European associates to form an 'Eastern Front' to block Hitler's designs for *Lebensraum*. In early 1937 the Popular Front leader Léon Blum began overtures to the Soviet Union for staff talks. But French military leaders remained divided, while France's East–Central allies maintained a deep distrust of the Soviet Union. French anxiety saw Stalin seeking greater cooperation with Paris in order to force France into confrontation with Germany, which would exhaust the fascist and capitalist powers and leave the Soviet Union arbiter of Europe. The French were beginning to regret their commitments in Eastern and Central Europe and the value of the Franco-Soviet Pact, particularly after Munich. Nevertheless, the Polish and Soviet agreements were maintained and even reaffirmed on 29 January 1939 as diplomatic deterrents. Appeasement was at its height as French and British leaders still hoped against hope that war could still be postponed or averted. But with Hitler's Prague coup of 15 March 1939 French policy was revitalized. Franco-British guarantees were showered on Eastern Europe and the Balkans and in mid-April France and Britain opened negotiations with Moscow for a mutual assistance treaty in which France took the lead in the face of British dilatoriness. But at the beginning of August French and British ministers were still haggling over travel arrangements for the military missions requested by the Russians. This left time for Hitler and Stalin to conclude the Nazi–Soviet Pact of 23 August 1939. With Russia's benevolent neutrality in the pocket, Hitler was freed from the traditional German nightmare of a two-front war.

The French were devastated, but they had not been unaware of the possibility of a rapprochement between the apparent polar opposites of fascism and communism. In 1936 they had heard from the British of illicit training in armoured warfare being given to panzer officers in the Soviet Union before Hitler's announcement of German rearmament in 1935. Their own Deuxième bureau had indicated Germany's urgent need for access to the plentiful raw materials of the Soviet Union and Stalin's need for manufactured goods. But they had not known of the serious political German–Soviet talks underway from mid-July, although the Americans were aware of them. The French had assumed, albeit after much hesitation and division, that an alliance with the Soviet Union would deter Hitler. It was too late. War seemed inevitable. Things were so different from 1914, when France had had the Russian steamroller on its side. 'Never in its history would France enter a war in such initially unfavourable conditions,' declared the head of French intelligence.[7] The value of the Russian ally was sorely underlined.

Post-war

Pressure on Germany from the Red Army after Hitler's attack on the Soviet Union in June 1941 – a stroke that assisted the powerful French Communist Party in resisting Vichy – revived for Resistance and Free French leaders the prospects of France regaining its 'traditional' counterweight to Germany in the east. This policy reversion was underlined by de Gaulle on 7 May 1944 in Tunis:

> Once the enemy has been routed, the French want to be a centre for direct and practical cooperation in the West and in the East, that is to say first of all to be a permanent ally of dear and powerful Russia.[8]

He explained in his war memoirs that Franco-Russian solidarity 'conformed to the natural order of things, as much in relation to the German danger as to Anglo-Saxon attempts at hegemony'.[9] On 2 December 1944 as head of the Provisional Government of the French Republic de Gaulle was invited to Moscow. He rejected Churchill's offer of a three-power treaty linking Russia, Britain and France, stating that, 'in relation to the German danger, Russia and France should contract a special agreement amongst themselves, because they were the most directly and immediately threatened'.[10] This led to a treaty with the USSR on 10 December 1944. On 21 December, talking of 'the philosophy of the Franco-Russian alliance', de Gaulle remarked: 'This pact is the sign by which Russia and France demonstrate their desire for close cooperation in all measures leading to the status of tomorrow's Europe.'[11]

De Gaulle's remarks marked a change in the value of the Russian alliance for France in the post-war world. It was intended to act not only as the traditional bulwark against the German threat, but also as a political counter-balance to 'Anglo-Saxon' power in Europe and the world. However, with General de Gaulle's disappearance from the political scene in France from 1946 and the onset of the cold war, the attraction of the Soviet Union diminished. Nevertheless, following Stalin's death in March 1953, détente seemed to occur in international relations. The Korean armistice was signed in July. The previous month for the first time Rassemblement du Peuple Français (RPF) Gaullist MPs were included in a Fourth Republic government. In a press conference on 12 November 1953 de Gaulle denounced the idea of a European Defence Community, referred to the Atlantic Alliance as an American protectorate and reminded his audience that France was still an ally of the Soviet Union and that Paris should seek 'an arrangement' with Moscow. De Gaulle like Moscow preferred a disarmed and divided Germany. De Gaulle also seemed to fear that Germany might be tempted to draw closer to the Soviet Union to regain its unity. The nightmare of a Germano-Soviet pact reared its head. But the Fourth Republic governments did not subscribe to such Gaullist views and were happy to go along with the Anglo-American position. Neither de Gaulle nor Moscow was happy with the Federal Republic of Germany's entry to the North Atlantic Alliance on 5 May 1955. Two days later the Soviet Union denounced the Franco-Soviet Pact. A week later it had established the Warsaw Pact with its East European satellites as a counter to NATO and called on East Germany to join it on 27 January 1956. The crystallization of the two blocs had hardened. However, in signing up to the North Atlantic Treaty and the Brussels Pact, the Federal Republic of Germany had committed itself 'never to use force to obtain the reunification of Germany'.[12] A negotiated reunification automatically assumed agreement by the two power-brokers in Europe, the

USA and the Soviet Union. For France, who feared reunification the most, this meant staying on good terms with both superpowers.

On returning to power in 1958, de Gaulle resurrected his policy of improving relations with the Soviet Union. As part of his bid to promote French glory and independence on the international scene, he invited the Soviet leader Nikita Krushchev to visit France in 1960. Although he was able to postpone the planned visit to the spring to follow the explosion of France's first nuclear test, things went no further. Of course, improved relations with Moscow did not mean that France dropped its guard against the Soviet Union militarily. On the contrary, development of France's nuclear arsenal was accelerated. Although the Soviet Union was never a designated target in any official defence documents, French nuclear strategy was predicated on the eventuality of having to riposte to a Soviet attack.

De Gaulle's attitude to European integration from the early post-war years to the 1960s was also predicated on the need to work more closely with the Soviet Union and was encapsulated in his reference to a Europe stretching from the Atlantic to Russia's Ural Mountains. His views on international relations were steeped in the perceptions of the balance of power prevalent before 1914. At the heart of his preoccupations remained the German question and the belief that Russia needed to be part of the European system to counter the power of Germany. This was most clear in the immediate post-war years, when it was still acceptable to speak of the German problem more openly. On 29 March 1949 he explained that, once Europe had been made on the basis of an agreement between France and the German states, 'we will be able to try, once and for all, to build a whole Europe with Russia too, should it change regimes'. At a press conference on 29 July 1963 he stated:

> France . . . has believed for a long time that the day may come when a real détente and even a sincere entente will allow relations between East and West in Europe to be completely changed, and it expects, if that day comes . . . to make constructive proposals concerning peace, the balance and the destiny of Europe.[13]

This would be François Mitterrand's view at the end of the cold war on the eve of German reunification.

From 1963 de Gaulle saw a rapprochement with Eastern Europe as part of his policy of French disengagement from NATO. It also coincided with his disappointment at Berlin's attitude, which, despite the Franco-German Treaty of the same year, was perceived as too committed to NATO and too pro-American. On the fortieth anniversary of the establishment of Franco-Soviet diplomatic relations in October 1924 a Franco-Russian commercial treaty was signed. At the same time de Gaulle and the Soviet head of state Nikolai Podgorny exchanged messages of cordiality. De Gaulle told his Soviet counterpart in typical sibylline manner: 'Despite the accidents of history, our two nations are deeply linked by a lasting friendship, by the conviction of sharing a certain common heritage and by a mutual and cordial interest.'[14] As always the German question was not far from de Gaulle's mind. In a press conference on 4 February 1965 he stated: 'the German problem is *par excellence* the European problem.' He explained that for France everything came down to three interlinked questions: 'Ensure that henceforth Germany be an element of progress and peace; under those conditions, help towards its reunification; take the path and choose the structure to get there.' A permanent solution to the German problem had to include all the European peoples. 'What needs to be done can only be done one day by agreement and concerted action of the peoples who have always been, who are and who will remain principally concerned by the outcome of their German neighbour, in short the European peoples.'[15] In that equation de Gaulle included the Russians, but excluded the Americans. Statements along these lines were repeated throughout 1965.

However, de Gaulle believed that it was necessary first to prove to the USSR that France was serious about disengaging from NATO. This was done by the press conference of 9 September 1965, in which he intimated that France would leave NATO by 1969. He then considered it important to show the USSR that it was in its interests to liberalize the regimes in Eastern Europe and to end the uncertain status of Germany by a joint declaration with France on the new status for Germany. From April to October 1965 relations with the Soviet Union were tightened considerably with an official visit to Paris from 26 to 30 April of the Soviet Foreign Minister, Andrei Gromyko, and the return visit of his opposite number Couve de Murville to Moscow from 28 October to 2 November 1965. It was also necessary to prepare French opinion for this change in French foreign policy. This explains de Gaulle's many declarations about reducing the Soviet threat, the renewal of Franco–Russian friendship and the development of relations with the East European countries. Thus he declared in words worthy of Delcassé that 'France shares . . . with Russia, over and above passing regimes, many natural affinities and many common interests.'[16]

Master of the theatrical and the symbolic, de Gaulle timed his visit to Moscow in June 1966 to coincide with France's withdrawal from NATO's integrated command structure. De Gaulle, who had had no meeting with an American president since Kennedy had come to Paris in 1961, now travelled to the Soviet Union to meet the Soviet leaders. The French President's Kremlin speech on 21 June confirmed his plan for a new European order overseen by Paris and Moscow. He called for more than peaceful coexistence but 'new relations aimed at détente, entente and collaboration' and stressed the need for disintegration of the two blocs based on the Atlantic and Warsaw pacts. Insisting again that the definitive settlement of Germany's status and the security of the European continent were a European problem, he added that, 'until the whole of Europe comes round to consulting, everything commits France and the Soviet Union to agree to it between themselves straight away'.[17]

The Franco-Russian alliance of the nineteenth century seemed on the point of resurrection. Agreement was reached on a common Franco-Soviet declaration for regular meetings on European and other international issues of common interest and a hotline was established to link the Kremlin to the Elysée. The treaty seemed almost a *réplique* to the 1963 Franco-German Treaty. Though not a formal treaty, it had the aura of a non-aggression pact.[18] Once again, in French eyes at least, France and Russia had come together as custodians of the European balance of power as the most interested parties in European security and the German 'question'.

De Gaulle's successor as President, Georges Pompidou, continued to entertain good relations with Moscow. In 1970 and 1971 Pompidou visited Moscow and Soviet leader Leonid Brezhnev went to Paris. After another visit by Pompidou to Moscow from 11 to 12 January 1973, a *communiqué* was issued reiterating Franco-Soviet friendship. Despite the Soviet Union continuing in military terms to appear France's potential enemy during the cold war, Paris was always reluctant to jeopardize their formal friendship. This could occasionally leave France out on a limb with other Western powers. Following the Soviet invasion of Afghanistan in December 1979 during Giscard d'Estaing's presidency, France was initially unwilling to condemn Moscow for this violation of Afghan sovereignty and reluctant to agree to any Western collective denunciation. The French ambassador was the only Western diplomat to attend the traditional Soviet 1 May parade in Red Square the following year. Indeed, a *communiqué* was published on 19 May explaining that informal discussions had taken place between the French President and Soviet leaders Brezhnev and Edward Gierek on the international situation and how to reduce present tension. France also decided, unlike other Western nations, not to boycott the August 1980 Moscow Olympic Games. In 1981, on the question of the prospect of a Soviet invasion of Poland to repress the unofficial Solidarity trade union struggling to have trade-union rights recognized, both Giscard d'Estaing and his successor François Mitterrand were ambivalent about expressing any view that might displease the Soviet Union.[19]

Ironically, the presence of communist ministers in the Mauroy government after Mitterrand's election to the presidency in 1981 would force the President to adopt a more objective position in relation to Moscow for fear of being seen as too pro-communist. Nevertheless, on 2 October 1985 France was the first state to receive the new Soviet leader Mikhail Gorbachev, with Mitterrand stating in Gaullist fashion that Franco-Russian relations were important 'for the search for the necessary balances in Europe and the world'. In 1986, in his book *Réflexions sur la politique extérieure de la*

France, Mitterrand stated in words reminiscent of Delcassé and de Gaulle: 'Our interests bring us together more often than one thinks. Russia has always represented in our history a useful counterweight, either at the European level, or at the global level . . . Russia feels in her bones what we feel.'[20]

In 1989, as soon as it was clear that German reunification was on the agenda, France approached the Soviet Union. In December 1989 Mitterrand visited Gorbachev in Kiev to discuss the reunification question and declared that French and Soviet views were broadly in line. Only later, when it became clear that Gorbachev was willing to give Russia's blessing to German reunification, in part because the USA supported it, would France move rapidly towards further European integration as a means of tackling the German question. Nevertheless, in the period from 1989 to 1991 Mitterrand, again in line with de Gaulle's positions about the German question being a European problem, repeatedly suggested that German reunification needed to take place through what he referred to as a 'European Confederation'. By this he meant through the institutions of the 1975 Helsinki Agreements for Cooperation and Security in Europe, which included Russia and which restricted European border alterations. When France was overtaken by the speed of the reunification process, it reverted to further European Community integration.

France's loyalty to its Russian friend was also in evidence as the former Soviet Union began to crumble with the ending of the cold war. Aware that complete collapse of the creaking Soviet economy could have dire conse-quences, Mitterrand pressed hard for a structure that would allow substantial funds to be channelled into Russia. At a special European Community Council of Ministers' meeting in Paris in mid-November 1989, Mitterrand pressed hard for the creation of a European Bank of Reconstruction and Development (EBRD). The bank was in place in record time by spring 1990. The French hoped that this would ensure that the Commonwealth of Independent States, and especially Russia, would obtain the necessary finance to remain afloat. As the British Prime Minister Margaret Thatcher explained: 'President Mitterrand and I finally put together a deal in 1990: I agreed that his protégé Jacques Attali would be the EBRD President and he agreed that the bank would be situated in London.'[21] Attali, Mitterrand's confidant and special adviser at the Elysée since 1981 and initiator of the EBRD project, was put in charge. The degree to which the French saw control of the EBRD as important was demonstrated by their insistence, following Attali's resignation in June 1993 after revelations about his profligacy, that his successor should remain French.

The twentieth century ended, as had the nineteenth, with France looking to the old *Franco-Russe* to provide the security guarantees against a powerful Germany in the heart of Europe. Similar to a century before, Russia's efficacy as a counterweight called for substantial loans. From one end of the twentieth century to the other, Russia remained of vital geo-strategic importance for France.

Notes

1 Quoted in Anne Hogenhuis-Seliverstoff, *Une alliance franco-russe: La France, la Russie et l'Europe au tournant du siècle dernier* (Brussels, Bruylant, 1997), p. i.
2 Quoted in Andrew, *Delcassé*, p. 13.
3 Girault, *Diplomatie européenne*, pp. 122–6.
4 P. Renouvin, *Histoire des relations internationales*, vol. VI, *1871–1914* (Paris, Armand Colin, 1955), p. 12.
5 M. J. Carley and R. K. Debo, 'Always in Need of Credit: The USSR and Franco-German Economic Co-operation, 1926–1929', *French Historical Studies*, 20/3 (summer 1997), pp. 315–56.
6 Quoted in Doise and Vaïsse, *Diplomatie et outil militaire*, p. 369.
7 Quoted in Adamthwaite, *Grandeur and Decline*, p. 223.
8 Carmoy, *Les Politiques étrangères*, pp. 14–15.
9 Charles de Gaulle, *Mémoires de guerre* (Paris, Plon, paperback edn., 1959), III, p. 54.
10 Carmoy, *Les Politiques étrangères*, p. 15.
11 Carmoy, *Les Politiques étrangères*, p. 18.
12 Carmoy, *Les Politiques étrangères*, pp. 66–7.
13 Quoted in Carmoy, *Les Politiques étrangères*, p. 354.
14 Quoted in Maurice Vaïsse, *La Grandeur: Politique étrangère du général de Gaulle, 1958–1969* (Paris, Fayard, 1998), p. 418.
15 Quoted in Carmoy, *Les Politiques étrangères*, p. 364.
16 Quoted in Carmoy, *Les Politiques étrangères*, pp. 366–8.
17 Quoted in Carmoy, *Les Politiques étrangères*, pp. 384–5.
18 Carmoy, *Les Politiques étrangères*, pp. 386–7.
19 Grosser, *Affaires extérieures*, pp. 284–7.
20 Quoted in Georges-Henri Soutou, 'La France et les bouleversements en Europe, 1989–1991, ou le poids de l'idéologie', paper given at the Franco-British Council conference, Royaumont (Sept. 1991), typescript, p. 4.
21 Margaret Thatcher, *The Downing Street Years* (London, Harper/Collins, 1993), p. 759.

8
Empire

France is a nation for whom imperial policy seemed both natural and justifiable. The universalist principles of the French Revolution implied that France had discovered Humanity's Holy Grail in the Rights of Man. Her altruistic purpose was therefore to bring the fruits of that discovery to all nations. The 'civilizing mission' was born.

Colonies had been a part of France's power base since the *ancien régime*. Under the Bourbons, from the 1690s to 1789, the territories of France's first colonial empire in the West Indies, Canada and India were continually fought over in a global struggle with Britain. This contest for naval, commercial and colonial supremacy was renewed in the Revolutionary and Napoleonic wars. By 1815 France was vanquished overseas, as she was in Europe. But her Empire, albeit reduced, was not lost completely. A second imperial expansion occurred in the late nineteenth century, prefigured by French seizure of Algeria in 1830. However, after France's crushing 1871 defeat by Germany, interest in empire was resuscitated, although not always sanctioned by governments in Paris. This brought about the acquisition of Tunisia (1881), the north of Indochina (1879–85) and Madagascar (1896). Writing in 1874, Paul Leroy-Beaulieu urged more overseas expansion, warning that without a big empire France's awful fate would be to fall below the rank of Spain or Portugal. In the 20 years from 1880 to 1900 the French Empire expanded tenfold in surface area and population to become the second largest colonial empire in the world after Britain's. Exuberant contemporaries proclaimed that what Rome had achieved in three centuries France had built in two decades.

Motivation for empire

Colonial expansion was no longer motivated by the desire to protect Catholic missionaries, as it had been. Yet even under the secular Third Republic protection for French religious orders abroad was rekindled when competing states' missionaries moved into an area, particularly British

Protestant missionaries. As in Britain, empire was the 'great game', providing outdoor activity for frustrated or ambitious civil servants and military personnel in search of adventure. However, until the last decade of the nineteenth century French public interest in colonial expansion was best summed up by Jules Ferry in 1889: 'All that interests the French public about the Empire is the belly dance.'[1] An expanding group of politicians, civil servants, writers, military and militants of colonial expansion intended to change that. Profiting from the notorious weakness of Third Republican governments and their indifference to foreign affairs, they became the inspirers and initiators of a series of grand designs, which dominated French expansion during the quarter century before the First World War. A measure of their success was their ability to get parliament to promote imperial expansion. The 'Colonial Group' of the Chamber began life in 1892 and quickly expanded to an inter-parliamentary group of some 90 to 100 members, which became known as the 'Parti Colonial'. It fostered imperialism despite this not always being official policy. However, the notion of 'party' belied its diffuse and undisciplined nature. Two-thirds of the group was from the left, and no particular interest group dominated other than that of the colonial cause.

Economic reasons were the most readily deployed to justify colonial expansion to public opinion and parliament. By the early 1880s the era of international free trade was drawing to a close. Economic protectionism took over, as many European states experienced what economists dubbed the 'Great Depression' from 1873 to 1896. Competition to secure raw materials and overseas markets increased. The scramble for Africa by the European powers was underway. In France, the leading exponent of colonial expansion Professor Paul Leroy-Beaulieu underlined in his influential book *On Colonial Expansion by Modern Peoples* (1874) the importance of colonies for commerce, industry, employment and the consumer in the mother country. In 1890 the colonialist, Premier and member of the republican governments from 1879 to 1885, Jules Ferry, put things more starkly: 'Colonial policy is the daughter of industrial policy.'[2] Protectionist legislation like the 1892 'Méline Tariff' encouraged French colonies to trade exclusively with the national market. However, there is little evidence to suggest that colonial expansion was undertaken for economic or financial reasons in the early stages. Despite heavy capital surpluses, most French financial institutions and private investors sought higher returns by investing in more developed economies. Indeed, one of the problems confronting the French Empire was under-investment, as exhortations to invest in the colonies by politicians such as Ferry revealed. Whereas 45 per cent of British foreign investment followed the flag before the First World War, the French Empire took only 9 per cent of French overseas investment and accounted for only 10 per cent of French external trade, even if a number of individual companies did extremely well.[3] However, in a major reassessment Jacques Marseille contested the basis on which the calculations for imperial investment were made and came up with a figure three times greater, roughly equivalent to sums invested in Russia.[4]

Whereas an expanding population in the Great Depression of the 1870s and 1880s encouraged many Britons to emigrate to the colonies, this was not the case with France. A stagnating population, a very low population density and relative wealth ensured that the French did not emigrate in significant numbers. The British white dominions peopled by millions of British emigrants gave the British people a sense of kith and kin with empire. The French did not have this. On the eve of the First World War the French overseas empire contained only 855,000 French people, of whom over 600,000 were in Algeria. Empire was not yet an integral part of Frenchness in the way that the British Empire was of Englishness.

Some hoped that empire could offer France the manpower it lacked most, soldiers. Napoleon III proclaimed: 'The most useful products Africa can supply to France are soldiers.' In 1857 the first battalion of *tirailleurs sénégalais* was formed and distinguished itself in the Franco-Prussian War. But successive Republican governments did not pursue this successfully in peacetime, despite Colonel Mangin's influential 1910 book *La Force noire*. In August 1914 only 30,000 *tirailleurs sénégalais* and 35,000 Algerians were under arms, whereas for Britain India was in Lord Salisbury's words 'an English barrack in the Oriental Seas', with a quarter of a million Indians under arms by that date.[5] Nevertheless, between 1914 and 1918 the colonies' contribution to the French war effort was substantial, supplying 500,000 troops and 200,000 industrial workers. Divisions were raised from across the Empire, most to fight in the mud and human slaughter of Flanders and Verdun.

Strong motivation for empire did come through France's belief in its universalist values. To be true to its destiny France must 'spread, wherever it is able, its language, its culture, its arms, and its genius'. Belief in its 'civilizing mission' bringing to all humanity the benefits of France's higher state of civilization was most easily justified in relation to more 'primitive' nations. On 28 July 1885 Jules Ferry declared: 'The superior races have a right vis-à-vis the inferior races ... because they have a responsibility, the responsibility to civilize the inferior races.'[6] Most European imperial powers claimed such rights, but the French model was different. It was, in French eyes, above all altruistic and uplifting, as a 1904 textbook for primary schoolteachers explained:

> Our patriotism is very different from that of other neighbouring countries, which seems founded on national pride, on ideas of territorial aggrandisement, on a notion of material grandeur that is debatable and precarious: their patriotism has something of the aggressive, the narrow and the mediocre.

By contrast, French patriotism was based on the 'moral superiority of its foreign policy', because the French ideal was a 'moral ideal of respect for others'. The widely used Lavisse *Histoire de France* primary school textbook explained: 'France is benevolent and generous to the peoples it has subjugated.'[7] The French believed that whereas other nations exploited their colonies France elevated them to a higher plane of civilization. The French model called for the colonized to be 'assimilated' into the French way of life. Theoretically, at least, because French civilization's values were universal, natives fortunate enough to find themselves under French rule were potential French citizens destined for full integration into French civilization irrespective of colour, creed or culture. Whereas Britons doubted that foreigners could ever learn British ways and therefore propounded the doctrine of 'self-government', the logical outcome of French colonization had to be French citizenship, the higher stage of civilization. This inexorable logic made decolonization more difficult than for Britain, as independence from France was *ipso facto* a retrograde step. By the First World War 'assimilation' had given way to a more flexible concept of 'association', in which cooperation between ruler and ruled was based on a degree of respect for native customs, beliefs and social structures, although they were to continue to receive the benefits of the French civilizing mission. Nevertheless, tensions between protagonists of the assimilationist and associationist models continued until decolonization was all but complete in 1962.

One of the strongest motivations for French colonization was political. The promoters of this imperial policy were mainly centrist republicans from Gambetta to Delcassé and Poincaré. After the humiliation of the Franco-Prussian War and the loss of Alsace-Lorraine, colonization became a compensation for apparent loss of great power status, a chance to rediscover greatness by other means. As Gambetta wrote to Ferry after the occupation of Tunisia in 1881: 'My dear friend . . . I thank you from the bottom of my heart . . . France is becoming a great power again.'[8] Other nationalists believed that, on the contrary, France should not be diverted by imperial adventure, but should concentrate on regaining Alsace and Lorraine and *revanche*. The ultra-nationalist Déroulède castigated Ferry in parliament: 'I have lost two sisters and you offer me twenty chambermaids!'[9] Bismarck certainly wished to encourage French imperial expansion as a distraction from *revanche*. Others saw in colonial expansion a social Darwinian means of ending political and social decadence; imperialism was a struggle for survival, which would restore France to great power status.

The vogue for exotic literature and adventure, or that which reinforced notions of racial hierarchy, also stimulated metropolitan interest in empire. The novels of Pierre Loti and Alphonse Daudet made the Empire into a familiar setting, whilst Jules Verne's best-selling hero, Captain Nemo, was the very stuff of colonial exploration. Tough, resourceful, adventurous, he drew upon science and technology to triumph over alien environments. Fiction and reality were mutually stimulated. Between 1871 and 1881 11 geographical societies were founded in France and two in Algeria with a membership of 9500.[10] Meetings, conferences and publications added momentum to colonial expansion among sections of the educated elite. Life imitated art.

Coordination of French imperial policy suffered from being shared and squabbled over by several bureaucracies. The Colonial Ministry, established in 1894 and from 1910 situated in the rue Oudinot, vied with the Quai d'Orsay and the Navy Ministry, which oversaw the administration of certain colonies. Competing interests and a plethora of colonial lobby groups from the Comité de l'Asie française to the Comité du Maroc often conspired to make colonial policy and administration a bear garden of intrigue and confusion for Republican governments, allowing colonial militants in the 'Parti Colonial' to pursue a forward policy. The French Empire was not the result of systematic imperial policy; it was more by accident than design.

The final phase

The 1919 peace treaties enlarged the Empire. The acquisition of Syria, the Lebanon and parts of Germany's former West African colonies, Togo and the rest of the Cameroons, marked the climax of French imperial expansion and was welcomed as an apparent enhancement of France's great power status. Most scholars believe that until the First World War France's Empire made a net economic and financial loss, whatever its prestige and strategic value. Between the wars, however, French trade and investments with the overseas territories markedly increased. By 1939–40, according to Jacques Marseille, the Empire was taking 50 per cent of French foreign investment and serious economic exploitation of the colonies was under way. The share of French total foreign trade increased substantially to 26.9 per cent of French imports and 27.2 per cent of French exports in 1938. Propaganda and promotion of the Empire by French governments matched economic activity. The colonial contribution to the war effort helped seal the bond between metropolitan France and the Empire. Empire had taken on a tangible form and post-war governments capitalized on it. The continuing development of a collective colonial consciousness was epitomized by the conversion of the Socialist party (Section française de l'internationale ouvrière (SFIO)) to the colonial cause. The SFIO leader Léon Blum revealed in 1924 how universalist ideals, patriotism and racial superiority could be, perhaps with unconscious hypocrisy, fused together in the colonial mission:

> We are too imbued with love of our country to disavow the expansion of French thought and civilization . . . We recognize the right and even the duty of superior races to draw unto them those who have not arrived at the same level of culture.[11]

The only remaining political opposition to colonialism came from the newly formed Communist Party, which represented only a small percentage of votes at this time. The colonial exhibitions of 1922 in Marseilles and 1931 in Paris drew millions of metropolitan visitors (eight million in the latter case) for whom overseas France had hitherto been an unknown quantity. The 1931 exhibition was a lavish, grandiose and spectacular marketing exercise. The image presented was a seductive one of a 'Greater France' with its 100 million inhabitants. Ethnically diverse the Empire might be, but it was politically unified under French guidance. However, this image of coherence, of grand imperial design and of the nation united behind the colonial mission was largely retrospective. According to Martin Evans, 'popular imperialism was something that happened *after* the scramble for colonies: the interest was in the defence of empire rather than its acquisition.'[12] Unlike the pre-First World War phase of expansion, now there was 'a colonial conscience', somewhat equating to Britain's. Dissidence there might be from communists and the Surrealist movement, but the official importance placed on empire percolated down through education, entertainment and the media to the average French person. Colonial figures, like Marshal Hubert Lyautey, the pioneer of colonial expansion in Morocco, became popular heroes for schoolchildren and adults alike.

Responsibility for the administration of the Empire was not straight-forward. The jewel in the French imperial crown was, of course, Algeria. Its status as an integral part of France, comprising three *départements* with MPs sitting in the Paris National Assembly, meant that the Interior Ministry administered it, like other parts of metropolitan France. The Foreign Ministry ran the North African protectorates of Morocco and Tunisia. The Colonial Ministry administered France's remaining colonial possessions, comprising Madagascar, Indochina, the French West Indies and the Pacific dependencies. The federation of French West Africa, founded in 1895 with its capital in Saint Louis in Senegal until 1902 then Dakar, linked Dahomey, Guinea, the Ivory Coast, Mauritania, Niger, Senegal and Upper Volta. French Equatorial Africa, founded in 1910, had its centre in Brazzaville and brought together the territories of Chad, the French Congo, Gabon and Oubangui-Chari. Finally, there were the mandates acquired from Germany, Togo and the Cameroons and those attributed to France by the League of Nations – Syria and Lebanon. The political and administrative division of responsibility for empire would be a source of problems.

As the threat of war increased with the rise of Nazi Germany, the Empire came to be presented even more positively in official circles. The French Empire became a source of comfort, hope and salvation, because, theoretically, it transformed a demographically enfeebled population of 42 million into an impressive 100 million colossus, towering above Germany's 60 million. This made colonial reform difficult even for enlightened administrations such as the 1936 Popular Front government. The proposed extension of voting rights to 25,000 Algerians was subsumed by the prospect of confrontation with fascism. In 1937 the Popular Front government even dissolved the leading party of Algerian nationalism, the North African Star, depicting it as analogous to the fascist leagues for the way it was undermining the Republic. By the late 1930s Algeria and the Empire had become an essential pillar of French security. Articles appeared in influential journals extolling the Empire's strategic value. 'Imperial policy will save France', boasted *Le Grand Echo* newspaper on 20 January 1939. However, a new-found love of empire in the 1920s and 1930s had not been translated into major investment in imperial defence, the Dakar and Mers-el-Kébir naval bases excepted. Indeed, the colonies were as much a defence liability as a strategic asset. They might have offered resources in time of war, but they required protecting. Defending the Empire as a whole proved beyond French capabilities in 1939–45. The combination of Nazi Germany, fascist Italy and Imperial Japan was too strong and too widespread. North Africa provided military reinforcements, but France had failed to develop military-industrial facilities in North Africa against the eventuality of defeat in Europe. North Africa was unable to act as the final redoubt for the French government in the face of the invading German armies. Vichy could do no more than guard the unoccupied status of North Africa after the 1940 armistice. As for Indochina, cut off from metropolitan assistance, it had to bow to Japanese will, becoming completely occupied by Japan in March 1945.

During the Second World War both Vichy and the Free French coveted the Empire. The Empire did not declare unanimously for Vichy or Free France. Most overseas territories were loyal to Pétain. For Vichy in 1940 and 1941, desperate to find a place in Hitler's New Order, imperial possessions were vital bargaining counters. In sub-Saharan Africa there was support in the summer of 1940 for de Gaulle. The New Hebrides, French Oceania, the five cities of French India and New Caledonia also rallied to his cause. For Free France, desperate to establish its legitimacy in the eyes of the French and the Allies, the Empire became central to Gaullist myth-making and ideology. By November 1942 the Empire had largely fallen under Free French control and subsequently made a crucial contribution to the war effort, supplying troops, financial and material resources as well as military bases. Free French troops based in Chad and the French Congo eventually swelled into the French corps that fought in Italy in 1943–44 and the Free French 1st Army under General de Lattre de Tassigny in France in 1944–45. By June 1942 de Gaulle was underlining the importance of the Empire, past and future: 'There is one element which, in these terrible trials, has shown the nation that it is essential to its future and necessary for its greatness. That element is the empire.'[13] Even before the war had ended the Empire loomed large as a pillar of post-war France. In January 1944 de Gaulle convened a conference at Brazzaville in French Equatorial Africa bringing together colonial governors and officials, though significantly not nationalist leaders, to consider the Empire's future role. It was also intended as a signal to the anti-colonial Americans that the French Empire was a united bloc where French authority would be unchallenged. Independence was emphatically denied. In the words of Marc Michel: 'The Empire was a vital element in the restoration of national prestige, just as it had been after 1870.'[14] In 1945 Gaston Monnerville, deputy for French Guyana and pre-war Under-Secretary of State for the Colonies, was appointed head of a commission to draft a new constitutional status for the overseas territories. Echoing Jules Ferry, he told the French National Assembly that the Empire had guaranteed France's status as a victor; without it it would be merely another liberated country.

Decolonization

In the immediate post-war years, France had very little to convince the international community that it was still a great power. However, in French eyes the Empire represented a material sign of greatness, still the second largest in the world. Consequently, they clung to it for more than it was worth. Just as the humiliation of defeat in 1870 motivated a scramble for empire, so the trauma of 1940 imposed its retention. Nationalist independence movements, which raised their heads from 1945, were brutally repressed. Ironically, France was fighting against the very logic that had legitimized de Gaulle's Free French: resistance against an army of occupation. Indigenous populations quickly lost hope that their part in the liberation of France would be matched by their own early liberation. In Algeria independence demonstrations on 8 May 1945 were violently repressed, resulting in anything up to 45,000 deaths. Three weeks later in Syria a general strike was countered by French shelling of Damascus for three days. A French bombardment of Haiphong in Indochina on 23 November 1946 was how the French military attempted to snuff out the nationalist movement. The March 1947 Madagascar uprising met with a fierce response. With the help of extra troops the insurgents were eventually isolated then starved into submission by December 1948 with the loss of 89,000 lives.[15] It was clear that empire would be retained at any cost. French commanders, still smarting from the humiliation of 1940, set their faces against further 'retreats and defeats'.[16] The mystique of empire had reached its zenith; it was soon to meet its nemesis.

At a political level, the problem was that none of the parties could conceive of independence and were unable to take on board the historical novelty of decolonization. As Martin Evans points out, for the SFIO indigenous emancipation was to be achieved not by independence but through the development of even closer unity with a democratic and socialist France. Thus the new Republic, based on the anti-fascism of the Resistance, would be the vehicle for progressive values amongst indigenous populations as well as a safeguard against local feudal despotism. Logically then, the colonies could not liberate themselves. In Martin Evans's words: 'Freedom emanated outwards from the metropole and not vice versa.' The civilizing mission was alive and well. Even the PCF had shed its pre-1936 anti-colonialism and argued that it was in the colonies' interests to remain attached to a socialist France as a bulwark against American imperialism. The largest party in France with 25 per cent of the vote in 1945 and a place in government happily cited the example of the Russian Empire being transformed into a union of socialist republics. Unity and assimilation were the watchwords. Unanimous political commitment to the Empire called for a new bond between France and the colonies. This was translated into reality in the new 1946 Fourth Republic constitution, which spoke of a 'French Union'. This comprised two elements: first, the indivisible republic, made up of metropolitan France, Algeria and other overseas departments; second, the French union itself, consisting of associated territories and states.[17]

The ideological justification for empire was reinforced by an economic one. The improvement in commercial relations with the Empire, apparent in the inter-war years, grew dramatically after the war, so that until 1960 the Empire remained France's most important trading partner. The high point was reached in 1952, when the colonies accounted for 42 per cent of French exports. Investment followed a similar pattern, with the French state funding infrastructure improvements. Empire meant more to France in the 1950s politically, economically and emotionally than it ever had before.

Yet there was growing opposition to French imperialism from within France and from within the Empire. Within France, because the political parties were unable to come to terms with the new idea of decolonization, anti-colonialism took a moral and intellectual form. With many of its roots in the struggle of Resistance leaders, it manifested itself in the press through new publications such as *France-Observateur* founded in 1950, *L'Express* in 1953 and in Catholic intellectual circles. But these intellectual movements took time to influence politics. Further military defeats would be needed before their hour would come. Within the Empire anti-colonialism fuelled the independence movements, which, far from having been extinguished by French repression, were increasingly determined.

Imperial tunnel vision had high opportunity costs. Unlike the pragmatic British, France stubbornly opposed decolonization and what it saw as another loss of face. Consequently, the enormous amounts of energy expended on retaining the Empire denied France the possibility of providing foreign policy leadership in Western Europe, of playing a full part in meeting the Soviet threat after 1949 and of upgrading its armaments and military doctrine. Worst of all, a fixation on empire blinded France to the strength and determination of opposition to its imperial rule.

The wars of French decolonization began in Indochina. From December 1946 France was at war with the Vietminh forces led by the revolutionary Ho-Chi-Minh. With the French preferring to fight rather than negotiate, the war increased in intensity. Although only professional soldiers were involved, the French were unused to the new guerrilla tactics of the Vietminh and were outmanœuvred. In a set-piece battle in the valley of Dien Bien Phu in May 1954, French forces were surrounded and defeated. Again France experienced humiliation and a blow to its national prestige. French public opinion's reaction ensured that Indochina was abandoned; to have continued would have meant weakening France still further, with the risk of losing the rest of the French Empire. Two months later France had withdrawn its forces and on 21 July ceded independence at the Geneva conference. Of the 12,000 French troops captured over 7000 would not return. Of those who did, several hundred French officers had learnt the hard way the meaning of dogged resistance, 'brain washing' and the potency of psychological warfare. In their eyes they had also experienced the ingratitude of the Republic. As their commander General Henri Navarre put it in 1956: 'It is from Geneva and not Dien Bien Phu that dates the humbling of France. It is the politicians and not the soldiers who should be held to account.'[18] The experience of that defeat ensured that the Republic died a little at Dien Bien Phu. Approximately 20,000 French soldiers, as well as 11,000 Legionnnaires, 15,000 Africans and 45,000 Indochinese died fighting the Viet Minh; the total death toll for both sides rose to between 400,000 and 500,000.[19] The army could not countenance another defeat. When imperial crisis resurfaced much closer to home in Algeria, in November 1954, the army responded with ruthless countermeasures partly learned in Indochina.

The defeat at Dien Bien Phu was a source of encouragement to other nationalist forces in other parts of the French Empire. Rebellions occurred in Morocco and Tunisia, but this time the enlightened Premier, Pierre Mendès-France, preferred to negotiate, which led to independence for both countries in 1956. Mendès-France was following the winds of change, not opposing them. Decolonization was an international phenomenon that came upon the post-war world rapidly and determinedly. Meeting at the Bandung conference of April 1955 in Indonesia, the newly independent nations of Africa and Asia established a rationale for decolonization that was more real than the logic that underpinned the French imperial model posited on the French civilizing mission. Linking the racism of Nazism with the racism of colonialism, it appealed to elements of a Western public, which had struggled against Hitler. The French were losing the intellectual battle against the unstoppable dynamic of decolonization. When their imperial reforms were introduced, they were too little too late. In June 1956 the Defferre law (named after the Minister for Overseas France) extended suffrage to all men and women in the Empire. It also allowed local assemblies greater powers and to vote on local budgets, thereby whetting the appetites of nationalists. When de Gaulle returned to power in May 1958, on the back of the revolt by settlers and the army in Algeria opposed to a 'sell-out', it was with a new concept for the relationship with the Empire, that of 'Community' to replace the old 'French Union'. This was a far more flexible and permissive arrangement, which even allowed for the possibility of leaving the 'Community'. It was accepted by most African nations in a referendum in September 1958 and was built into the Fifth Republic's constitution. But nationalists, especially in Black Africa, wanted more self-government and even independence. The Community had a short life. Between September 1958 and 1961 all African states, including Madagascar, acceded to complete independence, though most signed economic and defence cooperation agreements with France. Decolonization in sub-Saharan Africa occurred without a major crisis. Only in Madagascar in 1947 did tragedy strike when riots led to the death of 140 settlers, 1000 natives and brutal French repression calculated to have caused some 11,000 deaths. By 1960, the year France tested its first atomic bomb, de Gaulle understood that world rank was measured less in terms of square kilometres of empire than in mega-tonnage of nuclear weapons' yield.

Not everybody in France or the Empire agreed with de Gaulle's strategy of divestment of empire. In Algeria, in particular, opposition was virulent. The situation there was made worse by the fact that Algeria was not a colony but three departments of France, represented in the French parliament, with a million settlers living alongside nine million natives. Powerful elements within the French state were insistent about hanging on to this part of the Empire whatever the cost. Most determined and threatening of all was the French army, which refused to bow to another defeat. Fearful that the Fourth Republic's politicians would buckle again in the face of yet another colonial rebellion, the army was adamant that it had to win against the Algerian National Liberation Front, which had taken up the armed struggle from November 1954. Borrowing from tactics first experienced in Indochina, by 1957 the army, bolstered by reservists and totalling 350,000 men, was fighting a dirty war. In that 'savage war of peace' no holds were barred, not even that of toppling the Fourth Republic itself. When the military discovered that de Gaulle had 'betrayed' them by negotiating with the nationalists, they staged a military coup in April 1961. When that failed, rebel French officers and civilians went underground to form the Secret Army Organization (OAS) to lead a terror campaign in Algeria and metropolitan France, including numerous assassination attempts against de Gaulle himself. This polarized French and Muslim opinion still further, so that, when independence was finally granted on 3 July 1962 following the Evian

Accords, there was an immediate exodus of some one million *pieds noirs* settlers to France.

De Gaulle and decolonization had triumphed. The *pieds noirs* 'now became embarrassing untidy reminders of outdated colonial values'.[20] The Algerian War, the 'war with no name', uncommemorated and unacknowledged, became a taboo subject for the Gaullist regime. The war had caused enormous losses on both sides. Between 1954 and 1962 some two million French soldiers served in Algeria, most of them conscripts. In 1962 Paris admitted that 12,000 soldiers on the French side (9000 French, 1200 Foreign Legionnaires and 1250 Muslims) had been killed, as well as 2500 other sympathizers. French authorities put the Algerian death toll at 227,000 soldiers and 20,000 civilians. More recent statistics have put the combined dead at about half a million.[21] The scars have still not fully healed.

Post-colonialism

The French Empire mutated rather than disappeared. After decolonization there was a continuation of empire by other means. France spent much political and economic effort maintaining informal influence in the footprint of her old empire. Some of that was an insidious influence fostered by informal personal contacts through notoriously powerful figures such as de Gaulle's man in Africa, Jacques Foccart. He built a network of spies, informers and friends through which he ran African policy, bypassing the Quai d'Orsay. The first generation of African leaders preferred personal relationships to treaties and diplomatic links. Foccart encouraged them to see de Gaulle as a loving father, with the African Presidents as children who still needed guidance, 'Papa de Gaulle's children' in the words of *The Economist*. He became the African leaders' protector and kingmaker, deciding when France should intervene to prop up an ally and when it should allow a coup to remove a recalcitrant ruler. Foccart was said to keep signed letters from African Presidents in his drawer requesting French intervention to which he only needed to add the date. He was so influential that successive administrations down to Jacques Chirac, with the possible exception of Giscard d'Estaing, were obliged to call on his services to broker certain sensitive deals until his death in 1997. Occasionally the puppet master got it wrong. In 1965 he allowed Jean Bedel Bokassa, a former sergeant in the French army, to overthrow David Dacko in the Central African Republic in 1965. After 14 years of barbaric misrule, Bokassa was replaced by Mr Dacko, flown back to Bangui with an escort of 700 French paratroopers and Bokassa was given asylum in France.[22] The true extent and pervasiveness of France's informal network in Africa is only just coming to light at the beginning of the twenty-first century, as France is forced to relinquish its African grip. The 'Elf scandal' of the late 1990s involving massive illicit payments to

Mitterrand's close confidant and Foreign Minister Roland Dumas, and apparently other African politicians, from the funds of the hitherto state-owned Elf-Gabon oil company, is only the tip of the iceberg and has the potential to be one of France's greatest political scandals. Dumas is under judicial investigation and was forced to resign as President of France's Constitutional Council in 1999. Should a trial take place, it could bring what is left of France's African house of cards to the floor.

Overall, a vague notion of French worldwide outreach, a loose 'French Commonwealth', was established, which rested partly on informal political links, partly on the franc as a common currency, partly on the persistence of French as the lingua franca. French influence was buttressed by educational and cultural links as well as a network of military training and basing agreements, which gave France a role as 'gendarme' in Africa until the 1990s. Known officially as 'la Francophonie' ('those nations having in common the use of French'), this French Commonwealth has been criticized by detractors as mere French neocolonialism. Critics have seen it as propping up subservient local elites and despots, particularly in Black Africa, in exchange for French aid and international support. For France it has emblazoned its continuing great power pretensions, by affording it international voter support in international bodies, by maintaining the illusion of the French language as the basis of a world culture, by providing access to export markets and more importantly raw materials of a strategic nature, such as uranium ore from Central Africa and Congo-Kinshasa, and finally by providing it with strategic military bases across the world.

Nevertheless the confetti remains of empire have continued to create problems. In the 1970s the Comoros Islands in the Indian Ocean, former French Somaliland (now Djibouti), and the New Hebrides (now Vanuatu) were almost reluctantly granted independence. In New Caledonia, in the Pacific, tension between Melanesian Kanaks and French settlers burst into violence in 1988 with a total of over 30 deaths. The government was forced into a referendum, which promised a further vote on independence in 10 years. President Jacques Chirac's decision in 1995 to restart nuclear weapons testing in Mururoa atoll in French Polynesia sparked international condemnation and was criticized as a throwback to colonialism, even if the local administration supported it for the revenues it generated.

By the 1980s France had only 10 overseas outposts. These *départements et territoires d'outre-mer* (*DOM-TOMs*) are home to 1.8 million French citizens and total 120,000 square kilometres. They are legally part of France and rely heavily on French public-service employment and the generous social welfare system. Despite this, small but vocal dissident groups intermittently call for independence in Guadeloupe, Réunion and French Polynesia, sometimes violently. France, of course, gains from these possessions. New Caledonia is a precious source of nickel ore, French Polynesia until 1997 a valuable nuclear testing site, French Guyane the launching site for the European (French-dominated) space rocket Ariane. Strategically France gains a sovereign and internationally recognized presence in the Caribbean, the Indian and Pacific oceans and Antarctica. Prime Minister Raymond Barre once commented: 'Whatever their cost, the *territoires d'outre-mer* assure us of a world dimension which is fundamental for us.'[23] Under the Law of the Sea conventions they give France monopolistic rights to maritime resources in an exclusive economic zone of 200 miles off their coastlines, giving France the third largest maritime area in the world. As in the colonial past, any discussion of independence sees such advantages weighed in the balance. Because France traded heavily with its colonies in the post-war era, it ensured that they were granted preferential tariffs under the European Community's Yaoundé (1964–75) and Lomé (1976) accords. Even today the balance of trade between France and its African trading partners is, in general, favourable to France. Financial links are even closer. French banks have a strong tradition of lending to African governments and private enterprises. Since France established the African franc (the CFA franc) in 1947, pegging local currencies to the French franc at the rate of one CFA to two French centimes, currency stability is officially dependent on the Paris financial market and Bank of France. This has survived decolonization with 14 former French possessions in the franc zone. But France is increasingly finding such financial responsibility burdensome. In January 1994 France halved the CFA in value, devaluing the currency of some 80 million people in francophone Africa, thereby illustrating its partial financial disengagement from sub-Saharan Africa in the 1990s.[24]

On the positive side, the legacy of empire is present in a more multicultural France from literature and music to food and film. More negatively, large numbers of former settlers have since the 1980s voted for the extreme right National Front and its leader Jean-Marie Le Pen, who himself fought in Indochina and Algeria. Polling between 10 and 15 per cent of the vote since 1984, its policy is overtly racist, particularly in relation to immigrants from France's former colonies. In many ways this ambivalent attitude to empire seems indicative of a France uncomfortably caught between a colonial past and a post-colonial future.

Notes

1 Quoted in Andrew and Kanya Forstner, *France Overseas*, p. 17.

2 Quoted in Tacel, *La France et le monde*, p. 22.

3 Andrew and Kanya Forstner, *France Overseas*, pp. 14–15.

4 Jacques Marseille, *Empire colonial et capitalisme français, histoire d'un divorce* (Paris, Albin Michel, 1984).

5 Quoted in Andrew and Kanya Forstner, *France Overseas*, p. 13.

6 Andrew and Kanya Forstner, *France Overseas*, p. 26.

7 Quoted in Dominique Maingueneau, *Les Livres d'école de la République 1870–1914 (discours et idéologie)* (Paris, Le Sycomore, 1979), pp. 189–90, 186.

8 Quoted in Andrew and Kanya Forstner, *France Overseas*, p. 25.

9 Quoted in. Gooch, *Franco-German Relations*, p. 21.

10 Martin Evans, 'From Colonialism to Post-Colonialism', in Martin S. Alexander (ed.), *French History since Napoleon* (London, Arnold, 1999), p. 397.

11 Quoted in Evans, 'From Colonialism to Post-Colonialism', p. 402.

12 Evans, 'From Colonialism to Post-Colonialism', p. 406.

13 Quoted in Evans, 'From Colonialism to Post-Colonialism', p. 408.

14 Marc Michel, 'Decolonization: French Attitudes and Policies, 1944–46', in P. Morris and S. Williams (eds), *France in the World* (London, Association for the Study of Modern and Contemporary France, 1985), p. 83.

15 Figures from Evans, 'From Colonialism to Post-Colonialism', pp. 408–9.

16 Maurice Vaïsse, *1961: Alger, le putsch* (Brussels, Editions Complexe, 1983), pp. 51–3.

17 Evans, 'From Colonialism to Post-Colonialism', p. 409.

18 Henri Navarre, *Agonie de l'Indochine (1953–1954)* (Paris, Plon, 1956), p. 315, quoted in Jean-Pierre Rioux, *La France de la Quatrième République*, vol. 2, *L'Expansion et l'impuissance 1952–1958* (Paris, Seuil, 1983), p. 39 n. 2.

19 Robert Aldrich, *Greater France: A History of French Overseas Expansion*, (London, Macmillan, 1996), p. 286.

20 Evans, 'From Colonialism to Post-Colonialism', p. 411.

21 Aldrich, *Greater France*, p. 297.

22 Obituary 'Jacques Foccart', *The Economist*, 29 Mar. 1997.

23 Quoted in Jacques Dalloz, *La France et le monde depuis 1945* (Paris, Armand Colin, 1993), p. 181.

24 Aldrich, *France Overseas*, pp. 307–11, 321–2.

9
The post-cold war era

The ending of the cold war and the reunification of Germany have forced France, more than most powers, to rethink its relations with the wider world. France had always been critical of the 1945 Yalta settlement, which it saw as instrumental in producing the geopolitical freeze of the cold war. In French eyes it was at Yalta, and in France's absence, that the decision to divide Europe into two *blocs* was taken. Paradoxically, however, the Yalta settlement benefited France in a number of ways.

Cold war cosiness

First, it allowed France to carve out a niche between the superpowers, which enhanced its role on the international scene. This was most obvious under the presidency of General de Gaulle, who championed many a Third World country or weak nation against the superpowers. Thus smoke and mirrors enabled a medium-sized power to appear to have the status of an independent operator on the world scene, something of considerable benefit to the maintenance of, among other things, a neocolonial empire. This enhanced France's great power pretensions by a device unavailable to Britain, given the international perception of the latter being in America's pocket.

Second, in pretending to be aloof from the two *blocs* and the cold war, France could have its cake and eat it. It benefited from the US nuclear umbrella, yet remained on relatively good terms with the Soviet Union, thereby satisfying one of its traditional foreign policy objectives of having a 'friend' in Germany's back.

Third, the division of Europe into two *blocs* was fortuitous for dividing its old enemy Germany, arguably the single most important issue in French foreign policy since 1870. This satisfied a French war aim of 1918 and 1945: the dismembering of Germany. France achieved the long-standing objective of seeing its old enemy reduced to manageable proportions without the stigma of having brought it about itself. Not only did the cold war perpetuate that division; it also prolonged French military occupation rights in Germany.

Fourth, the cold war justified France's possession of nuclear weapons. The nuclear deterrent was seemingly held to defend the national 'sanctuary' against a Soviet attack, although the latter was never designated as a target in any of the five-year defence programme laws until the 1980s. Nuclear weapons acted as a badge of great power status as well as being an additional guarantee of security against Germany. Thus the cold war became the fig leaf for the ultimate defence against Germany, because, according to post-war treaties, Germany could never possess nuclear armaments, as Premier Pierre Mendès France pointedly told Cabinet in December 1954.

Fifth, the cold war indirectly justified France's other outward sign of greatness, a permanent seat on the United Nations Security Council. While the Soviet Union was the adversary of the Western powers, it was unlikely that those powers would give up their numerical superiority among the permanent members of the Security Council, or 'Big Five'. France's permanent seat on the Security Council, like Britain's, was therefore guaranteed for the cold war's duration. Moreover, with a divided and weakened Germany, there could be no serious challenge to France – or Britain – retaining their seats, despite their medium-power status and lesser economic influence than either Germany or Japan. Furthermore, Germany's divisions, its lack of self-confidence and reluctance to play an international role made the European Community a Franco-German club in which France remained the dominant partner, notably on international issues.

Germany

The ending of the cold war and unification of Germany in 1990 disturbed France's cosy position in the international system and brought old questions to the fore; prominent among them was the German question. The writer François Mauriac once quipped that he loved Germany so much that he was delighted there were two of them. Certainly, since the 1963 Franco-German friendship treaty, fear of Germany had been the fear that dare not speak its name. The embarrassed silence was broken in 1989. Admittedly, in the early 1970s France had been wary of Germany's *Ostpolitik*, designed to move towards reunification of the two Germanys. In 1978 François Mitterrand, then head of the French Socialist Party, remarked: 'Without ignoring what unification can represent politically and morally for the Germans, I shall stick to the rigorous criteria of the European balance, the security of France, the maintenance of peace: I think it is neither possible nor desirable.'[1] Given traditional French anxiety about German might, it was not surprising that six days after the fall of the Berlin Wall, French Foreign Minister Roland Dumas declared: 'We know that reunification is not a question for today.' In December 1989 President Mitterrand declared that, without being hostile to the idea, 'reunification is not on the agenda'.[2] The French ambassador to the

German Federal Republic remarked in undiplomatic fashion that the real fear of unification was that it 'would give birth to a Europe dominated by Germany, which no one, in the east or west, wants'.[3] The old demon of the German threat with its roots in the nineteenth century and in three wars was moving to centre stage. Thrown off balance by the prospect of unification, French policy was in a state of flux; old reflexes were displayed. France, together with Britain, and partly Russia, attempted to block German re-unification, at least until it could be secured on terms acceptable to Paris and London. They failed and France reverted to the old ploy of drawing Germany closer to restrict its freedom of manœuvre. As Raymond Aron once quipped, 'when the French don't trust the Germans they make them compatriots'.

According to Hubert Védrine, France's Foreign Minister in 2000, France 'reinvented' its foreign policy after the fall of the Berlin Wall.[4] Margaret Thatcher recounted how the immediate prospect and then the reality of German reunification was to 'fuel the desire of President Mitterrand and M. Delors for a federal Europe which would "bind in" the new Germany to a structure within which its preponderance would be checked'. In her words, 'the French were federalists on grounds of tactics rather than conviction'.[5]

When Helmut Kohl announced his plan for a vague federation between the two Germanys on 28 November 1989, he received a very negative reaction from France. At the European summit in Strasbourg on 9 December, Mitterrand insisted that reunification needed to take place democratically on the basis of the collective security principles inherent in the 1975 Helsinki agreements: 'It should take place in the context of European integration.'[6] Forced by the sheer momentum of events into accepting that German unification was inevitable, France insisted that it could only be contemplated in the context of further European integration. To secure the prize of re-unification, Kohl was ready to concede to Mitterrand's desire for a common foreign and security policy, first mooted in 1985, now to be integrated into what was to become the Maastricht Treaty. These compromises led to a letter from Kohl and Mitterrand to their European partners on 16 October 1991 setting out many of the Maastricht ideas. The French conceded to Germany's request that the Western European Union (WEU) develop closer links with NATO. In this way the WEU would become both the instrument of European Union defence and the European pillar of NATO. The French hoped that a 35,000-strong Franco-German army corps would be placed under WEU command to begin creating a European defence outside NATO. Only much later would the French accept that the Eurocorps be placed at the WEU's disposal and, when necessary, ready for NATO's operational use.[7]

French fears about proximity to a Greater Germany had never evaporated completely, even if rarely uttered in public. French anxiety about demo-graphic and economic inferiority re-emerged in popular circles. With the

Iron Curtain raised, the new united Germany rediscovered its traditional geopolitical position in the centre of Europe. A new Janus-like Germany facing east and west, with increased trading possibilities, greater political reach and influence unnerved Paris. Fears that Germany need no longer depend so exclusively on Western Europe, and France, chilled French policy-makers. The 'German problem' was again a topic for discussion and polemic. Germany's Gross National Product was referred to as being equivalent to France's and Britain's combined, while Germany's population was, as Clemenceau remarked after the Versailles settlement, 'still 20 million too many'. In 1990 the senior editor of the influential French weekly *L'Express* penned the book *France-Germany: The Return of Bismarck*. It referred to the years after 1945 as a 'historical reprieve' and hoped that this time Germany would not succumb to former 'megalomania'. He was stung most by the 'arrogant' remark of a former German Foreign Minister in the 1960s: 'When will the French stop travelling in first class with a second class ticket?'[8] Little did he know that in 1998 that German Foreign Minister would become Chancellor Gerhard Schröder, whom the French press dubbed Britain's not France's friend.

Anxiety did not disappear even after the initial shock of reunification. In a book published in 1996, Jean-Pierre Chevènement, Socialist Party parliamentary deputy for Belfort – an ancient fortified city bordering Germany – and Defence Minister from 1988 to 1991, warned that Europe's geopolitics had been overturned by German reunification. Referring to France's old counterbalance to German power, he warned that the situation was worsened by the Soviet Union's implosion. He calculated that the scenarios facing France were: 'A Europeanized Germany, a German Europe or an American new world order.' Chevènement quoted Mitterrand three years after reunification responding to the question: 'Isn't Germany going to regain its dominant influence in Central Europe?' with the words, 'It already has'.[9] Certainly, a more self-confident Germany no longer seemed embarrassed about intervening in the hitherto French reserved domain of European Community foreign policy to contradict the French position. The break-up of Yugoslavia from summer 1991 saw Germany championing the right of self-determination for Slovenes, Croats and Bosnians, to Mitterrand's public disapproval, while France supported the status quo. For Chevènement, a self-proclaimed opponent of the Maastricht Treaty, Maastricht was a way for Germany to dress up a return to power in European colours. 'What Germany could not obtain in two world wars – continental preponderance – it is on the point of acquiring by finance and in peace, in the name of a liberal and technocratic conception of Europe.'[10] Chevènement embarrassed the French authorities again in May 2000 when, as Interior Minister in the Socialist Jospin government, he stated in an interview that Germany had not overcome its Nazi past, prompting calls for his resignation despite his apology.

The old German problem had resurfaced. France had little alternative but to bind it closer through further European integration. Maastricht is how Mitterrand had attempted to emasculate Germany. But that risked allowing a more powerful Germany to dominate the European Union, as Chevènement and others on the Gaullist right, such as Charles Pasqua and Philippe Séguin, exclaimed during the run-up to Maastricht in 1992. The Central Committee of the French Communist Party also denounced 'this supranational Europe dominated by Germany'.[11] The dilemma was clearly reflected in the 20 September 1992 referendum results on Maastricht (coincidentally the two-hundredth anniversary of the defeat of invading Prussians by a French revolutionary army) with 51 per cent in favour and 49 per cent against. A year later a poll showed that, if the referendum were held again, 56 per cent would vote against Maastricht. Fear as to whether partnership with Germany meant French subservience resonated in the 1990s as it had a century before. This was demonstrated graphically in spring 1993 during international speculation against the franc, attributed to the German Bundesbank's refusal to lower interest rates in the name of a strong mark policy to defeat post-unification inflation. France claimed it was subsidizing reunification. Gaullist ex-minister François Guillaume's warnings resonated strongly with many opposed to the Maastricht Treaty when he claimed that Europe was succumbing to the 'American diktat' with 'German Europe rearing its head behind'.[12]

Personalities committed to the Franco-German partnership have always helped overcome difficulties between Paris and Bonn. This was true of de Gaulle and Adenauer, Giscard d'Estaing and Schmidt, Kohl and Mitterrand. Cracks were papered over by images of solidarity: Chancellor Helmut Kohl and President Mitterrand in 1985, arms linked, paying respects to the war dead of 1939–45, or the two men taking the salute of the Franco-German brigade as it participated in the 1995 Bastille Day (the first German troops to parade in Paris since Hitler's conquering armies in 1940). However, Mitterrand and Kohl marked the end of the war generation of political leaders in Paris and Bonn with personal memories of Franco-German conflict. The election of the Gaullist Jacques Chirac to the presidency in 1995, followed by the Socialist Lionel Jospin to the premiership in 1997, erased that personal experience of Franco-German conflict. The election of the Social Democrat and proclaimed Anglophile Gerhard Schröder to the chancellorship in 1998 provoked nervousness about Franco-German friendship. Chirac's speed in inviting the chancellor-elect to visit Paris in September 1998 spoke volumes about concerns over the future direction of Franco-German relations and the mutual need to demonstrate a cordial working relationship. But the French forced the pace and revealed old anxieties. French officials saw Schröder being tempted in three possible directions – turning Germany more in on itself; focusing foreign policy further to the east with EU enlargement; attempting to bring Britain more into a triangular partnership of the Big Three European nations. Any combination risked reducing France's weight in the European Union. The changeover in Bonn came at a time of stagnation in Franco-German relations. 'It has always been a marriage of reason not love', observed one official.[13] Differences range from political control over the Euro, attitudes to Nato and the emphasis on enlargement as well as increasingly sensitive topics such as reform of the Common Agricultural Policy and the size of Germany's EU budget contribution. Since then Lionel Jospin has stolen a march on Schröder by seeking to draw closer to Britain's Labour Prime Minister, Tony Blair, notably in joint initiatives on European defence cooperation. The old reflex of the Paris–London axis to counterbalance an unwieldy Germany lives on.

The Anglo-Saxons

In the post-cold war era France remains ambivalent towards the Anglo-Saxons. Following the disappearance of the Soviet threat French relations with the USA remain unclear. Gaullist rhetoric notwithstanding, France always called for an American presence on the European continent after the First and Second World Wars to bolster French security; reluctance characterized the American position. During the cold war France benefited from the protection of the American nuclear umbrella while professing anti-Americanism. It profited from a strong Western alliance without paying the full costs of Western discipline. Beneath the veneer of scepticism towards Washington's role on the European continent is an old French fear, present in many other European nations, that the USA will return to isolationism, or that its geopolitical interests will not always allow it to intervene on behalf of European interests. Consequently, France should organize its own security alone or collectively with other European powers. An article in the military and security review *Défense nationale* in 1993 pointed to the little noticed Canadian decision of 27 February 1992 to withdraw all its forces from Europe by 1995 signalling, in the view of the authors, a North American 'disengagement' from Europe. The article called for a Franco-British rapprochement proportionate to an American withdrawal from Europe, particularly in the nuclear weapons field.[14] However, France has not always found Britain a willing partner. Nevertheless, in the last decade of the twentieth century, London was prepared to work more closely with Paris on military cooperation in everything from joint armaments production to the development of rapid reaction forces, like the Franco-British 'air corps' based at Northwood outside London. With British support NATO made a further gesture to the French by working out ways of detaching NATO forces – 'separable but not separate', in the jargon – for possible Europe-only operations, notably in the Balkans, where NATO forces intervened in March

1999 to deny Serbian persecution of Albanians in the southern Yugoslav province of Kosovo. London and Paris have worked well together in these NATO Combined Joint Task Forces, allowing greater European roles in peacekeeping as well as strengthening the European pillar of NATO. Ever-closer cooperation was clearly demonstrated at the December 1998 Saint Malo summit, where Tony Blair and Lionel Jospin agreed to give the European Union a real defence policy. However, London continues to insist that increased Franco-British cooperation, and especially European defence cooperation, notably a European Rapid Reaction Force outlined in November 2000, cannot be at NATO's expense.

Despite France's closer cooperation with Washington since the end of the cold war, suspicion of American hegemonism has not disappeared. On the eve of the Gulf War France's socialist Defence Minister, Jean-Pierre Chevènement, remarked in the best Gaullist tradition that neither France's interests nor its geography coincided with America's. In his book *Le Pari sur l'intelligence*, published in 1985, Chevènement stated that, although American colonization was less disagreeable than a Soviet invasion, the latter was improbable whereas the former was happening every day. It was partly his opposition to France joining in the American-led operation *Desert Storm* to push Iraqi troops out of Kuwait in February 1990 in conformity with UN resolutions that led France to hesitate so long about joining in the operation. Paris preferred an embargo rather than war and an international conference on Middle Eastern affairs. When it eventually joined the allied forces, committing only 10,000 troops compared to Britain's 35,000 and America's 540,000, the Gulf War experience heightened its sensitivity to American power. It became acutely aware of its largely conscript army's unsuitability to fight an overseas high-tech war, the inferiority of its Mirage fighters (not fitted with night vision) and in particular its dependence on US satellite intelligence for virtually every aspect of the war. Perceived dependence on the Americans was a massive fillip to the French to develop their satellite intelligence at enormous cost.

In the post-cold war era France sees American hegemony increasing in all areas from economics and culture to military power. France can no longer play one superpower off against the other. Influential international relations commentators such as Professor Alain Joxe, brother of the former socialist Defence Minister, Pierre, charged the USA with dragging the West into a new bipolar conflict along an axis that is no longer East–West but North–South. France is described as perched on the fault line between the prosperous North and the impoverished South running along the southern Mediterranean rim, with the USA always able to withdraw into its safe North American haven.[15] Paris felt this to be so in 1993 during the Bosnian civil war, which opposed Serbs and Muslims. France was the largest contributor to the peacekeeping United Nations Protection Force. But, when

Paris called for US air and ground support to stop increasing aggression against Bosnian Muslims, Washington refused to commit ground forces. American public opinion was unwilling to countenance casualties in a far-off Balkan war. At the beginning of 1994 Franco-American tensions ran high. Although Washington finally agreed to limited NATO air strikes against Serb positions, Paris believed this proved that American protection could never be counted on.

Frustration with the USA was vented in early 1997, when President Jacques Chirac attacked the USA declaring: 'The United States has the pretension to want to direct everything, it wants to rule the whole world.'[16] In March 1997 in Gaullist vein Chirac embarked on a major tour of Washington's traditional sphere of influence, Latin America, accompanied by businessmen and bankers in a show of defiance to American commercial and political interests.

The old Gaullian belief that American support for Europe is unreliable and American withdrawal inevitable leaves Paris committed to a European defence that does not rely solely on an Anglo-Saxon-dominated NATO. Despite France reintegrating certain strategic NATO committees and participating more fully in NATO operations in the early 1990s, Paris still refused to reintegrate the Defence Planning Committee and the Nuclear Planning Group. But by 1995 it was using the prospect of full reintegration as leverage to effect change in NATO's organization and priorities. From 1995 to 1997 President Chirac attempted to reposition NATO's eastwards strategic focus southwards to satisfy French anxieties about risks from rogue states across the Mediterranean (the 'Club Mad'). In December 1995 Chirac set as conditions for reintegration that a European (read French) officer became commander of NATO's southern command forces (AFSOUTH) based in Naples and that a new equilibrium be established over duties and responsibilities between the USA and NATO-Europe. Optimism about a French return was demonstrated on 13 June 1996 after a North Atlantic Council meeting attended by the French Defence Minister. NATO's Secretary-General, Javier Solana, opened the press conference in French, unheard of for years. The final communiqué spoke of the rapprochement with France as 'a historic event'.[17] But the Clinton administration was reluctant to put AFSOUTH and the US Sixth Fleet in the Mediterranean under European command. Chirac prematurely declared in early September 1996 that the USA was ready to concede to French aspirations only to be contradicted by Clinton on 26 September 1996. Rejection cooled French enthusiasm for NATO and France returned to its rhetoric on American hegemonism. French support for US-led NATO enforcement of the 1995 Dayton peace agreement on Bosnia weakened. Traditional reluctance to support US policy positions out of the NATO area returned, notably for the 1998 Israel–Palestine Wye Accords and UNSCOM enforcement in Iraq.

France's position vis-à-vis NATO was best summed up on 2 December 1997 by socialist French Defence Minister Alain Richard, who described France as being 'in, but not integrated'. France practises what *Le Monde* newspaper's defence correspondent called 'à la carte cooperation with NATO', with French officers participating in NATO Combined Joint Task Forces. But, as the former Chief of the French Defence Staff, General Douin, remarked in December 1997: 'France will not return to NATO like an errant school-boy to class.'[18]

In many ways the USA has become the scapegoat for France's difficulty in coming to terms with globalization at the beginning of the twenty-first century. Remarkable press and media consensus reigns over the evil of US-led 'ultra-liberalism'. In December 1999 a Roquefort cheese-waving sheep farmer José Bové, violently opposed to 'MacDomination' (a reference to the ubiquitous American hamburger chain), became a folk hero for taking his fight for *l'exception française* in agriculture to the 'Anglo-Saxon-dominated' World Trade Organization's meeting in Seattle. But French theory does not always square with practice, as the number of MacDonald restaurants in France continues to soar, with some 790 in 410 towns by 1998. By the end of the twentieth century even the European Union, hitherto seen as a bastion of French interests, was depicted as having sold out to Anglo-Saxon free-market tyranny in its attack on cherished French traditions such as the state monopoly on public services, huge farm subsidies and unpasteurized cheeses. Nevertheless, a malicious pride is taken in France's once sleepy state-owned monoliths matching the Anglo-Saxons at their own global game. New privatized French giants have emerged such as Total-Fina-Elf oil and Renault, which at the end of 1999 took a controlling share in Japan's second largest car producer Nissan, followed by a 70 per cent stake in South Korea's Samsung Motors. The globalizing drive of certain French multinationals is symptomatic of a new business self-confidence in certain circles. As Renault's chairman, the Swiss-born, ENA-educated, Louis Schweitzer remarked: 'The French are much less frightened of Anglo-Saxon manners, dominance, language or whatever than they were 10 years ago.'[19] This is the exception that proves the rule, although the private sector's willingness to adapt to the forces of globalization may be France's salvation.

The French language

The decline of the French language internationally – portrayed as a victim of hegemonic English – is seen by some as a metaphor for the decline of France in the world. Not surprisingly, a good deal of effort is put into attempting to stem the tide. In 1966 the Haut comité de la langue française was established to find new words to replace invading English terms. In 1984 an international francophone television station was set up, TV5, financed by

France, Quebec, Wallonia and Switzerland. In February 1986 President Mitterrand created the first Francophone summit in Paris with 42 delegations. In June 1988 the Rocard government established a Minister for Francophonie to organize and promote the French language in the world. French is an official language in Belgium, Luxembourg, Switzerland, Canada, Louisiana, Haiti and the former states of sub-Saharan Africa that were members of the French Union, as well as Zaïre and Madagascar. There are said to be in total some 120 million French-speakers in the world, yet in 1992 French was only the eleventh most spoken language. The teaching of French and cultural exchanges abroad are organized by the General Directorate for Cultural Scientific and Technical Affairs in the Foreign Ministry (absorbing about a third of the foreign affairs budget) and in the Education Ministry. The official vehicles for French language and culture abroad are the 10 or so French institutes, such as the Ecole française de Rome, and the 83 French *lycées*. There are also thousands of Catholic schools in numerous countries, and the old Third Republican organization created in 1902 the Mission laïque française with some 20 schools. Finally, there is the Alliance française, founded in 1883 and still going strong with its 1300 local committees based in most countries. Overall some 85,000 French *agents culturels* operate abroad, of whom 28,000 are civil servants. Official defenders of the French language subscribe to the credo that their mission is justified by the nature of the concepts of which the French language is the vehicle – liberty, justice, equality and fraternity encapsulated in the Rights of Man. France sees itself as the home and guardian of such values and official speeches never miss the opportunity of reiterating that glorious heritage dating from the French Revolution. Here is the justification for French universalist foreign policy and France's world role.[20] The threat from the English language is much more than just a linguistic struggle; it strikes at the heart of France's *raison d'être* in the world. France's Minister of Culture and *Francophonie* declared pointedly in 1994, as he prepared a bill to limit the use of English in France: 'the use of a language is not innocent. It becomes . . . an instrument of domination, an agent of uniformity . . . '. He went on to proclaim that the French must 'remain faithful to our culture and to the universality which is the thousand-year-old mission of France.'[21]

   In the 1980s legislation restricted the use of English in advertising. But this is little more than a finger in the dyke. French television was obliged to show 44 per cent of French films, but satellite stations have undermined this. The introduction in 1981 of private radio stations in France allowed American and British rock and popular songs to gain a strong foothold with French audiences. In January 1996 a law obliged radio stations to devote 40 per cent of their air time to French songs. Now the fear is of the virtual monopoly of English on the Internet. The struggle is as vain as it is prolonged. By 1997 the French were spending nearly $1 billion a year promoting French language and culture, despite (or because) Chinese, Arabic, Spanish, Portuguese – and of course – English being spoken more than French.

France's imperial idea, which once underpinned French claims to grandeur and world status, has been repackaged to emphasize defence of cultural particularisms, not retention of territory. Asserting French cultural specificity in the face of Americanization was one of the roles assigned to the Secretary-General of *la Francophonie*, the former UN Secretary-General, Boutros Boutros-Ghali, on this post's creation in 1997. When the seventh Francophone summit conference met in Hanoi that year, 46 countries (many of whom had only tenuous links with French, as in the case of Portuguese-speaking Sao Tomé) attended it. As in the nineteenth century the organizers claimed that English was the language of commerce, but French, they asserted, was the language of 'culture and fraternity'. But it is significant that France is moving from the maximalist position of striving to promote French as a world language, to the lesser position of claiming that French should be defended in the name of cultural particularisms. France has become the self-proclaimed champion of these values in bodies like the World Trade Organization. However, the retraction of French as an international language is perceived as eroding France's legitimacy to play a world role. With democracy's gradual triumph across the world from the nineteenth to the twentieth century the *raison d'être* of France's claim to being an international model has been eroded, along with Britain's and even the USA's. Since the end of the cold war, for the first time in world politics the number of democratic states has overtaken undemocratic ones; in 1993 of 187 states 107 were democratic. The French democratic model, like the British, has lost its exclusivity. In international eyes France is merely associated with the French language, no longer perceived as a world language, but increasingly a quaint and endangered species.

Despite the hostile rhetoric to the perceived Anglo-Saxon monolith, since the end of the cold war Franco-British relations with their annual summits have continued to improve, notwithstanding occasional differences such as the late 1990s 'beef crisis'. In October 1994 a joint military air command was planned to support international peacekeeping and humanitarian operations; four months earlier discussions focused on France and Britain sharing the burden of nuclear deterrence through joint ballistic missile submarine patrols. Economic relations are very close, as they have been since the nineteenth century. Britain continues to be France's second largest export market after Germany, while France is Britain's third largest market after the USA and Germany. Since 1997 defence relations have tightened further. Franco-British cooperation was crucial to military operations and peace making in the Bosnian and Kosovo crises. The French military programme bill for 1997–2002 spoke of a 'privileged partnership' with Britain. It also planned for Franco–British cooperation on armaments projects to rise from 2.5 per cent of total arms programmes in 1996 to 13.9 per cent in 2002. In 1998 Prime Minister Tony Blair called for a strong European foreign policy backed by a real 'defence capability'. This was music to French ears after London's opposition in the 1980s to Paris championing the WEU's revival.

In moments of strategic difficulty Paris and London still display the old reflex of drawing closer together. Both Mitterrand and Prime Minister Margaret Thatcher acted in concert to thwart German reunification. At two private meetings organized at Mitterrand's behest at the December 1989 Strasbourg summit, the two opponents of reunification discussed the lessons of Germany's role in European history. Mitterrand stressed that 'in history the Germans were a people in constant movement and flux', while Thatcher produced 'a map showing the various configurations of Germany in the past, which were not altogether reassuring about the future.' Mitterrand was critical of Chancellor Helmut Kohl's handling of events and stated 'that at moments of great danger in the past France has always established special relations with Britain and he felt such a time had come again'.[22] The British Prime Minister called for papers to be drawn up to strengthen Anglo-French cooperation. Meeting at the Elysée on 20 January 1990 Mitterrand was more pessimistic about the possibility of stopping reunification, though sharing Thatcher's worries about 'the Germans so-called "mission" in central Europe'. The decision for British and French defence ministers to concert more closely on reunification was overtaken by events. Margaret Thatcher explained that Mitterrand switched from wishing to block German reunification with Britain's help to tying Germany down with further European integration. As General de Gaulle's Prime Minister, Georges Pompidou, once declared, France 'by its geography and its history is forced to play the European card'.[23]

The Mediterranean

In the post-cold war era the Mediterranean has regained the geo-strategic importance it once held for France. Louis Blanc, the 1840s influential French socialist leader, called for France's civilizing mission to be extended to the North African peoples, and looked forward to the whole Mediterranean becoming a 'French lake'.[24] Half a century later, Delcassé underlined the Mediterranean's importance in French geopolitics. French security and the Mediterranean surfaced again during the inter-war period and again during the 1954–62 Algerian War. Then French security was thought to rest on a defence line along the axis Paris–Algiers–Brazzaville, encapsulated in General Salan's remark that the Mediterranean runs through the French Empire like the Seine through Paris. This conviction was not limited to the military or politicians of the right. The French National Assembly heard on

30 September 1957 how it was necessary to tell 'the allies, who have not quite understood – perhaps because they have not been made to understand – that the Mediterranean, and no longer the Rhine, is the true axis of our security and thus of our foreign policy'.[25] These words spoken by France's former Justice Minister, François Mitterrand, were similar to post-cold war debates about rethinking French geo-strategic priorities. Until the cold war's end, it had been overlooked that France was still a prominent Mediterranean power with a neocolonial empire along the 1957 axis. In the mid-1980s France's African ex-colonies still swallowed most of the overseas-aid budget; the 14 countries in sub-Saharan Africa grouped into the Communauté financière africaine (CFA) took 54.5 per cent and North Africa 12.4 per cent. France's trade patterns continue to reflect flows established in the Empire's heyday.

With the disappearance of the immediate threat from the east, a new threat loomed to the south across the Mediterranean. The scenarios painted were of economic or political 'boat people' fleeing poverty and oppression or, in the light of the Gulf War, a direct armed attack on a southern French city like Marseilles from a hostile southern Mediterranean power equipped with ballistic missile technology capable of delivering nuclear, chemical or biological weapons. Given the availability of such technology from parts of the former Soviet Union, China or North Korea and the fact that France's defences had been largely geared to an attack from the east, France refocused its strategic priorities southwards. The fear was first expressed by the extreme right Front National party, which in its 1993 legislative elections manifesto called for an anti-ballistic missile defence system to counter any attack from the south.[26] Continuing violent turmoil in Algeria from 1992 widened the fear of that state falling to Islamic fundamentalism and threatening French interests through direct attack, or more surreptitiously through sympathetic elements in the Algerian community in France as a base for terrorist attacks. An opinion poll commissioned by the French Defence Ministry in May–June 1991 had already shown that 58 per cent of interviewees believed that France's principal threat came from the south. The threat from regional hegemons from the south also prompted a significant shift in French policy on nuclear proliferation. In 1995 France finally signed up to the 1968 Nuclear Non-Proliferation Treaty and became one of its warmest supporters. In a Senate debate on 18 May 1993, the Gaullist Prime Minister Edouard Balladur stated that focus on Eastern Europe should not be to the detriment of France's Atlantic and Mediterranean interests. In the same debate Interior Minister Charles Pasqua remarked, 'Europe has three dimensions: Mediterranean, continental, Atlantic', and France was 'the only country in the Community to have been, and to be, an active player in all three'. He went on to stress that European construction was 'for the moment too continental'.[27] This recalled General de Gaulle's 1948 appeal for some

European framework to guarantee French security, because France's 'dignity' and 'duty' required that it be 'the centre and key' of a group of states 'having as its arteries the North Sea, the Rhine and the Mediterranean'.[28]

Perception of a threat from the southern Mediterranean was not restricted to the right. The left-wing socialist Defence Minister Jean-Pierre Chevènement resigned on 29 January 1991 on the grounds that the Gulf War was a war against an Arab nation and therefore a historical and geo-political error contrary to French interests. Certain Gaullists reiterated the General's pro-Arab diplomacy and the need for France to stay on good terms with its southern Mediterranean neighbours. Chevènement had long been a proponent of a New Deal for the Maghreb countries to maintain and develop allies in the region and avoid demographic expansion and extreme poverty fuelling Islamic fundamentalism. This strategy would avoid France becoming embroiled in a North–South struggle by basing its security on 'a diplomacy of development', which also fitted snugly into the age-old 'civi-lizing mission'. This strategy has been applied, except that France has used the European Union to develop a Euro-Mediterranean economic area. The 1992 Lisbon European Council stressed the Mediterranean's importance in the development of a Common Foreign and Security Policy. Alain Juppé, French Prime Minister from 1995 to 1997, cautioned the European Union: 'It is good of course to focus on the problems of eastern Europe, but we must not neglect what is happening on our southern frontiers.'[29] The November 1995 Barcelona conference established a partnership agreement between the Maghreb countries and the European Union aimed at encouraging peace, stability and prosperity in the region for security reasons. A more overtly military initiative was the 1994 maritime cooperation agreement between France, Italy and Spain to deal with a potential threat from the southern Mediterranean. With French pressure the southern Mediterranean is increasingly regarded as Europe's 'backyard'.

Since the end of the cold war the south has resumed its strategic importance as potentially a new front line resulting from a domino-like fall of regimes to Islamic fundamentalism along the southern Mediterranean rim and even sub-Saharan Africa. Africa has always been France's 'backyard' or *pré-carré*. Since the early 1960s France intervened some 20 times in Africa, usually after a technical invitation from the country concerned and using the justification of protecting European expatriates and property (or under the guise of UN peacekeeping or 'humanitarian interventions', as in the con-troversial deployments in Zaïre in 1991 and Rwanda in 1994). However, France has found this increasingly difficult to sustain alone. Until the early 1990s, France maintained some 8000 troops and 1200 military advisers around Africa, reaffirming its claim that francophone Africa remained within its sphere of external influence. However, in 1994 France ended its commit-ment to unconditional support for sub-Saharan African countries. In 1997 a

40 per cent reduction in French troop levels was announced, linked to President Chirac's decision to end conscription in favour of a smaller professional army by 2002. An attempt was made to put a brave face on this. Foreign Minister Hubert Védrine touchily denied that these cutbacks marked a 'retreat', insisting that France merely sought to move 'to a smaller, more flexible and more effective force'.[30] In October 1997 Védrine embarked on a whistle-stop tour of sub-Saharan Africa to explain France's new 'modernized' and 'adapted' African policy, underlining that links between francophone countries were 'indestructible'. What this meant in reality was that France was cutting its military cooperation budget in Africa by 4.9 per cent and moving to a position where it shared more of its traditional defence liabilities in Africa with Britain and the USA, but with the emphasis on Africans solving their own problems. To that end France offered to contribute a million dollars to establish a conflict prevention and resolution centre and a further $30 million to establish regional military academies and increase equipment stocks to enable African troops to carry out their own conflict resolution. Britain was to do the same thing for East Africa.[31] This apparent carving-up of the African continent into spheres of influence by former colonial powers was evidence of the desire to find a way of extricating themselves from military commitment to the continent.

Inability to act independently in Africa has forced France to collaborate. In March 1999 Foreign Minister Hubert Védrine and his British counterpart Robin Cook flew to Africa to open a Franco-British ambassadorial conference on the continent. Loss of French influence in sub-Saharan Africa has been eroded by the death of staunchly francophile and long-serving African leaders such as Presidents Houphouët-Boigny of the Ivory Coast and Jean Bedel Bokassa of the Central African Republic. The French economy has found it increasingly difficult to prop up the franc zone, as the 50 per cent devaluation of the CFA franc in January 1994 showed. The need to refocus France's strategic priorities southwards as part of collective action was demonstrated by its 1995 claim for NATO's southern flank (AFSOUTH) to be put under European or even French command.

Rethinking strategy, defence and identity

France, more than any other great power, has had to rethink its strategic priorities in the post-cold war era. During the cold war French defence was predicated on the idea of a major conflict close to metropolitan France with an emphasis on static national defence. Although France's first genuinely post-cold war reforms appeared in the 1992–4 *Loi militaire*, they were only limited adjustments. In September 1992 France's Defence Minister, Pierre Joxe, demanded a rethinking of France's nuclear deterrent hitherto based on massive retaliation. With the Gulf War and potential threats from regional hegemons in mind, he stated that France's nuclear strategy would need to cope with new threats 'other than those connected with massive deterrence, which has dominated until now' and he called for France to develop 'more flexible, lighter and more precise arms systems'.[32] Since the end of the cold war French defence contractors like MATRA revived research into a French neutron bomb likely to be of greater use against a small Mediterranean state than France's inflexible nuclear arsenal geared to massive retaliation. France was invited to participate in the American Global Protection against Limited Strikes programme, an offshoot of the Strategic Defence Initiative (Star Wars), intended to protect against a strike from a regional power. French military planners are conscious of France being within firing range of 'Club Mad' rogue states. There has been a switch of emphasis from massive deterrence based on the *faible au fort* (weak to the strong) to a more surgical one based on the *fort au fou* (the strong to the mad).

These ideas were taken further in the 1994 Defence White Paper and the 1996 military programme bill for the years 1997–2002. Overturning France's nuclear strategy since the 1960s, the National Assembly's Defence Commission produced a 150-page report setting the tone for the 1994 Defence White Paper. It demanded that France's

> nuclear arms must be conceived in such a way as to offer a range of actions intended to defend our fundamental interests, and no longer just our vital interests. Deterrence can no longer be limited to the deterrence of the weak against the strong and we must possess the capability for limited and very precise strikes.[33]

The 1997–2002 military programme bill overhauled France's defence posture since the Second World War and established new military priorities. These were, first, to professionalize the French army and do away with compulsory military service by 2002 to allow France greater flexibility and force projection in traditional roles of defence against aggression in Europe and the resolution of crises further afield with up to 50,000 troops. Second, to restructure France's defence capability by developing international and, especially, European partnerships in armament production (international cooperation agreements in general were set to rise from a mere 16 per cent to 34 per cent). The intention was also to restructure the national arms industry's 5000 firms and 200,000 employees and to reduce the state's role. Third, to reduce France's nuclear forces by closing the *plateau d'Albion* missile site and scrapping the Hades missiles by 1998 (reducing military nuclear expenditure from 31.4 per cent of the defence budget in 1990 to less than 20 per cent in 2002). This was intended to focus on more flexible air and sea capabilities, notably with four nuclear submarines with a second strike capability and by increasing the number of aircraft carriers by bringing into service the *Charles de Gaulle*. Fourth, to build a common defence policy for the European Union that will also reinforce the European pillar of the Atlantic Alliance. Most remarkable of all was the call for France's defence to be less self-reliant than ever before. France declared its willingness to give a more European dimension to its independent nuclear deterrent and talked of 'concerted deterrence'. The document also called for French defence to take account of new risks presented by certain regional powers, the pro-liferation of weapons of mass destruction, nationalist and terrorist move-ments, organized crime, drug and arms traffickers. To monitor such activities, and aware of French deficiencies in intelligence gathering during the Gulf War, the bill called for better intelligence through further development of the collaborative HELIOS and HORUS satellite programmes. The document clearly stated France's willingness to participate fully in reform of the Atlantic Alliance, implying that this was conditional on how much responsibility was given to the Europeans in any new Atlantic partnership.[34] However, erosion of France's post war great power attributes looks likely to continue. On 14 April 2000 the Russian parliament finally signed up to the second treaty of the Strategic Arms Reduction Talks (START-2) to reduce nuclear warheads in the USA and Russia from the START-1 ceiling of 6000 to 3500 by 2007. Britain and France have thus far avoided being included in the drive towards disarmament. However, the prospect of the US–Russian START-2 being rapidly followed by a START-3 deal will put pressure on the three smaller nuclear powers, Britain, France and China, to join in multilateral disarmament.[35] If so, one of the mainstays of France's claim to great power status, its ability to maintain an independent nuclear deterrent, may disappear.

The ending of the cold war wrought greater havoc with France as a world power than with any other. It was forced to relinquish a Gaullist conception of foreign policy and defence. It has 'denationalized' many aspects of defence and orientated French forces towards European and international roles. Its armed forces have at last been reduced, reorganized and professionalized. The Gaullist emphasis on the nation state, independence, the national sanctuary and intergovernmentalism is slipping from its world outlook. But France is still in a transitional phase. Many of the defence reforms will not be fully implemented until 2015. Thus far France has lost a reasonably privileged position and not yet found a new world role. Unsurprisingly, its first reaction to the ending of the cold war was to resort to old geo-strategic reflexes: the desire to block German reunification by summoning up past allies and counterweights – Britain and Russia. When that failed, Europe provided the solution. Few French people would disagree with Giscard d'Estaing's confession: 'It is in France's interest to drive the European organization.'[36] That was fine as long as it could do so. That it still can is no longer evident with a more self-confident Germany and a bigger community. France remains uncertain about its role in world affairs. It remains ambivalent about Europe, NATO, Germany, Britain and the USA. Some suggest it should learn to live more comfortably alongside the remaining superpower. Others suggest that fostering an independent Europe based on a French model is where its salvation lies. Professor Alain Joxe hopes that Europe will develop according to what he calls the 'French school', 'which wants the international order around France to be compatible with the survival of republican principles' based on the nation state, *jus solis* and *laique* citizenship, in the face of what he calls the 'German' school (based on small independent communities), and the 'American' school (a single imperial order). The French school 'spread across the world . . . like a call addressed as much and more to Voltaire, to Rousseau, to Victor Hugo and, now, to de Gaulle, as well as to living Frenchmen'. It is, he explains, the national Republican tradition on which the unity and success of the Third Republic was built and which today is common to left and right.[37] Certainly many of France's elite remain attached to the old universalist ideals of the eighteenth and nineteenth centuries. History is summoned to the rescue. The disorientation of the post-cold war era still sees France, at the beginning of the twenty-first century, looking back to the future.

A world role is linked to identity. At the beginning of the twenty-first century all nation states, particularly Western ones, are questioning their national identities. States with pretensions to an international identity and world role are having to do so more acutely. World powers had identities that the international community could recognize. Britain was a world empire promoting notions of self-government, free trade and the rule of law; the USA was the champion of liberal democracy and freedom; the Soviet Union was the mother of communist revolution; France was the foyer of the universalist values of the Rights of Man, the French language and culture. But today those personalities have disappeared, are contested or have withered.

Following his election victory in 1997 Prime Minister Tony Blair called on marketing experts to reinvent Britain's image in the world: 'Cool Britannia' was the pale outcome. But what does France represent to the international community in the era of globalization? It may be the third most important tourist destination in the world, receiving some 36 million visitors in 1986, but few would explain their motivation to visit the country as a desire to share grandiose French values. Is France any longer a world personality? Is it recognized as having a legitimate and distinct world role? Is it still a great power? In General de Gaulle's words, should it not continue to behave like a great power precisely because it no longer is one?

To a large extent since the Second World War France's world role has been 'performative', to use the terminology of cultural studies. France defined its great power status less by physical characteristics than by what it believed itself to be, and then acted out the role. The international community largely accepted the personality and performance France ascribed to itself on the world stage. Centred squarely on the nation state, France cultivated a French model based partly on what it believed it stood for, the Rights of Man and the French language, and partly on what it was not, the American model. With the ending of the cold war, the extension of globalization and the decline of the nation state, France is no longer clear what its role is and how it should perform it. It has begun to define itself most by what it is not, rejecting the American model and championing 'cultural particularisms'. It is conscious of being first and foremost a European nation, but is wary about blending its identity into a European model over which it has less and less control. How it resolves that question may decide whether it remains a world power.

Notes

1 Quoted in Soutou, 'France et bouleversements', p. 5.
2 Quoted in Soutou, 'France et bouleversements', p. 7.
3 Quoted in Alistair Cole, *François Mitterrand: A Study in Political Leadership* (2nd edn, London, Routledge, 1997), p. 152.
4 'France against the World', *Financial Times*, 25 July 2000.
5 Thatcher, *Downing Street*, pp. 759–60.
6 Quoted in Soutou, 'France et bouleversements', p. 7.
7 Georges-Henri Soutou, *L'Alliance incertaine: Les Rapports politico-stratégiques franco-allemands, 1954–1996* (Paris, Fayard, 1996), pp. 402–11.
8 Quoted in Valance, *France-Allemagne*, p. 147.
9 Quoted in Jean-Pierre Chevènement, *France-Allemagne: Parlons franc* (Paris, Plon, 1996), p. 36.
10 Quoted in Chevènement, *France-Allemagne*, pp. 38–9; for continuing evidence of these neuroses, see Joseph Rovan, *Bismarck, l'Allemagne et l'Europe Unie, 1898–1998–2098* (Paris, Editions Odile Jacob, 1998), esp. pp. 129–231; Pierre M. Gallois, *La France, sort-elle de l'Histoire? Superpuissances et déclin national* (Lausanne, L'Age d'Homme, 1998), esp. pp. 105–35, 137–58.
11 Quoted in Robert Gildea, *France since 1945* (Oxford, Oxford University Press, Opus paperback, 1997), p. 214.
12 'Guillaume repart a l'assaut', *Le Point*, 13–19 Mar. 1993, p. 5.
13 'French Embrace Schröder before he can Turn his Head', *Financial Times*, 30 Sept. 1998.
14 H. Coze and J. Puq, 'L'Avenir de la dissuasion nucléaire', *Défense nationale*, 50 (Feb. 1993), p. 18.
15 Alain Joxe, 'Autonomie stratégique de l'école française', in *Un Nouveau débat stratégique: Actes du colloque* (Paris, La Documentation française et le Ministère des affaires étrangères, 1993), p. 117.
16 Quoted in James Petras and Morris Morley, 'Contesting Hegemons: US–French Relations in the "New World Order"', *Review of International Studies*, 26 (2000), p. 66.
17 'OTAN: La France participera aux travaux de planification', *Le Monde*, 15 June 1996.

18 *Le Monde*, 5 Dec. 1997.
19 'The Unlikely Emperor', *Financial Times*, 29–30 Apr. 2000, p. 15.
20 Tacel, *France et le monde*, pp. 261–2.
21 Jacques Toubon, 'L'Esprit des langues', *Le Monde*, 24 Feb. 1994.
22 Thatcher, *Downing Street*, pp. 796, 798.
23 Quoted in Alfred Grosser, *Affaires extérieures: La Politique de la France 1944–1984* (Paris, Flammarion, 1984), p. 193.
24 Quoted in Andrew, *Delcassé*, p. 54.
25 Quoted in Grosser, *Affaires extérieures*, p. 134.
26 'Le Programme des principales forces en présence', *Elections législatives de mars 1993 (Le Monde, Dossiers et Documents*, 1993), pp. 52–3.
27 *Le Monde*, 20 May 1993.
28 Quoted in M. Wise, 'France and European Unity', in R. Aldrich and J. Connell (eds), *France in World Politics* (London, Routledge, 1989), p. 40.
29 Quoted in A. Aghrout, *From Preferential Status to Partnership: The Euro-Maghreb Relationship* (Aldershot, Ashgate, 2000), ch. 5.
30 *Financial Times*, 31 July 1997, p. 2.
31 'La France veut "moderniser" sa politique africaine', *Le Monde*, 14 Oct. 1997.
32 Pierre Joxe, 'Discours d'ouverture', in *Un nouveau débat stratégique*, p. 9.
33 *Le Monde*, 4 Feb. 1994.
34 'Projet de loi relatif à la programmation militaire pour les années 1997 à 2002', Exposé des motifs and Rapport Annexe, Ministère de la défense, SIRPA, 1996.
35 'Russian Vote to Cut Arms Boosts Nuclear Reduction', *Financial Times*, 14–15 Apr. 2000.
36 Quoted in Dalloz, *France et le monde*, p. 180.
37 Alain Joxe, 'Autonomie stratégique', pp. 109–21.

Conclusion

There is a series of continuities in France's relations with the rest of the world that have their source in the defeat of 1871. It is the contention of this work that study of France's twentieth-century external relations must therefore be a history of the 'long century'. The preceding chapters have discussed themes that emerge from that period and have arrived at a number of provisional conclusions. Analysis of the machinery of foreign policy making suggests that ultimate power for France's relations with the outside world resided with the same agents. Fluctuations in their degree of influence, notably as regards the President of the Republic and the Foreign Minister, have been more the result of personalities and styles of leadership than constitutional prerogatives, that is until the Fifth Republic formally concentrated power in the President's hands. On the question of strategy and defence, one of the detectable continuities is the overall absence of co-ordination between foreign and defence policy, often with disastrous consequences. Once again, it is only with the Fifth Republic that the two were aligned satisfactorily under the auspices of the President. Intelligence has been a 'missing dimension' in France's twentieth-century history in more ways than one. The stigma of the Dreyfus Affair ensured that intelligence assessments to this day are not effectively fed into the decision-making process, despite France's intelligence agencies having often performed well in gathering data and even analysing them.

If one is to ask in which single area French foreign, defence and intelligence efforts were concentrated over the long century, then the answer must be Germany. The 'long century' is primarily the history of relations with France's German neighbour. From the end of the Franco-Prussian War and German unification in 1871 to the reunification of Germany a century and a quarter later, it is the story of France's search for continental security. Even the second phase of French imperial expansion from the 1880s is partly a wounded reaction to the defeat of 1871. From then on the organization, formulation and execution of foreign policy were geared principally to dealing with the German 'question'. Defence and strategy were planned with the

German threat clearly in mind, even during the cold war, if one takes into consideration the development of France's nuclear weapon as the ultimate defence against a resurgent Germany. France's search for allies since the 1870s until the end of the 'long century' is largely to do with the perceived need for collective security against a powerful Germany. France has tried many ways of dealing with the German question, which over the period have proceeded in cycles from a desire to crush, contain, conciliate and even collaborate with its eastern neighbour.

France's relationship with the so-called Anglo-Saxons has been ambivalent, particularly since 1917 when to a certain extent an 'American problem' is discernible. While desirous of having Britain and the USA as allies against a powerful Germany (and later the Soviet Union), France also felt the need to retain some independence in order not to succumb to an 'Anglo-Saxon' world order politically, economically and culturally. As the chapter devoted to relations with Russia suggests, here too there is ambivalence. Once the ideological posturing is swept away, over the long term Russia is regarded as sharing with France fundamentally similar geopolitical conceptions of a European order. In French eyes, the crux of the matter has been the shared fear of a too powerful Germany to the east of France and to the west of Russia. The chapter devoted to empire explored France's imperial motives, which chimed in with universalist principles emanating from the Enlightenment and the French Revolution and justified the 'civilizing mission'. But empire was also a means for France to supplement its world power aspirations. For that reason decolonization was particularly difficult in the aftermath of a humiliating French defeat in 1940. Many of the themes and continuities described above came to a head with the ending of the cold war. France, more than most powers, found it difficult to adjust to the new post-cold war era. That process of adjustment is still underway and touches on two more important questions. The first is the overall pattern of France's world role over the 'long century'; the second is the extent to which adjusting to the New World Order will require a shift in France's self-perception and perhaps its national identity.

At the beginning of the twentieth century France was one of the eight great powers in the world with Britain, Germany, Russia, Austria-Hungary, Italy, Japan and the USA. Indeed, it was probably one of the top three in terms of actual economic and military power. At the beginning of the twenty-first century it is arguably still in third position among what might be considered to be the seven world powers: the USA, Russia, Britain, Germany, Japan and China. Today France is the fourth economic power and the third nuclear power in the world. It is one of only five permanent members of the United Nations Security Council, a leading member of the European Union and a member of the exclusive G8 club of the most powerful industrial nations. It still controls the African Francophone area economically and to a certain extent politically, and still possesses colonial outposts in every ocean of the world. For a country that represents only 0.37 per cent of the world's land mass and less than 1 per cent of the world's population, this is some achievement.

What this apparent consistency from one end of the twentieth century to the other masks is both decline and renewal. Over those 100 years France's power has declined relative to the strongest power in the group, which some have interpreted as its decline to medium-power status. Jean-Baptiste Duroselle, using Clausewitz and Raymond Aron, defined a great power as 'a political unit capable of ensuring its own security alone against any other political unit'.[1] That was virtually France's case in 1914 in relation to each of the other seven powers, barely the case in relation to the other six in 1939 and not the case in relation to the two superpowers after 1945. Today there is only one hyperpower, which dwarfs all others.

The other feature of France's position as a great power since 1870 is the remarkable fluctuations that affected it. Unlike Britain's position, which was one of slow and consistent decline in terms of relative power, France's international fortunes have fluctuated considerably, even violently. Ever since the defeat in 1871 and the three years of German occupation that followed, France's foreign policy was characterized by two aims: to ensure its continental security and to restore its world status. From the relative power and security of its pre-1914 alliances, it entered a war from which it emerged proportionally the worst hit of all the victorious nations and arguably one of the weakest of the great powers. It was able to climb back up the great power ladder, managing eventually by 1940 to deploy considerable armed forces. However, its morale had been sapped during the inter-war years by internal strife and its military strategy was steeped in the past. This contributed to its defeat in 1940 and to the lowest ebb of its great power status. From 1940 to 1944 it ceased to exist as an independent power. Nevertheless, its potential power remained great, which explained Churchill's desire to see post-war France restored to world power status. The story since then has been of an unsteady climb back to international power respectability, albeit marred by occasional dips owing to turbulent decolonization from 1954 to 1962 and military instability in 1958 and 1961, which, in the eyes of some, brought it to the brink of civil war.

Gaullist policies subsequently gave France greater freedom of manœuvre on the international stage, backed by a strongly expanding and modernized economy, so that by the 1970s France had overtaken Britain in most of the measurements of great power status from economics to nuclear weaponry. How France will fare in the post-cold war era is still unclear, with Britain appearing to have caught up again. Although France took more time to adjust than most other powers to the new international order, it appears at the beginning of the twenty-first century to be managing the transition effectively. Its economy is at last adapting to a global market and throwing off the shackles of state control; its defence is being modernized with a wholly professional army from 2002 and its foreign policy is forsaking the Gaullist shibboleth of independence for independence's sake. France continues to use the European Union most effectively as an extension of its national power. It may have doubts about how far it should be committed to further European integration, but it firmly believes that its future lies in an integrated Europe. As François Mitterrand stated during the 1992 Maastricht referendum campaign: 'France is our *patrie*, Europe our future.'[2]

In many ways the history of France and the world in the twentieth century is similar to Britain's: a great power that has had to adjust to medium power status. France too lost an empire, but did find a role. It projected itself from 1958 as an independent, and almost intentionally curmudgeonly, power twixt the two superpowers. Exceptionalism became a virtue. Unlike Britain it improved economic performance by modernizing from the 1940s to buttress its international role. It skilfully used the European Community to enhance its international position. Overall, since the 1960s its world policy has been remarkably imaginative. Unlike the more pragmatic, evolutionary and stolid British performance, France attempted leaps of faith and was rewarded. Of course there is often more of the conjuring trick than the traditional indices of power in France's seemingly impressive world presence. But then international power has always been much more than merely the sum of its diplomatic, military and economic parts. France more than any other power has 'performed' its international role with typical garrulousness. Almost two centuries ago the counter-revolutionary writer Joseph de Maistre had understood what was unique in French power. 'There is in the power of the French, there is in their character, there is above all in their language a certain proselytising force which passes imagination. The whole nation is no more than a vast propaganda.'[3] Inventing the French nation was a principal preoccupation of its elites since the Revolution. They were remarkably successful. Even in the late twentieth century France was perceived as being a nation state with one of the clearest senses of national identity. But there are signs that that old identity of the 'one and indivisible Republic' is wearing thin. In August 2000 bold plans to give greater autonomy to a turbulent Corsica provoked the resignation of the Interior Minister amid warnings that this would bring similar claims for greater recognition of regional identities and autonomy. France's multicultural identity is beginning to break through the Republican façade of the unitary state, helped by globalism and deeper European integration. Attempts have been made to stem the tide. Since the Revolution the Republic has used 'spectacle' as a means of giving public visibility and legitimacy to the otherwise abstract notion of the nation state. In recent years France, more than most other powers, has resorted to spectacle on a grand scale to reaffirm and redefine its collective identity, from the 1989 bicentennial commemoration of the French Revolution to the 1998 World Cup and latterly the year 2000 millennial celebrations. These performances were a response to a general insecurity about France's identity and place among the leading nations of the world. Through them an attempt was made to turn the sources of its insecurity – globalization, multiculturalism, European integration – into something positive by linking all three to French universalism.[4] For the moment the conjuring trick remains at the level of spectacle. Whether at a lower level French society can repeat the trick and adapt to the necessary changes is the real question. How the 'one and indivisible French Republic' integrates the new forces of globalization, regionalization, multiculturalism and the 'right to difference' and blends them to reinvent its identity will have a profound effect on France's place in the world in the twenty-first century.

Notes

1   Jean-Baptiste Duroselle, Introduction to Jean-Claude Allain (ed.), *La Moyenne Puissance au XXe siecle: Recherche d'une définition* (Paris, FEDN-IHCC, 1989), pp. 12–13.

2   Quoted in Philippe Moreau Defarges, *La France dans le monde* (Paris, Hachette), 1994, p. 181.

3   J. de Maître, *Correspondance, 13 Dec 1815*, in *Œuvres complètes . . . Nouvelle édition ses oeuvres posthumes et toute sa correspondance inédite* (Lyons, 1884–7).

4   Michael F. Leruth, 'Themes of the French Year 2000 Celebration', in *Modern and Contemporary France* (forthcoming); Régis Debray, *L'Etat séducteur. Les Révolutions médiologiques du pouvoir* (Paris, Gallimard, 1993).

Bibliography

Adamthwaite, Anthony, *France and the Coming of the Second World War 1936-1939* (London, Frank Cass, 1977).

—— *Grandeur and Misery. France's Bid for Power in Europe 1914–1940* (London, Arnold, 1995).

Aghrout, Ahmed, *From Preferential Status to Partnership: The Euro-Maghreb Relationship* (Aldershot, Ashgate, 2000).

Aldrich, Robert, *Greater France: A History of French Overseas Expansion* (London, Macmillan, 1996).

Alexander, Martin, 'Did the Deuxième Bureau Work? The Role of Intelligence in French Defence and Strategy 1919–1939', *Intelligence and National Security*, 6/2 (1991), 293–333.

—— *The Republic in Danger: General Maurice Gamelin and the Politics of French Defence, 1933–1940* (Cambridge, Cambridge University Press, 1992).

—— (ed.), *Europe since Napoleon* (London, Arnold, 1999).

—— 'The French Experience 1919–62: French Military Doctrine and British Observations, from World War One to the Algerian War', in J. Gooch (ed.), *The Origins of Contemporary Doctrine* (Camberley, SCSI, no. 30, 1997), 32–51.

Allain, Jean-Claude (ed.), *La Moyenne Puissance au XXe siècle: Recherche d'une définition* (Paris, FEDN-IHCC, 1989).

Amalvi, Christian, *Les Héros de l'histoire de France* (Paris, Editions Phot'œil, 1979).

Andrew, Christopher, *Théophile Delcassé and the Making of the Entente Cordiale* (London, Macmillan, 1968).

—— 'France and the German Menace', in Ernest May (ed.), *Knowing one's Enemies: Intelligence Assessment before the Two World Wars* (Princeton, Princeton University Press, 1984).

—— *Secret Service: The Making of the British Intelligence Community* (London, Sceptre, paperback edn, 1992).

—— and Kanya Forstner, A. S., *France Overseas: The Great War and the Climax of French Imperial Expansion* (London, Thames & Hudson, 1981).

—— and Mitrokhin, Vasili, *The Mitrokhin Archive: The KGB in Europe and the West* (London, Allen Lane/Penguin, 1999).

Bédarida, François, 'La "Gouvernante anglaise"', in René Rémond and Janine Bourdin (eds), *Edouard Daladier, chef de gouvernement (avril 1938–septembre 1939)* (Paris, FNSP, 1977).

—— 'Postface', in Douglas Johnson, François Bédarida and François Crouzet (eds), *Britain and France: Ten Centuries* (Folkestone, Dawson, 1980),

Bell, P. M. H., *France and Britain, 1900–1940: Entente and Estrangement* (London Longman, 1996).

Beloff, Max, 'The Anglo-French Union Project of June 1940', in *Mélanges Pierre Renouvin: Etudes d'histoire des relations internationales* (Paris, PUF, 1966).

Binion, Rudolph, *Defeated Leaders*, New York, Columbia University Press, 1960.

Braudel, Fernand, *L'Identité de la France*, vol. 1, *Espace et histoire* (Paris, Arthaud-Flammarion, 1986).

—— *L'Identité de la France*, vol. III, *Les Hommes et les choses*, part 2 (Paris, Arthaud-Flammarion, 1986).

Butler, Rohan, and Bury, J. P. T. (eds), *Documents on British Foreign Policy 1919–1939* (*DBFP*), 1st series, vol. XII (London, HMSO, 1960).

Carley, M. J., and Debo, R. K., 'Always in Need of Credit: The USSR and Franco-German Economic Cooperation, 1926–1929', *French Historical Studies*, 20/3 (Summer 1997), 315–56.

Carmoy, Guy de, *Les Politiques étrangères de la France 1944–1966* (Paris, La Table Ronde, 1967).

Caron, François, *An Economic History of Modern France* (London, Methuen, 1979).

Carroll, E. M., *French Public Opinion and Foreign Affairs, 1870–1914* (London, Frank Cass, 1931).

Chevènement, Jean-Pierre, *France-Allemagne: Parlons franc* (Paris, Plon, 1996).

Cole, Alistair, *François Mitterrand: A Study in Political Leadership* (2nd edn, London, Routledge, 1997).

Coze, H., and Puq, J., 'L'Avenir de la dissuasion nucléaire', *Défense nationale*, 50 (Feb. 1993).

Dalloz, Jacques, *La France et le monde depuis 1945* (Paris, Armand Colin, 1993).

Dansette, A., *Histoire des Présidents de la République* (Paris, 1953).

Debray, Régis, *L'Etat séducteur. Les Révolutions médiologiques du pouvoir* (Paris, Gallimard, 1993).

De Gaulle, Charles, *Discours et messages*, vol. 1, *Pendant la guerre: Juin 1940- Janvier 1946* (Paris, Plon, Livre de Poche, paperback edn, 1970).

—— *Mémoires de guerre* (Paris, Plon, paperback edn, 1959).

—— *Vers l'armée de métier* (Paris, Presses Pocket, 1989).

Doise, Jean, and Vaïsse, Maurice, *Politique étrangère de la France: Diplomatie et outil militaire 1871–1991* (Paris, Seuil, paperback edn, 1992).

Duroselle, Jean-Baptiste, 'Changes in French Foreign Policy since 1945', in Stanley Hoffman, *In Search of France* (New York, Harper Torchbooks, 1963).

—— *La Décadence 1932–1939* (Paris, Imprimerie Nationale, 1979).

—— *Tout empire périra: Une vision théorique des relations internationales* (Paris, Publications de la Sorbonne, 1981).

Evans, Martin, 'From Colonialism to Post-Colonialism', in Martin S. Alexander (ed.), *French History since Napoleon* (London, Arnold, 1999).

Faligot, Roger, and Krop, Pascal, *La Piscine: Les Services secrets français 1944–1984* (Paris, Seuil, 1985).

Fontaine, André, *Un seul lit pour deux rêves: Histoire de la 'détente' 1962–1981* (Paris, Fayard, 1981).

Faupin, Alain (General), 'L'Otan, un moyen au service de l'Europe politique', in *La Revue internationale et stratéqique*, Special issue 'Quel avenir pour l'OTAN?', 32 (1998), 59–65.

France, 1996 (Paris, La Documentation française et le Ministère des affaires étrangères, 1996).

Frank, Robert, 'Vichy et le monde; le monde et Vichy: Perceptions géopolitiques et idéologiques', in Jean-Pierre Azéma and François Bédarida (eds), *Le Régime de Vichy et les français* (Paris, Fayard, 1992).

Frankenstein, Robert, *Le Prix de réarmement français, 1935–39* (Paris, Publications de la Sorbonne, 1982).

Gallois, Pierre M, *La France, sort-elle de l'Histoire? Superpuissances et déclin national* (Lausanne, L'Age d'Homme, 1998).

Gaudemet, Yves-Henri, *Les Juristes et la vie politique de la IIIe République* (Paris, PUF, 1970).

Gildea, Robert, *France since 1945* (Oxford, Oxford University Press, Opus, paperback edn, 1997).

Girardet, Raoul, *Mythes et mythologies politiques* (Paris, Seuil, 1986).

Girault, René, *Diplomatie européenne et impérialismes, 1871–1914* (Paris, Masson, 1979).

Godfrey, John F., *Capitalism at War: Industrial Policy and Bureaucracy in France, 1914–1918* (Leamington Spa, Berg, 1987).

Gooch, G. P., *Franco-German Relations, 1871–1914: The Creighton Lecture, 1923* (New York, Longman, 1923).

Gordon, David C., *The French Language and National Identity* (The Hague, Mouton, 1978).

Gordon, Philip, *France, Germany and the Western Alliance* (Boulder, Colo., Westview, 1995).

Gregory, Shaun, *French Defence Policy into the Twenty-First Century* (London, Macmillan, 2000).

Grosser, Alfred, *La IVe République et sa politique extérieure* (Paris, Armand Colin, 1961).

—— *La Politique extérieure de la Ve République* (Paris, Seuil, 1965).

—— *Affaires extérieures: La Politique de la France, 1944–1984* (Paris, Flammarion, 1984).

Gueslin, A., *L'Etat, l'économie et la société française XIXe–XXe siècle* (Paris, Hachette, 1992).

Hamilton, K. I., 'Britain and France', in F. H. Hinsley (ed.), *British Foreign Policy under Sir Edward Grey* (Cambridge, Cambridge University Press, 1977).

Hayward, J. E. S., *Governing France: The One and Indivisible French Republic* (2nd edn, London, Weidenfeld & Nicolson, 1983).

Herrman, Michael, *Intelligence Power in Peace and War* (Cambridge, Cambridge University Press, 1996).

Hoffmann, Stanley, *Sur la France* (Paris, Seuil, 1976).

Hogenhuis-Seliverstoff, Anne, *Une alliance franco-russe: La France, la Russie et l'Europe au tournant du siècle dernier* (Brussels, Bruylant, 1997).

Horne, Alistair, *The French Army and Politics 1870–1970* (London, Macmillan, 1984).

Howorth, Jolyon, 'The President's Special Role in Foreign and Defence Policy', in Jack Hayward (ed.), *De Gaulle to Mitterrand: Presidential Power in France* (New York, New York University Press, 1993), 150–89.

Jackson, Peter, 'French Intelligence and Hitler's Rise to Power', *Historical Journal*, 41/3 (1998).

Jardin, Pierre, 'Le Renseignement français en Allemagne au lendemain de la Seconde Guerre Mondiale (1940–55)', in *Cahiers du Centre d'etudes d'histoire de la défense*, no. 1, *Le Renseignement* (Paris, Centre d'études d'histoire de la défense, 1996), pp. 62–7.

Johnson, Douglas, 'Entente and Mésentente', in Douglas Johnson, François Bédarida amd François Crouzet (eds), *France and Britain: Ten Centuries* (Folkestone, Dawson, 1980), 265–73.

Joxe, Alain, 'Autonomie stratégique de l'école française', in *Un nouveau débat stratégique* (Paris, La Documentation française et le Ministère des affaires étrangères, 1993), 109–21.

Keiger, J. F. V., `Jules Cambon and Franco-German Détente 1907–1914', *Historical Journal*, 26/3 (1983), 641–59.

—— 'Omdurman, Fashoda and Franco-British Relations', in Edward Spiers (ed.), *Sudan: The Reconquest Reappraised* (London, Frank Cass, 1998).

—— 'Une perception britannique du renseignement français', in Pierre Lacoste (ed.), *Le Renseignement à la française* (Paris, Economica, 1998).

—— *France and the Origins of the First World War* (London, Macmillan, 1983).

—— *Raymond Poincaré* (Cambridge, Cambridge University Press, 1997).

Kennedy, Paul, *The Realities behind Diplomacy: Background Influences on British External Policy, 1865–1980* (London, Fontana, 1981).

—— *The Rise and Fall of the Great Powers* (London, Unwin Hyman, 1988).

Keylor, W. R., 'France's Futile Quest for American Military Protection, 1919–22', in M. Petricioli and M. Guderzo (eds), *A Missed Opportunity? 1922: The Reconstruction of Europe* (Berne, Peter Lang, 1995).

—— *The Twentieth Century World: An International History* (New York, Oxford University Press, 1984).

Kolodziej, Edward A., *Making and Marketing Arms: The French Experience and its Implications for the International System* (Princeton, Princeton University Press, 1987).

La Défense: La Politique militaire française et ses realisations, Notes et Etudes Documentaires, no. 3343, 6 Dec. 1966, Paris, La Documentation française et le Ministère des affaires étrangères, produced by the Ministry for Armed Forces Information Service.

Lacouture, Jean, *De Gaulle*, vol. III, *Le Souverain* (Paris, Seuil, 1986).

Laqueur, Walter, *A World of Secrets: The Uses and Limits of Intelligence* (New York, Basic Books, 1985).

Leruth, Michael F., 'Themes of the French Year 2000 Celebration', in *Modern and Contemporary France* (forthcoming).

Livre blanc sur la défense (Paris, Sirpa, 1994).

Maingueneau, Dominique, *Les Livres d'école de la République 1870–1914 (discours et idéologie)* (Paris, Le Sycomore, 1979).

Maître, J. de, *Correspondance*, in *Œuvres complètes … Nouvelle édition, contenant ses œuvres posthumes et toute sa correspondance inédite* (Lyons, 1884–7).

Marion, Pierre, *La Mission impossible: A la tête des service secrets* (Paris, Calmann-Lévy, 1991).

Marseille, Jacques, *Empire colonial et capitalisme français, histoire d'un divorce*, (Paris, Albin Michel, 1984).

Mayeur, Jean-Marie, *La Vie politique sous la Troisième République 1870–1940* (Paris, Seuil, 1984).

Mendl, W., *Deterrence and Persuasion: French Nuclear Armament in the Context of National Policy, 1945–1969* (London, Faber, 1970).

MI5. The Security Service (2nd edn, London, HMSO, 1996).

Michel, Marc, 'Decolonization: French Attitudes and Policies, 1944–46', in P. Morris and S. Williams (eds), *France in the World* (London, Association for the Study of Modern and Contemporary France, 1985).

Moreau Defarges, Philippe, *La France dans le monde* (Paris, Hachette, 1994).

Navarre, Henri, *Agonie de l'Indochine (1953–1954)* (Paris, Plon, 1956).

Néré, J., *The Foreign Policy of France 1914 to 1945* (London, Routledge, 1975).

Nicolson, Harold, *Diplomacy* (London, Thornton Butterworth, 1939).

Paillole, Paul, *Services Spéciaux (1935–1945)* (Paris, Robert Lafont, 1975).

Parodi, Maurice, `Histoire récente de l'économie et de la société françaises, 1945–1970', in Georges Duby (ed.), *Histoire de la France* (Paris, Larousse, 1970).

Passy, Colonel, *Souvenirs: Deuxième bureau Londres* (Monte Carlo, Raoul Solar, 1947).

Péan, Pierre, *Le Mystérieux Docteur Martin (1895–1969)* (Paris, Livre de poche, 1993).

Pennetier, Jean-Marc, 'The Spring-Time of French Intelligence', *Intelligence and National Security*, 11/4 (Oct. 1996), 780–98.

Petras, James, and Morley, Morris, 'Contesting Hegemons: US–French Relations in the "New World Order"', *Review of International Studies*, 26 (2000), 49–67.

Philpott, William, *Anglo-French Relations and Strategy on the Western Front 1914–18* (London, Macmillan, 1996).

Pickles, Dorothy, *The Government and Politics of France*, vol. II, *Politics* (London, Methuen, 1973).

—— *The Uneasy Entente: French Foreign Policy and Franco-British Misunderstandings* (Oxford, Oxford University Press, 1966).

Poidevin, Raymond, and Bariéty, Jacques, *Les Relations franco-allemandes 1815–1975*, (Paris, Armand Colin, 1977).

Poincaré, Raymond, *L'Idée de patrie* (Paris, 1910).

Porch, Douglas, *The March to the Marne: The French Army 1871–1914* (Cambridge, Cambridge University Press, 1981).

—— *The French Secret Services: A History of French Intelligence from the Dreyfus Affair to the Gulf War* (New York, Farrar Strauss Giroux, 1995).

'Projet de loi relatif à la programmation militaire pour les années 1997 à 2002', Exposé des motifs and Rapport Annexe, Ministère de la défense, SIRPA, 1996.

Renouvin, Pierre, *Histoire des relations internationales*, vol. VI, *1871-1914* (Paris, Armand Colin, 1955).

—— and Duroselle, Jean-Baptiste, *Introduction à l'histoire des relations internationales* (2nd edn, Paris, Armand Colin, 1966).

Rioux, Jean-Pierre, *La France de la Quatrième République*, vol. 2, *L'Expansion et l'impuissance 1952–1958* (Paris, Seuil, 1983).

Rosenblum, M., *Mission to Civilize: The French Way* (San Diego, Harcourt Brace Jovanovich, 1986).

Rovan, Joseph, *Bismarck, l'Allemagne et l'Europe Unie, 1898–1998–2098* (Paris, Editions Odile Jacob, 1998).

Saint Aulaire, Comte de, *Confession d'un vieux diplomate* (Paris, 1953).

Simonian, Haig, *The Privileged Partnership: Franco-German Relations in the European Community, 1969–1984* (Oxford, Oxford University Press, 1985).

Soutou, Georges-Henri, 'La France et les bouleversements en Europe, 1989–1991, ou le poids de l'idéologie', paper given at the Franco-British Council conference, Royaumont (Sept. 1991), typescript.

—— *L'Alliance incertaine: Les Rapports politico-stratégiques franco-allemands, 1954-1996* (Paris, Fayard, 1996).

Stevens, Anne, 'The President and his Staff', in J. Hayward (ed.), *De Gaulle to Mitterrand: Presidential Power in France* (New York, New York University Press, 1993), 76–100.

Tacel, Max, *La France et le monde au XXe siècle* (Paris, Masson, 1989).

Taylor, A. J. P., *The Struggle for Mastery in Europe 1848–1918* (Oxford, Oxford University Press, paperback edn, 1971).

Thatcher, Margaret, *The Downing Street Years* (London, Harper/Collins, 1993).

Thomas, Martin, 'France in British Signals Intelligence, 1939–1945', *French History*, 14/1 (2000), 41–66.

Tombs, Robert, *France 1814–1914* (London, Longman, 1996).

Tomlinson, Philip (ed.), *French Classical Theatre Today: Teaching, Research, Performance* (Amsterdam, Rodopi, 2001).

Trachtenberg, Marc, *Reparation in World Politics: France and European Economic Diplomacy, 1916-1923* (New York, Columbia University Press, 1980).

Vaïsse, Maurice, 'Post-Suez France', in W. R. Louis and R. Owen (eds), *Suez 1956: The Crisis and its Consequences* (Oxford, Oxford University Press, 1989).

—— *1961: Alger, le putsch* (Brussels, Editions Complexe, 1983).

—— *La Grandeur: Politique étrangère du général de Gaulle, 1958–1969* (Paris, Fayard, 1998).

Valance, Georges, *France-Allemagne: Le Retour de Bismarck* (Paris, Flammarion, 1990).

Venier, Pascal, 'Delcassé et les relations franco-britanniques pendant les débuts de la guerre de Boers', in Rémy Paech, Claudine Pailhes and Louis Claeys, *Delcassé et l'Europe à la veille de la Grande Guerre* (Toulouse, forthcoming).

Wark, Wesley K. (ed.), *Spy Fiction, Spy Films and Real Intelligence* (London, Frank Cass, 1991).

Warusfel, Bertrand, 'Le Contre-espionnage français', in *Cahiers du Centre d'études d'histoire de la défense*, no. 1, *Histoire du renseignement* (Paris, Cahiers du Centre d'études d'histoire de la défense, 1996).

Weber, Eugen, *Peasants into Frenchmen: The Modernization of Rural France* (London, Chatto & Windus, paperback edn, 1979).

Williams, Philip, *Wars, Plots and Scandals in Post-War France* (Cambridge, Cambridge University Press, 1970).

Williamson, Samuel, 'Joffre Reshapes French Strategy, 1911–1913', in Paul Kennedy (ed.), *The War Plans of the Great Powers, 1880–1914* (London, Unwin Hyman, 1979).

Willis, F. Roy, *France, Germany and the New Europe 1945–1963* (Stanford, Calif., Stanford University Press, 1965).

Wise, M., 'France and European Unity', in R. Aldrich and J. Connell (eds), *France in World Politics* (London, Routledge, 1989).

Young, John, *France, the Cold War and the Western Alliance, 1944–1949: French Foreign Policy and Post War Europe* (Leicester, Leicester University Press, 1990).

Young, Robert J., 'The Aftermath of Munich: The Course of French Diplomacy, October 1938 to March 1939', *French Historical Studies*, 8/2 (Fall 1973).

—— *France and the Origins of the Second World War* (London, Macmillan, 1996).

Zervoudakis, Alexander, 'Nihil mirare, nihil contemptare, omnia intelligere: Franco-Vietnamese Intelligence in Indochina, 1950–1954', in Martin Alexander (ed.), *Knowing your Friends: Intelligence inside Alliances and Coalitions from 1924 to the Cold War* (London, Frank Cass, 1998).

Index